The Worship Mall

Founded in 1897, the Alcuin Club seeks to promote the study of Christian liturgy and worship in general with special reference to worship in the Anglican Communion. The Club has published a series of annual Collections, including *A Companion to Common Worship*, volumes 1 and 2, edited by Paul F. Bradshaw, a new edition of the classic text *Christian Prayer through the Centuries*, by Joseph Jungmann (SPCK 2007) and most recently *An Evangelical Among the Anglican Liturgists*, by Colin Buchanan (SPCK 2009). The Alcuin Liturgy Guide series aims to address the theology and practice of worship, and includes *The Use of Symbols in Worship*, edited by Christopher Irvine, and two volumes covering the celebration of the Christian Year: *Celebrating Christ's Appearing: Advent to Christmas*, and *Celebrating Christ's Victory: Ash Wednesday to Trinity*, both by Benjamin Gordon-Taylor and Simon Jones. The Club works in partnership with GROW in the publication of the Joint Liturgical Study series, with two studies being published each year.

Members of the Club receive publications of the current year free and others at a reduced rate. The President of the Club is the Rt Revd Michael Perham, its Chairman is the Revd Canon Dr Donald Gray CBE, and the Secretary is the Revd Dr Gordon Jeanes. For details of membership and the annual subscription, contact The Alcuin Club, 5 Saffron Street, Royston, SG8 9TR, or email: alcuinclub@gmail.com

Visit the Alcuin Club website at: **www.alcuinclub.org.uk**

The Worship Mall

*Contemporary responses to
contemporary culture*

Bryan D. Spinks

*Goddard Professor of Liturgical Studies and Pastoral Theology,
Yale Institute of Sacred Music and Yale Divinity School*

Alcuin Club Collections 85

Church Publishing
NEW YORK

Library of Congress Cataloging-in-Publication Data

Spinks, Bryan D.
 The worship mall : contemporary responses to contemporary culture / Bryan D. Spinks.
  p. cm.
 Originally published: London : Society for Promoting Christian Knowledge, 2010.
 Includes bibliographical references (p.   ) and index.
 ISBN 978-0-89869-675-2 (pbk.) -- ISBN 978-0-89869-677-6 (e-book) 1. Public worship.
2. Postmodernism--Religious aspects--Christianity. I. Title.
 BV15.S64 2011
 264.009'051--dc22
                          2010050680

First published in Great Britain in 2010
Society for Promoting Christian Knowledge
36 Causton Street
London SW1P 4ST
www.spckpublishing.co.uk

First published in North America in 2011
Church Publishing, Incorporated.
445 Fifth Avenue
New York, New York 10016
www.churchpublishing.org

Typeset by Kenneth Burnley, Wirral, Cheshire
Cover design by Laurie Klein Westhafer

Printed in the United States of America

To Care
My Beloved
Who has enabled me to smile again inside

For lo, the winter is past, the rain is over and gone. The flowers appear on the earth; the time of singing has come, and the voice of the turtledove is heard in our land.

Song of Songs 2.11–12.

Contents

Preface

This study has grown out of a course of the same title that I offered at Yale Divinity School, first in Spring 2007, and again in Spring 2009. The time seemed ripe to look at what is going on in liturgy in this post-modern era. Some worship forms try to be consciously postmodern, some are just 'contemporary', and some are consciously counter-cultural. My British background and my American domicile have meant that I have attempted to present a study that is transatlantic, though some may view the result as being simply lost at sea. I am acutely aware that each chapter in this book either has been, or ought to be, a book in its own right, but at the very least I hope it may inspire others to do that work, and in so doing, present a fuller and more focused picture than I have been able to do here. I am grateful to the Alcuin Club for inviting this work as one of their volumes.

In 2007 I was assisted by teaching assistant, Dr Glen Segger, and I am grateful for his ideas and suggestions regarding internet material, and especially YouTube material. A teacher always learns much from his or her students, and since most in the class have been Gen X and Gen Y, their knowledge of, and comments on, pop music and contemporary Christian music have been invaluable. It is also rewarding to be able to cite my own former students – the work of Sarah Koenig and Melanie Ross in *Worship*, and Irene Ai-Ling Sun in *Studia Liturgica*, as well as the work of the Revd Lucas Grubbs and Jooil Park for the Master of Sacred Theology degree. I am also indebted to conversations with John Baldovin on Roman Catholic worship; Peter Ward on 'Praise and Worship', and 'alt.worship'; and Sally Morgenthaler on 'emergent' worship. Canon Bill Hall, the Revd Paige Blair and Fr Simon Rundell kindly provided material on the Duke Ellington Mass, U2charist and an alt.mass respectively. My thanks also to the Chapel Ministers at Yale Divinity School who allowed me to celebrate a 'blended, simplified High Mass in the Anglican tradition' in Marquand

Chapel. I am also grateful to Alan Murchie for including an explanation for the setting of the sung Gospel used in that service. The Conant Fund of the Episcopal Church kindly gave a grant to cover research during my sabbatical leave which enabled me to visit Cityside Baptist Church, Auckland, New Zealand; Hillsong Church, Baulkham Hills, Sydney, Australia; and, Hillsong Church UK in London. With the departure of my research assistant Mary Farag to pursue her Coptic studies in Germany, I was left without a research assistant. My wife, the Revd Care Goodstal-Spinks, came to the rescue, and dedicated many hours correcting and improving my grammar, checking the quotations and completing the bibliography. This work is dedicated to her.

BRYAN D. SPINKS
Christ the King 2009

Acknowledgements

The author and publisher gratefully acknowledge permission to reproduce copyright material. Every effort has been made to trace and acknowledge copyright holders. The publisher apologizes for any errors or omissions that may remain and, if notified, will ensure that full acknowledgement is made in a subsequent edition of this book.

Extracts from *The Hip Hop Prayer Book with Holy Bible Stories* by Timothy Holder, Church Publishing, Inc., New York, 2006, used with permission.

The English translation of 'Gloria in excelsis' from *The Roman Missal* © 2008, is used with permission of the International Committee on English in the Liturgy, Inc. All rights reserved.

The English translation of 'Gloria in excelsis' (1970) by the International Consultation on English Texts is used with permission.

Extracts © The Iona Community are taken from *The Iona Abbey Worship Book*, Wild Goose Publications, Glasgow, 2007.

The author extracts cited by Dong-sun Kim, from *The Bread for Today and the Bread for Tomorrow: The Ethical Significance of the Lord's Supper in the Korean Context*, Peter Lang, Frankfurt am Main, 2001, are used with permission.

Extracts from *Moot Community Little and Compline Services* (Pocket Liturgies Series), edited by Ian Mobsby, Mark Mcleary, Carey Radcliffe and Mike Radcliffe, published by Proost, are reproduced with permission.

Extracts from *Celtic Daily Prayer: A Northumbrian Office* © 2005 by the Northumbria Community are reproduced by permission of HarperCollins Publishers Ltd.

Extracts from songs on 'Wonder Working God' by Andy Park are used by permission.

The translation of 'They are blessed those who pray' from *Modern African Spirituality: The Independent Holy Spirit Churches in East Africa 1902–1976* by Ane Marie Bak Rasmussen, I. B. Tauris & Co. Ltd 1996, is reproduced by permission.

Lyrics from *The Soaking Room* by Laura Rhinehart are used by permission.

The Plan of St Gregory Nyssa, San Francisco, from *Searching for Sacred Space: Essays on Architecture and Liturgical Design in the Episcopal Church*, edited by John Runkle, Church Publishing, Inc., New York 2002, is used with permission.

Extracts from *Celtic Worship Through the Year* by Ray Simpson, copyright © 1997 by Ray Simpson; Morning Worship © 1997 Ray Simpson and Mark Slater, reproduced by permission of Hodder & Stoughton Ltd.

Lyrics from 'Let Your Glory Fall' used by permission from Vineyard Music. <www.VineyardMusic.com>

Lyrics from 'Dreams', from the Kiss of Heaven album by Darlene Zschech are used by permission. <www.darlenezschech.com>

Introduction: Postmodernity, malls and worship

One of the problems with the word 'culture' is that everyone lives in one, or several, and does so quite happily without being able to define and explain it. It has been likened to speaking one's native language. We just do it, and do not agonize over the grammar. Indeed, the best English grammar books, for example, have been written by foreigners who have had to learn the language as outsiders. Why, though, should we want to stop and ponder culture? John Drane asks:

> Are our efforts at cultural analysis truly describing what is there in any objective sense at all, or are we merely deluding ourselves with the thought that, if we are able to name a thing, we can also be in control of it, and therefore it becomes less of a threat to our familiar systems and lifestyles?[1]

The title of Drane's book is inspired by one dominating influence in the contemporary world, which is American in origin but is now part of global culture – McDonald's. He, in fact, took it over from a book by George Ritzer, *The McDonaldization of Society*.[2] Drane says that McDonaldization is 'the process by which the principles of the fast-food restaurant are coming to dominate more and more sectors of American society as well as the rest of the world'.[3] And he lists the characteristics as efficiency, calculability, predictability and control – all four of which are crucial ingredients in a consumer-based society.

---

1 John Drane, *The McDonaldization of the Church: Consumer Culture and the Church's Future* (Smyth & Helwys Publishing Inc., Macon GA, 2001), p. 2.
2 George Ritzer, *The McDonaldization of Society*, rev. New Century edn (Pine Forge Press, Thousand Oaks CA, 1995).
3 Drane, *The McDonaldization of the Church*, p. 32.

But McDonaldization is taking place in what is now commonly called either late modernity or postmodernity. Like the word 'culture', 'postmodern', 'postmodernism' and 'postmodernity' are slippery terms that can be dropped into conversations, learned papers and books, but that conceal far more than they reveal.[4] Stanley Granz cited Charles Jencks's claim that 'Postmodernism was born in St. Louis, Missouri, on July 15, 1972, at 3:32 P.M.' This was when the Pruitt-Igoe housing project, a landmark of modern architecture, was razed to the ground with dynamite, because the functionalism of modernism had failed as an experiment.[5] In fact the terms postmodern and postmodernism had been around for some time in the art world, and in the world of architecture and design. Later they would creep into linguistic analysis and textual studies, and then into historiography, and be associated with the names of Michel Foucault, Jean-François Lyotard, Frederic Jameson, Jacques Derrida and Jean Baudrillard (to name but a few), and in between would embrace more popular cultural art forms such as pop music and fashion.[6] All these are intellectual expressions. Most people do not drop the word 'postmodernity' into their conversations, but, like speaking one's mother tongue, just live in its popular everyday expressions without agonizing reflection or analysis. In the more popular culture it is the world of the internet and computers, of cell phones, iPods, BlackBerries, DVDs, MTV, Disney make-believe, virtual worlds, music, and contemporary fashion with teenage markets. But it is a culture where the methods and legacies of modernity and tradition still find a place. Furthermore, in so far as it is based around consumerism, it is a global corporate culture. The majority of those who do reflect on the change suggest that between the 1960s and the 1990s a crucial shift in how we *feel* about things began to occur. Drane gives a helpful, but rather general, summary:

> we are discovering that the rational-materialistic worldview handed down to us from the eighteenth, nineteenth and early

---

4 For the difference in these terms, see David Lyon, *Postmodernity*, second edn (University of Minnesota Press, Minneapolis, 2005), p. 10.

5 Stanley J. Grenz, *A Primer on Postmodernism* (Eerdmans, Grand Rapids MI, 1996), p. 11, referring to Charles A. Jencks, *The Language of Post-Modern Architecture*, fourth edn (Academy Editions, London, 1984), p. 9.

6 Steven Connor, *Postmodernist Culture: An Introduction to Theories of the Contemporary*, second edn (Blackwell, Oxford, 1997); Gerard Delanty, *Modernity and Postmodernity: Knowledge, Power and the Self* (Sage Publications, London, 2000).

twentieth centuries has led to lives that are fractured and broken, and has created personal dysfunction on the grand scale.[7]

This, of course, is an oversimplification. At the risk of further oversimplification, the following characteristics of modernity and postmodernity are often suggested. Modernity had the belief that progress was unending (a grand or metanarrative), and was optimistic about the ability of the human mind to solve major world problems. It elevated the rational and scientific methods, and also placed faith in 'experts'. It preferred simplified linear connections and relationships, and searched for universal norms. It emphasized mind over body, and concepts and words over the visual and experiential. In contrast, postmodernity is suspicious of grand narratives and denies notions of unending progress. It stresses that meaning is dependent upon relationships, and that there are few universal all-encompassing theories. It questions metaphysical realities and objective truth. It places mind and body together, and prefers the visual and experiential over concepts and words. David Lyon notes that postmodernism is about deposing reason, nature and progress, but 'in everyday life, the postmodern may be seen as a blurring of boundaries between "high" and "low" culture; the collapse of hierarchies of knowledge, taste and opinion; and the interest in the local rather than the universal'.[8]

Two crucial ingredients of this culture – be it popular or the more intellectual reflection – are simulacra/simulation, and bricolage. Simulacra – things look real, but are not – and we can list here things ranging from virtual reality on computer screens to theme parks, where castles are not castles; and bricolage or eclecticism – things from different cultures and different epochs placed side by side without any feeling that such things are out of context.

CONSUMERISM AND THE MALL

If there are dislocations between modernity and postmodernity, there are also constants and continuities, and first among them is the fact that both modernity and postmodernity are consumer cultures. Indeed, David Lyon commented, 'If postmodernity means anything, it means the consumer society.'[9] Of course, in broad strokes it is possible to see

7 Drane, *The McDonaldization of the Church*, p. 26.
8 Lyon, *Postmodernity*, p. 10.
9 Lyon, *Postmodernity*, p. 88.

consumerism as being born in the Enlightenment, where the Industrial Revolution put the final nails in the rural agrarian culture's coffin, hastening the growth of both urban sprawl and the breakdown of the old social order. Yiannis Gabriel and Tim Lang note:

> It is mainly since the Roaring Twenties in the United States that the meaning of consumption broadened still further to resonate pleasure, enjoyment and freedom . . . Living life to the full became increasingly synonymous with consumption.[10]

They note further: 'The major players in the consumerist game, the transnational corporations, are global players, the stakes are global, and the implications of the game itself are global.'[11]

Modern advertising makes no secret of its aims to stimulate desire rather than to propose the means for satisfying needs. John Clammer observed:

> Shopping is . . . adventure, safari, carnival, and contains unexpected 'risks' in what you may find and who you may meet. It is a kind of self-discovery. And by its very nature it possesses theatricality: one dresses up to go out and one shops to acquire the new persona, to modify the old one or to perfect the setting in which one is seen and known.[12]

He indicates that 'Shopping is not merely the acquisition of things: it is the buying of identity.'[13] Zygmunt Bauman noted: 'Reality, as the consumer experiences it, is a pursuit of pleasure. Freedom is about the choice between greater and lesser satisfactions, and rationality is about choosing the first over the second.'[14] It is, of course, the concern of any producer to effect desire rather than complete satisfaction, so that whatever one purchases, it is not enough – it is the desire that produces the excitement and satisfaction, not the goods themselves. Take for

---

10 Yiannis Gabriel and Tim Lang, *The Unmanageable Consumer: Contemporary Consumption and Its Fragmentation* (Sage Publications, London, 1995), p. 7.
11 Gabriel and Lang, *The Unmanageable Consumer*, p. 10.
12 John Clammer, 'Aesthetics of the Self: Shopping and social being in contemporary urban Japan' in Rob Shields (ed.), *Lifestyle Shopping: The Subject of Consumption* (Routledge, London, 1992), pp. 195–215, pp. 203–4.
13 Clammer, 'Aesthetics of the Self', p. 195.
14 Zygmunt Bauman, *Intimations of Postmodernity* (Routledge, London, 1992), p. 50.

example the iPod, which is forever being updated and improved, and the new ones integrate a phone with music, internet access and video entertainment features. Tomorrow something even more spectacular will come along – buy one today, but next year you will be enticed to upgrade to something newer. James Farrell notes that the contemporary slogan is, 'I consume, therefore I am: Credit Card instead of Descartes'.[15] In addition, there are designated times during the year when retailers can be particularly seductive and alluring about certain things. The mall calendar is, after all, very much like a liturgical calendar – for example, in February there are sales for winter clearance, housewares and spring pre-season sales; there are promotions for Valentine's Day, and for spring colours and fashions; and in this month occur also in the USA Groundhog Day, President's Day, Bachelor's Day, frequently Mardi Gras, and Black History Month.[16]

Whether it is the Mall of America in Bloomington, Minnesota, USA, or Lakeside at West Thurrock or the Gateshead Metro Centre in England, or Souk Sharq Mall in Kuwait City in the Middle East, the mall takes its place as a centre for the consumer. Malls emerged in the era of modernity, taking the place of the older department store and its successor, the galleria. With the decentralization of the city, a different consumerist solution was required, hence the out-of-town mall, the first perhaps being Southdale Center in Edina, Minnesota in 1960. Farrell observes that the USA 'has more shopping malls than high schools, and in the last forty years, shopping center space has increased by a factor of twelve'.[17] Architects put a great deal of thought into the design of each space, both macro and micro. Writing on good retail design, architect Charles Kober claims to address the 'task of attracting a fickle consumer, keeping that person at the center longer, stimulating impulse purchases, appealing to the customer's self-image and aspirations, and making the shopping experience safe, convenient, and fun to ensure a return visit'.[18] The importance of lighting, colour and intentional music cannot be underestimated. Farrell claims that malls reinforce American values of individualism and choice. He writes: 'Shopping centers still contain such utopian promises of peace and plenty, stuff and sociability.

15 James J. Farrell, *One Nation Under Goods: Malls and the Seduction of American Shopping* (Smithsonian Books, Washington DC), 2003, p. 261.
16 See Farrell, *One Nation*, Table 3, pp. 48–9.
17 Farrell, *One Nation*, p. xi.
18 Farrell, *One Nation*, p. 16.

Malls embody the values and ideals of what we might call "commercial utopianism" – freedom, abundance, leisure, happiness, individualism, and community.'[19] He goes on: 'It emphasizes opportunity, but not equality. It evokes passion, but not much compassion . . . Malls sell "the good life", not the good society.'[20]

Both the variety of stores and the design of individual stores make the mall, born in modernity, an equally postmodern phenomenon. Gabriel and Lang comment:

> The reassuring quality of its anchor supermarket at one end, the familiar array of boutiques next to the intriguing shop selling Peruvian parrots and Colombian hammocks, the bars, the restaurants, the soft background music, the discreet lighting, the comfortable climatization, the instantly meaningful signs – this is a synthetic oasis, and none the less stimulating for being designed with people like you in mind. It is a clean, genial, graffiti-free space, where a cultural oxymoron can be acted out, [with] relaxed exploration. There are no worries here, no pushy salesman, no invisible pickpockets, goods have fixed price-tags and are covered by the Trades Description Act; if you run short of cash, plastic money is welcome. To be sure, this is a fantasy world; it brings exotica to the consumer instead of taking the consumer to the exotica.[21]

If Gabriel and Lang give the macro view, Farrell homes in on the Rainforest Café for the micro. It is, he says, Disney's Jungle Cruise as a dining experience, with the appeal to sight, sound, smell, touch and taste.[22] 'It is virtual tourism, a postmodern pilgrimage, a way of going everywhere without going anywhere, except, of course, to the mall.'[23] But like all consumerism, modern and postmodern, the mall is, says Farrell, the place where we let other people know who we are; 'at the mall, we're often just looking at ourselves by looking at commodities'.[24]

David Lyon asked the searching question: 'The dazzling displays of the shopping malls and TV ads may seem to offer a consumer cornu-

---

19 Farrell, *One Nation*, p. 265.
20 Farrell, *One Nation*, p. 266.
21 Gabriel and Lang, *The Unmanageable Consumer*, pp. 68–9.
22 Farrell, *One Nation*, pp. 238–9.
23 Farrell, *One Nation*, p. 235.
24 Farrell, *One Nation*, p. 144.

copia, but shall "we" henceforth discover our identity and integration in the market-place alone?'[25] One hopes the answer is no, because the gospel is concerned with humanity discovering its identity in God (*imago Dei*) and its integration into the koinonia of the Trinity. The Church, too, is in a marketplace, selling not just the good (God-like) life, but also the good society, and the fulfilment of desire.[26] It too attempts to woo the consumer, and the main commodity it offers is worship. But how does, or how might, postmodernity and the present generation that was born into a postmodern world impinge on the commodity of worship?

THE PRESENT SPIRITUAL CLIMATE AND GENERATION Y

At one point John Drane writes, 'the church as we know it is in decline. On the other [hand], there is the equally incontrovertible fact that we live in a time when the overt search for spiritual meaning has never been more intense than it is now.'[27] What Drane says here needs to be qualified. First, there are differences across the globe and across religions. While urbanization seems to go hand in hand with religious decline, clearly Islamic cities, however westernized, still give the appearance of a solid monolithic Islamic spirituality that is alive and well. In Africa and South America, Christianity is expanding rapidly. This contrasts with Europe, where religion is in retreat; however, in spite of all the talk of separation of Church and State, America remains quite religious, though here too there has been a decline since the 1960s. Yet, so many sociologists argue, if organized religion seems in decline, interest in spirituality is a growth industry. Here care has to be taken as to what the term 'spirituality' actually means. It has become an 'in' word, and covers everything from different moral and ethical codes to a diverse range of esoteric, sometimes occult, practices influenced by Eastern religions and New Age movements. Researchers point to the interest in films and books concerning ghosts, the supernatural, angels and miracles. However, since much of this is produced for entertainment (and consumption) it is sometimes difficult to separate the entertainment value

---

25 Lyon, *Postmodernity*, p. 92.
26 See Vincent J. Miller, *Consuming Religion: Christian Faith and Practice in a Consumer Culture* (Continuum, London and New York, 2005).
27 Drane, *The McDonaldization of the Church*, p. 65.

and interest from belief and conviction. A study undertaken by Heelas and Woodhead in Kendal, England, considered not only churchgoing in all the denominations represented (most of which are in decline) but also the para-spiritual activities, from mediums to aromatherapy, Wicca and astrology.[28] The findings of that study suggest an upsurge in what they termed 'spirituality'. Their definition was broad, and as subsequent studies have noted, they did not highlight the statistical fact that many patrons of New Age-type material happened to be women in their forties and fifties, or that there was less interest by young people. This raises the question of whether or not postmodernism is friendly to religion and spirituality, and more particularly, is the postmodern generation – Gen Y – open to spiritual things?

According to Karl Mannheim,

a 'generation' refers to a group of people who experience and respond to specific socio-historical conditions in common ways, depending in part on age. In other words, people growing up, living through and responding to particular historical events, political structures, dominant ideologies and technical developments together form a generation with a shared world view that distinguishes them from other generations.[29]

Sociologists and cultural analysts tend to identify the following generations:

- the World War Generation, born between 1901 and 1924 (not many alive now)
- the Builder or Silent Generation, born 1925–45
- The Boomer Generation, born 1946–63
- Generation X, born 1964–81
- Generation Y, born 1982–present (but perhaps we are already into a Gen Z).[30]

---

28 Paul Heelas and Linda Woodhead et al., *The Spiritual Revolution: Why Religion is Giving Way to Spirituality* (Blackwell, Oxford, 2005).
29 Karl Mannheim, 'The Problem of Generations' in *Essays on the Sociology of Knowledge*, cited in Sara Savage et al., *Making Sense of Generation Y: The World View of 15–25-year-olds* (Church House Publishing, London, 2006), pp. 5ff.
30 Mannheim, 'The Problem of Generations', pp. 5–7.

Given that Gen Y is supposed to be postmodern, and open to stories and images, and less concerned with rationalism, are they more spiritual than Boomers and Gen Xers?

We have to distinguish between the USA and the UK, and here I refer to two studies, that of Sara Savage et al., previously cited, and Lyn Schofield Clark's *From Angels to Aliens: Teenagers, the Media and the Supernatural*.[31] The UK study suggests that belief in God is an optional matter, a consumer choice. If belief works, fine, if not, drop it. The supernatural, from Harry Potter to *Lord of the Rings* and TV sci-fi, suggests that it is valued for its entertainment worth. Young people use videos and DVDs to create meaning in their own lives. Films and soaps are a means of escaping into another world, and anticipating what the storyline may be. Valued are the qualities of strength of character, authenticity and good looks. Music plays a big part in their lives, but it is generally chosen to reflect what they already feel. It reflects rather than informs their attitudes, and it provides a comforting backdrop rather than a demanding presence. Important are:

- Consumerism. This is the first 100 per cent consumer generation. We are what we buy. At the heart is choice, as its emblem and core value.
- Electronic media. This generation has seen the move from book to screen.
- Globalization, and the collapse of time and space through the internet.

The research confirmed that conservative churches, particularly those that embrace charismatic spirituality, that engage the emotions as well as the rational mind, seem to have more appeal to young people than those of a more liberal and non-charismatic persuasion. However, overall young people in the UK show a great deal of fuzziness and uncertainty concerning traditional Christian beliefs. The research concluded that there was no evidence to suggest that Gen Y in the UK is a generation of spiritual seekers. This latest report does part company with some earlier reports, and perhaps what the cumulative evidence suggests is that while Gen Y is not *per se* a generation of spiritual seekers, the postmodern

---

31 Lyn Schofield Clark, *From Angels to Aliens: Teenagers, the Media and the Supernatural* (Oxford University Press, New York, 2003).

culture itself allows more openness to spirituality, and consequently young people themselves may be more open to spirituality.

The US study is one person's study, and utilized a much smaller sample of selected persons. Schofield Clark noted the supernatural in popular TV programmes, citing *Buffy the Vampire Slayer* as a good example of a postmodern production. She also notes *Smallville*, *Charmed*, *Roswell* and *The Matrix*, which all illustrate the interest in the supernatural.[32] Schofield Clark grouped the young people she interviewed as follows:

- The 'Resisters', who love supernatural legends but hate organized religion.
- The 'Mystical' teens, who blurred the boundaries between religions and fictional legends. They remain believers of a sort, and are intrigued by the realm beyond the material world.
- The 'Experimenters', who appreciate both religion and the legends of the supernatural.
- The 'Traditionalists', who affirm the boundary between religion and the media.
- The 'Intrigued' teens who wish to separate religion and legend, but have difficulty doing so.[33]

The conclusion was that young people often know precious little about the traditions of religion. This conclusion is reinforced by the analysis of Robert Wuthnow and a survey by David Kinnaman and Gabe Lyons.[34]

So what is the value of these studies? We live in a postmodern culture, which in theory is less rationalistic and more open to faith claims; but the culture is neutral, and has inherited the anti-religious bias of modernity. Thus, although in theory young people should be more open to religion than Boomers and Gen X, in fact many do not have the knowledge or experience to be more open to spirituality and faith.

---

32 Schofield Clark, *From Angels to Aliens*, p. 69.
33 Schofield Clark, *From Angels to Aliens*, *passim*.
34 Robert Wuthnow, *After the Baby Boomers: How Twenty- and Thirty-Somethings are Shaping the Future of American Religion* (Princeton University Press, Princeton NJ, 2007). David Kinnaman and Gabe Lyons, *UnChristian: What a New Generation Really Thinks about Christianity . . . and Why It Matters* (Baker Books, Grand Rapids MI, 2007). See also Ken Ham and Britt Beemer, with Todd Hillard, *Already Gone: Why Your Kids Will Quit Church and What You Can Do to Stop It* (Master Books, Green Forest AR, 2009); Christian Piatt and Amy Piatt, *MySpace to Sacred Space: God for a New Generation* (Chalice Press, St Louis MO, 2007).

THE WORSHIP MALL

It is this context in which the invitation is made to look at the worship mall. Robert Wuthnow writes:

> Young adults are no longer born into faith communities that embrace them fully and command their allegiance over a lifetime. It becomes necessary to shop for a place of worship, rather than simply inheriting the congregation in which a person is raised.[35]

If people 'shop' for worship, the trends in contemporary worship can be described as a 'worship mall' on at least two accounts. First, religion is in competition with all the leisure and entertainment industries, and consumerism is both leisure and entertainment. The mall is open on Sundays and competes with the Church, and people have to make a choice. Consumerism promises desire and satisfaction. Faith offers satisfaction through desire for the Other. And we only need to remind ourselves of the mall's liturgical calendar which is a parody of the Church's liturgical calendar.

Second, the very fact that there are different trends in contemporary worship suggests that worship styles too represent a mall, offered by different churches to suit your personal taste or spirituality, all enticing in different ways, and in competition with one another. Who are they for? Who do they appeal to? Are they postmodern, or expressions of modernity? What is in them that might appeal to Gen Y? Are they worship, or something other than worship? Is current Roman Catholic rethinking of Vatican II really postmodern, or is it something else? Why is there great interest in Celtic spirituality and Celtic worship? Is it really Celtic, or is it like Disney – a simulacrum? What about blended services and alt.worship – are these just bricolage, or is bricolage OK? Is emergent worship really postmodern? Saddleback Church, Willow Creek and other megachurches appeal to the corporate achiever and to Boomers, but do they sell out to the culture, and are they survivals from modernity masquerading in postmodern disguise? And in the many praise and worship services, do contemporary music styles make the service postmodern? Where do snake-handling sects in Appalachia and the Amish fit in to the new high-tech world of the internet? The chapters that

---

35 Wuthnow, *After the Baby Boomers*, p. 124.

follow are an invitation to walk through the worship mall and look around at some of what is on offer in the postmodern global culture. Unlike the real mall, though, apart from the purchase of this book, you shouldn't need your credit card.

Chapter 1

Blended, fusion or synthesis worship

Exactly what may or may not constitute this form of contemporary worship is difficult to define with any precision. According to the late Robert Webber, he and Chuck Fromm, the CEO of Maranatha! Music, first coined the term 'blended' worship in 1987, and the style was initiated at a conference they subsequently organized at Irvine, California. They had discussed the idea that if traditional and contemporary (praise and worship music) styles of worship represented thesis and antithesis, the likelihood was that a synthesis between the two would occur – and so 'blended' worship was born.[1] In response to Robert Webber, Sally Morgenthaler was of the opinion that the term 'blended' was too tame, and indicated that 'fusion' would be a better term. Synthesis is also appropriate; however, these terms themselves beg the question of what is being blended, fused or synthesized.

In an earlier book Webber had set out in more detail what he meant by 'blended' worship, and how it might be achieved. The subtitle, 'The Creative Mixture of Old and New', provided a clue.[2] Webber had migrated from an evangelical background to the Episcopal Church, though he never entirely abandoned his original constituency, and it was to the American evangelical constituency that he addressed much of his writings. He was convinced that in a postmodern culture, the older Billy Graham model was no longer working, and that the younger evangelicals (Gen Y) wanted something more traditional and more deeply mystical in worship.[3] His view was that the classical structures of

---

1 Robert Webber, 'Blended Worship' in Paul A. Basden (ed.), *Exploring the Worship Spectrum: 6 Views* (Zondervan, Grand Rapids MI, 2004), pp. 175–91, pp. 178–9.
2 Robert Webber, *Planning Blended Worship: The Creative Mixture of Old and New* (Abingdon Press, Nashville TN, 1998).
3 Robert Webber, *The Younger Evangelicals: Facing the Challenges of the New World* (Baker Books, Grand Rapids MI, 2002).

the eucharistic liturgy which had been reappropriated by the Liturgical Movement, and typified in the Episcopal Book of Common Prayer, were more appealing than revival style worship. He identified the ritual as a journey, moving from Gathering, to Word, to Thanksgiving, and on to Dismissal or Sending. Traditional or classical worship had the Trinity as its object of worship, and combined the language of mystery (Father) with the languages of story (Son) and symbol (Spirit). These needed to be blended carefully with contemporary praise and worship music, which, when used properly, also conveys a journey through the gates of the Temple, to the outer courts, inner courts and into the Holy of Holies. Webber gives an example of a blended act of gathering:

Gathering Songs

Entrance Hymn with Procession	The experience of coming before God
Greeting, Call to Worship, and Invocation	
. . .	
Songs of Praise and Worship	The experience of God's transcendence
. . .	
Confession and Forgiveness	The experience of God's forgiveness and relationship
. . .	
Opening Prayer	Transition to the Word.[4]

Examples of Gathering Songs include 'God is Here' (Fred Pratt Green), 'King of the nations' (Graham Kendrick), 'We Bring the Sacrifice of Praise' (Kirk Dearman) and 'Lord, I Lift Your Name on High' (Rick Founds).[5] Entrance Hymns might range from 'Praise to the Lord, the Almighty' (Joachim Neander), to 'The Lord is Present' (Gail Cole), and 'Make Way' (Graham Kendrick). The Call to Worship might be divided between leader, people and all together, and might be presented with an

---

4 Webber, *Planning Blended Worship*, p. 60.
5 Webber, *Planning Blended Worship*, p. 66.

overhead projector.[6] The confession of sin may be said, but may be followed by a song of lament ('Purify my heart', Jeff Nelson).[7]

Webber was very critical of the idea that blended worship was simply singing hymns and choruses, and not a seriously planned amalgamation of two styles of liturgical journeys. However, ultimately what he put forward as blended worship appears to many to be a Eucharist of the classical shape, interwoven with hymns or choruses which are sung to contemporary music styles. Sally Morgenthaler, who was concerned to explain 'emergent worship', noted that postmodern culture likes pastiche, and emphasizes panchronicity and pangeography, and might prefer a less linear model to the one proposed by Webber.[8] Her suggestion of 'fusion' might suggest more flexibility and much wider music resources than Webber envisaged. The question might be asked, for example, is a folk Mass a blended service? How far does the music determine whether a rite is blended or not? These are not easy questions to answer, and it is difficult to draw hard and fast delineations. I would suggest that a 'fusion' or 'synthesis' service might be one where music and prayer texts are carefully woven to appeal to the contemporary spiritual desire of openness, without surrendering the deep structures of the liturgical tradition. This can best be illustrated by the following examples of what I would describe as blended, fusion or synthesis worship.

THE FINNISH LUTHERAN THOMAS MASS

This service was first celebrated in April 1988 in the Mikael Agricola Church, Helsinki, which has subsequently been the home of this rite, where in the winter months it is celebrated every Sunday, in the evening. It is also celebrated monthly in other major towns – but it is an urban rite, and has not been successful in rural areas. Juha Kauppinen explains:

> In comparison with traditional church services, the St Thomas Mass places a particular emphasis on prayer and music. Whereas the aim has been to modernize the language of prayer and music, they nevertheless reflect the ancient traditions of the Christian Church. Every mass includes the celebration of the Eucharist, as

6 Webber, *Planning Blended Worship*, p. 69.
7 Webber, *Planning Blended Worship*, p. 75.
8 Sally Morgenthaler, 'An Emerging Worship Response' in Paul Basden (ed.), *Exploring the Worship Spectrum* (Zondervan, Grand Rapids MI, 2004), pp. 208–13, p. 212.

well as an opportunity for confession and anointing with oil. The sermon is not as central as in a traditional service. The mass is also significantly longer than a traditional service: it may last approximately two hours.[9]

The Thomas Mass is named after doubting Thomas, and is aimed at lapsed communicants; a high percentage of Finns are confirmed in the Evangelical Lutheran Church of Finland, but only a small percentage regularly attend church. This rite was aimed at attracting those aged between 25 and 40. It takes the form of a traditional Lutheran Mass, slightly reordered, with informal additions and contemporary music from many sources, including Taizé, South Africa and the Finnish mission areas, as well as Finnish folk music. Preparation is undertaken by between 20 and 40 laity, who take part in the processions in and out, all carrying candles. On the occasion I attended this service, about 12 clergy also participated. After the choir and band had sung and played 'warm-up' music, there was a robust introit, during which the lay planners and clergy processed in carrying candles, preceded by a large Taizé cross. After the celebrant prayed the traditional *confiteor*, the choir responded with a dignified Kyrie. Then two lay people in turn led a more informal confessional, each time responded to by the choir singing the Kyrie. After this came the time of prayer, counselling, confession and anointing. People left their pews and went to side altars or side prayer tables (which were furnished with a cross or an icon, and candles). There they wrote down prayers which they placed in baskets – or they filed up to the communion rail for counselling and anointing. Meanwhile the choir and band sang and played appropriate meditative music. That part of the service may last up to 20 minutes. At a particular point, those in charge of the side altars brought the baskets with the written prayers to the centre where, from a microphone, a selection of those prayers was read aloud, and after each reading the choir sang a response. The unread petitions were placed into one container and taken up to the altar. Lections followed and an informal sermon was given. The Eucharist followed, with robust music for the Sanctus, and a more restrained Agnus Dei. Usual attendance in Helsinki is between 700 and 1,300.

Because of the high degree of lay planning and the use of live, professional musicians, this is very much an urban rite, and those who attend

---

9 Juha Kauppinen, *The St Thomas Mass: Case Study of an Urban Church Service*, Publication no. 43 (Research Institute of the Lutheran Church in Finland, Tampere, 1992), p. 6.

are mainly middle class.[10] A survey discovered the importance of music in the celebration:

> Many of those who attended the mass pointed out that the songs did not have the function of linking different parts of the mass together. They were experienced as significant and independent parts of the mass. The songs had the nature of preaching, prayer, and meditation. This was a new experience for many.[11]

This rite is very much 'blended' or 'fusion'. Formal Lutheran mass prayers are juxtaposed with colloquial, informal, personal prayers and petitions. There is great lay participation at every stage, though many clergy are also involved. The music is global, and the use of candles and icons provides a meditative atmosphere. The overall service is colourful and filled with sound and movement.

THE U2 EUCHARIST/U2CHARIST

The appropriateness of rock music in Christian worship continues to engender very different responses. John Blanchard and Dan Lucarini stress the negative associations of this music genre – drugs, sexual immorality, concern with the occult, and an anti-Christian stance. They argue that rock music in worship encourages worldliness, self-promotion, is purely entertainment, dilutes holiness, and widens the generation gap in church, and therefore needs to be kept out of the Church.[12] However, Mark Joseph draws attention to a whole number of singers and bands who, rather than being consciously 'Christian bands', inhabiting a Christian subculture, have preferred to compete in the secular market and marry lyrics reflecting a Christian world-view with rock music.[13] Such bands as Creed, Jars of Clay, and Delirious? do not withdraw from contemporary culture, but live, move and have their faith commitment within it. One of the most prominent and successful of such bands is U2. Using their lyrics and music, the 'U2 Eucharist' or 'U2charist' has evolved. This is not simply a blending of liturgical rite

10 Kauppinen, *The St Thomas Mass*, p. 12.
11 Kauppinen, *The St Thomas Mass*, p. 35.
12 John Blanchard and Dan Lucarini, *Can We Rock the Gospel? Rock Music's Impact on Worship and Evangelism* (Evangelical Press, Darlington, 2006).
13 Mark Joseph, *Faith, God and Rock + Roll, from Bono to Jars of Clay: How People of Faith are Transforming American Popular Music* (Baker Books, Grand Rapids MI, 2003).

with any rock music or with rock songs as per the Webber model; it quite specifically blends the more overtly Christian lyrics and social challenges of this particular band with the traditional liturgy. Beth Maynard points out that U2

> are simply artists who find it natural to draw on Biblical imagery and raise religious issues in their work . . . They wrestle with spiritual themes and set nuggets of Scripture in the midst of their work, but they compete in the marketplace rather than preach to the choir.[14]

For example, '40' from the 1983 album *War* is named after its inspiration, Psalm 40, and has a refrain from Psalm 6.

The band is Irish, and Bono (Bonovox, Paul Hewson) came from a mixed Catholic/Church of Ireland marriage. He, together with The Edge (David Evans), and Larry Mullen, found faith with Shalom, a non-denominational charismatic community, but after their initial success, members of Shalom suggested that their vocation was to give up rock music. The band decided instead to leave Shalom, and take their Christian commitment to the world. The fourth member of the band, Adam Clayton, came much later to endorse Christian values. Bono wrote an introduction to the publication of the Psalms from the version of Eugene H. Peterson.[15] He has also been the spokesperson, and most vocal member, about the convictions and messages found in the lyrics. Commenting on U2's 2001 Elevation tour to *Rolling Stone* magazine, Bono said:

> It feels like there's a blessing on the band right now. People are saying they're feeling shivers – well, the band is as well. And I don't know what that is, but it feels like God walking through the room, and it feels like a blessing, and in the end, music is a kind of sacrament; it's not just about airplay or chart positions.[16]

---

14 Beth Maynard, 'A Brief History of U2 for Novices' in Raewynne J. Whiteley and Beth Maynard (eds), *Get Up Off Your Knees: Preaching the U2 Catalog* (Cowley Publications, Cambridge MA, 2003), pp. 167–76, p. 167.

15 See Eugene H. Peterson, *The Message//Remix: The Bible in Contemporary Language* (NavPress Publishing, Colorado Springs, 2003). Those used to other versions of the Bible may miss the biblical inspiration of many of the lyrics in the U2 songs.

16 Cited in Steve Stockman, *Walk On: The Spiritual Journey of U2* (Relevant Books, Orlando, 2005), pp. xi–xii.

The scriptural allusions and reflections in this band's songs may be illustrated by reference to just a few:

- 'Peace on Earth' – which mentions heaven being needed on earth now, and how the singer is sick of hanging around waiting for it.
- 'Grace' – which plays with the word as a girl's name, and also something that changed the world, and which makes beauty out of things that are ugly, and which hurt and sting.
- 'Gloria' – which is about trying to sing and finding wholeness in 'you', and includes the Latin words Domine, Exultate as well as Gloria.

Christian Scharen has commented:

> A glance down the list of scriptural quotes and allusions in songs from 'I Will Follow' to 'Grace' makes clear that although U2 is deeply shaped by the world of scripture, they also commonly use scripture in such a way that their songs are iconic, pointing toward deeper things, toward the soul, rather than speaking directly and simply about issues of faith as so much of contemporary Christian music does.[17]

However, it is important also to add that U2 has remained outside any particular church, and is suspicious of organized religion. The band's collective spirituality has found concrete expression in their work for AIDS and relief of debt in the Global South. They see the gospel as blossoming in peacemaking and justice, and thus their songs have a social message too; as Trenton Merricks commented, many of the songs 'shove the problem of evil right in your face'.[18] And it has been argued that the poetry of the songs reflects the postmodern condition.[19]

---

17 Christian Scharen, *One Step Closer: Why U2 Matters to Those Seeking God* (Brazos Press, Grand Rapids MI, 2006), p. 26.
18 Trenton Merricks, 'U2 and the Problem of Evil' in Mark A. Wrathall (ed.), *U2 and Philosophy: How to Decipher an Atomic Band* (Open Court, Chicago IL, 2006), pp. 99–108, p. 101.
19 Iain Thomson, 'Even Better than the Real Thing? Postmodernity, the Triumph of the Simulacra, and U2' in Wrathall (ed.), *U2 and Philosophy*, pp. 73–95.

A U2 Eucharist utilizes the lyrics and music (and often the actual recordings) of U2 in the context of a traditional eucharistic liturgy, usually aimed at youth, but because of the widespread popularity of the band, actually being 'all-age' worship. U2 gives permission for the use of its music on the understanding that all offerings go to relief of poverty. Although not claiming to have invented the U2 Eucharist, Paige Blair, a priest of the Episcopal Church USA, in the diocese of Maine, has certainly pioneered and developed it, and has been a consultant in sharing the 'how to do it' with many other churches, both Episcopal and non-Episcopal. Paige Blair held her first U2 Eucharist at St George's Church, York Harbor, Maine on 31 July 2005. She has explained her pioneering work thus:

> The background in brief: my parishioners and I noticed that U2 was popping up in conversation at the church in many different settings – adult education classes, meetings, coffee hour – and we kept finding ourselves talking about how U2 had been important on our spiritual journeys. I had just read *Get Up off Your Knees* , a collection of sermons based on U2 lyrics, and floated the idea of a service in which all the music, from hymns to 'service music' (like the Gloria or Kyrie) would be by U2, and a number of parishioners in different generations were really excited. So we built a team to design the liturgy and choose the music, and to ask questions like, 'How do we get the sound loud enough?' and 'How do we play the music?' A DJ? A CD? Powerpoint? We chose powerpoint since we figured we'd want the lyrics visible and for people to be hands-free for dancing and clapping if possible. Powerpoint slides with the lyrics of the music and also the rest of the service on them, coordinated with the playing of the music, has been the best tool to allow full participation from the audience. We have provided a paper bulletin with the same information as the powerpoint slides.[20]

Blair adds:

> By February 2006, we had done three such services, the last of these being a baptism U2 service – it was incredibly moving. In March

---

20 Paige Blair, 'What is a U2 Eucharist (or U2charist) as celebrated at St. George's Episcopal Church' at <http://s3.amazonaws.com/dfc_attachments/public/documents/414/What_is_a_U2charist.pdf>.

2006 we began 'taking the service on the road' to other churches that had heard about our U2charist service and wanted us to bring it to them (such as the service in Providence, Rhode Island). We did two in March and four in May 2006, and the summer and fall of 2006 are looking busy. The liturgy itself is pretty traditional – it has all the usual required elements: A Gospel reading, prayers, and communion from an authorized prayer book. The music is really what is different. And yet not so different. It is rock, but it is deeply and overtly spiritual.[21]

A sample outline for a U2 Eucharist suggests:[22]

Preludes: 'Allelluiah', 'Pride' ('In the Name of Love') and 'Where the Streets Have No Name' from *Vertigo 05 Live from Chicago* (African flags at the end of this piece are a powerful lead in to the Millennium Development Goals [MDG] theme of the liturgy).

Opening Hymn: 'Mysterious Ways' (as a hymn to the Spirit this is a particularly appropriate song in the season after Pentecost).

Opening Acclamation, Collect for Purity.

Song of Praise: 'Elevation'.

Collect for the Day, Readings, Sermon.

Sermon Response: 'One'.

Creed, Prayers of the People (addressing the MDG).

Collect after the prayers: '40'.

Confession and Absolution.

Celebration of Absolution: 'When Love Comes to Town'.

The Peace.

Offertory: 'Love and Peace or Else'.

The Great Thanksgiving.

Communion Hymns: 'Yahweh', 'Miracle Drug'.

Post Communion Prayer and Benediction.

---

21 Blair, 'What is a U2 Eucharist'.
22 <http://www.e4gr.org/pray/u2services.html>. (Note: the sample services on this website have since been replaced by a recipe for a U2 service at the following website: <http://www.e4gr.org/u2charists/howto.html>.

Closing Hymn: 'Beautiful Day'.

Dismissal.

Postlude: 'Peace on Earth/Walk On' from *America: Tribute to Heroes* (sends the congregation out on Alleluias).

My own experience of a U2 Eucharist is that there is a large disconnect when the texts of the Episcopal Book of Common Prayer (1979) are followed slavishly – the U2 lyrics cry out for a more flexible and less turgid style of language, perhaps those from *Enriching Our Worship*, or from other sources, such as the Roman Catholic Eucharistic Prayer for Reconciliation, or material from *A New Zealand Prayer Book*.

DUKE ELLINGTON MASS

There is nothing startlingly new about a jazz Mass or even jazz Vespers. Rather like a 'rock Mass', jazz is a musical genre, and again, like rock, it has been regarded with suspicion by some because of its dual origins, partly in African American Spirituals, but equally in secular music of saloons and brothels, and thus 'of the devil'.[23] In defence of its use in worship, Reid Hamilton and Stephen Rush argue that the spiritual and improvizational aesthetic of jazz is a metaphor for the values of creativity, co-operation, and artistic quality that they believe are necessary for meaningful worship, and they provide a range of settings they have used within celebrations of the Episcopal eucharistic liturgy.[24] A special 'high culture' variation of this type of celebration is perhaps the Eucharist celebrated at the Cathedral Church of Saint John the Divine on 5 October 2008 for the feast of St Francis, where the musical accompaniment was by the Paul Winter Consort, a consort that combines classical and world music with jazz.[25] However, whereas Reid and Rush have in mind local churches with willing musicians, the Paul Winter Consort points to a more professional and potentially costly celebration. The Duke Ellington Mass is within this second category, but what it has in common with the U2 Eucharist is that it is not simply a jazz Mass, but quite specifically uses Duke Ellington's Sacred Concerts.

---

23 For the spirituality/sacramentality of jazz, see David Brown, *God and Grace of the Body: Sacrament in Ordinary* (Oxford University Press, Oxford, 2007).

24 Reid Hamilton and Stephen Rush, *Better Get It in Your Soul: What Liturgists Can Learn from Jazz* (Church Publishing Inc., New York, 2008), p. 5.

25 For the Paul Winter Consort, see <http://www.livingmusic.com/biographies/pwconsort.html>.

The Duke Ellington Mass has been celebrated/staged[26] at Durham, Ely and St Paul's, London, Cathedrals, and at Dewsbury. The inspiration for these celebrations came from Bill Hall, a jazz enthusiast who became the full-time Chaplain to the Arts and Recreation in north-east England.[27] Through this ministry, Hall met Will Gaines, a dynamic exponent of be-bop, the high-speed style of tap dancing associated with jazz. Gaines worked with Ellington and his orchestra at a concert in Bristol, which was part of Ellington's Seventieth Birthday Tour. Gaines danced to a piece from Ellington's 1963 show, *My People*, entitled, 'David Danced', suggested by 2 Samuel 6.[28] It was only in the 1980s that Hall realized the significance and possibilities of this, and he began to investigate the place of the Sacred Concerts in Ellington's life. Ellington wrote three Sacred Concerts, 1965, 1968 and 1973, and he claimed that they were the most important things he had ever done. Ellington was indebted to his mother for a deep, biblical faith, and he professed that his education had been threefold – the street, school and the Bible. He wrote:

> My mother started telling me about God when I was very young . . . She was mainly interested in knowing and understanding about God, and she painted the most wonderful word pictures of God. Every Sunday she took me to at least two churches, usually to the Nineteenth Street Baptist, the church of her family, and to John Wesley A.M.E. Zion, my father's family church.[29]

Ellington later said:

> There have been times when I thought I had a glimpse of God. Sometimes, even when my eyes were closed, I saw. Then when I tried to set my eyes – closed or open – back to the same focus, I had no success of course. The unprovable fact is that I believe I

---

26 As will be apparent, the word 'staged' is appropriate in this context.

27 Bill Hall, 'Jazz – Lewd or Ludens?' in Jeff Astley, Timothy Hone and Mark Savage (eds), *Creative Chords: Studies in Music, Theology and Christian Formation* (Gracewing, Leominster, 2000), pp. 194–209. I am indebted to Bill Hall for information, orders of service, and the CD *Duke Ellington: The Durham Connection. Selection from the Sacred Concerts, Stan Tracey Orchestra* (2000).

28 Hall, 'Jazz – Lewd or Ludens?', p. 199.

29 Edward Kennedy Ellington, *Music Is My Mistress* (Da Capo, New York, 1973), pp. 12–14.

have had a glimpse of God many times. I believe because believing is believable, and no one can prove it unbelievable.[30]

The Sacred Concerts, though inspired by the Bible, were not worship but concerts, and were performed as concerts. In the programme of the first Sacred Concert performed in Grace Cathedral in 1965, Ellington wrote:

> As I travel from place to place by car, bus, train, plane . . . taking rhythm to the dancers, harmony to the romantic, melody to the nostalgic, gratitude to the listener . . . receiving praise, applause and handshakes, and at the same time, doing the thing I like to do, I feel that I am most fortunate because I know that God has blessed my timing, without which nothing could have happened – the right time or place or with the right people. The four must converge. Thank God.[31]

He added:

> If a man is troubled, he moans and cries when he worships. When a man feels that that which he enjoys in his life is only because of the grace of God, he rejoices, he sings, and sometimes dances (and so it was with David in spite of his wife's prudishness).[32]

Thus the Sacred Concerts expressed a deep personal Christian faith. The biographer Derek Jewell explained: 'although it was scarcely surprising that the world outside did not suspect the beliefs of the emergent hip entertainer, those who were close to him were always aware of Duke's faith.'[33]

In the light of what he considered to have been a less than successful performance of the third Sacred Concert when performed in St Paul's Cathedral, in 1982, it occurred to Bill Hall that the best setting for pieces from Ellington's Sacred Concerts might be a liturgical eucharistic setting. Will Gaines introduced Hall to Stan Tracey, the jazz pianist, who liked the idea. Peter Baelz, then Dean of Durham Cathedral, gave

---

30 Ellington, *Music Is My Mistress*, p. 260.
31 Ellington, *Music Is My Mistress*, pp. 261–2.
32 Ellington, *Music Is My Mistress*, p. 262.
33 Derek Jewell, *Duke: A Portrait of Duke Ellington* (W. W. Norton & Co. Inc., New York, 1977), p. 26.

full support to the project, though much fundraising had to be undertaken for the venture to come to fruition. Hall notes:

> The musicians engaged by Stan Tracey always read like a who's who of British modern jazz, including both a range of major soloists and some of the foremost section players. The premiere in Durham Cathedral on 6 October 1990 was no exception. With Stan Tracey on piano were saxophonists Peter King, Jamie Talbot, Art Themen, Alan Skidmore, with baritone saxophonist Dave Bishop; trumpeters Guy Barker, Henry Lowther, John Barclay and Alan Downey; trombonists Malcolm Griffeths, Chris Pyne and Geoff Perkins; bassist Dave Green and drummer Clark Tracey. The choir [Durham Cathedral choir] was augmented by jazz vocalist Tina May, who sang some of the solo parts, and of course, Will Gaines was engaged to dance the *David* piece.[34]

As this was to be public worship, no admission charge could be made, though the actual undertaking was quite costly, and relied on grants from a number of sources. The eucharistic liturgy was the texts of the then new rite of the Church of England, *The Alternative Service Book 1980*. Rather like a U2 Eucharist, pieces were chosen to interlock or blend with the liturgy. The order of service for 6 October 1990 began with a rubric explaining, 'Today the orchestra, the soloists and the choir will offer the music and dance and we make the service our own by sharing in that offering.' The Entry was in silence, but the preparation began with 'In the Beginning, God', and after the Opening Greeting and Collect for Purity, 'Ain't but the One', which takes up the theme of the Summary of the Law. The Confession and Absolution were interspersed with 'Will You Be There?', and 'Don't Get Down On Your Knees to Pray Until You Have Forgiven Everyone', followed by 'Father, Forgive'. In place of the Gloria in Excelsis, 'Praise God and Dance' was played, sung and danced. After an appropriate Collect, 'Come Sunday', 'Books of the Old Testament', and 'Books of the New Testament' were sung, and 'Something 'bout Believing' took the place of the Creed. The Communion from the Offertory to Dismissal had far less musical interjection, with 'Come Sunday' as an orchestral piece at the Offertory, followed by 'The Lord's Prayer', and a piano solo meditation. After the Dismissal, 'David Danced Before the Lord' was played and danced. Bill Hall explained:

---

34 Hall, 'Jazz – Lewd or Ludens?', pp. 202–3.

My aim of bringing together jazz and the cathedral choral tradition of music had worked well because of the high quality of each and through mutual respect. It was a triumph both for Stan and for James Lancelot [Master of the cathedral choristers], who by now was very enthusiastic and eager to repeat the experience. Over the next few days, we received very many letters of appreciation . . . When we play jazz, or influence its playing by our receptive listening, we can be tuning in to something very precious and at the very depths of our being. When this takes place in church we can be consciously or unconsciously aware that *homo ludens* is truly made in the image of *Deus ludens*.[35]

The Duke Ellington Mass, therefore, is not simply a jazz Mass, but a careful selection of words and music from Duke Ellington – words and music which he himself thought were divinely inspired, and divine gifts – to which the CD recording testifies. This, too, is a 'blended' worship service, yet what makes it very different from the U2 Eucharist is the demand for a high degree of professionalism on the part of the live musicians and dancers involved, as well as the costs to mount such a venture. Few places, other than a cathedral with financial grants, could mount such an enterprise. But it remains a powerful 'cathedral usage' 'blended' service.

THE HIP-HOP EUCHARIST

Hip-hop is more than just a style of music; it is a culture. It has been described thus:

True Hip-hop is a term that describes the independent collective consciousness of a specific group of inner-city people. Ever growing, it is commonly expressed through such elements as: Breakin' (dance), Emceein' (rap), Graffiti (aerosol art), Deejayin', Beatboxin', Street Fashion, Street Knowledge, and Street Entrepreneurialism. Discovered by Kool DJ Herc in the Bronx, New York around 1972, and established as a community of peace, love, unity, and having fun by Afrika Bambaataa through Zulu Nation

---

35 Hall, 'Jazz – Lewd or Ludens?', pp. 204 and 208, with a reference to Johan Huizinga, *Homo Ludens* (Paladin, London, 1970).

in 1974, Hip-hop is an independent and unique community, an empowering behavior, and an international culture.[36]

Afrika Bambaataa was a disc jockey in the Bronx, and a driving force behind the development of rap music. He was a former gang member, and believed that the arts could be used to combat street violence. Hip-hop culture thus embraces rap music within a wider cultural context. In so far as it has been described as 'postsoul', it is a postmodern subculture which has emerged into the arena of postmodern global culture. Within this music world, MCs and DJs have key roles – particularly the former:

> You can learn a lot about various ethnic and urban street cultures through the emcee. He or she must be knowledgeable of urban street language, style and culture in order to earn the right to be listened to. Hip-hop listeners want to know what's really going on in the street. They want to know who's keeping it real . . . The emcee is telling the listener what's really going on from their perspective, and they are presenting a way of living within urban culture.[37]

The MC has the microphone and chants verses that rhyme, or verses that don't rhyme, but that rhythmically flow from the music. The net result is that hip-hop has its own language and vocabulary.

DJs and MCs have overlapping roles, but the DJ originally mixed the records. A technique developed thereby while one record was spinning and people were dancing, a record on another turntable was used as an instrument to create effects that complemented the beat – 'scratching'. Similarities have been seen between the secular MC and DJ, and the African American preacher and worship leader. The migration of hip-hop into worship services was perhaps inevitable, though with a repudiation of the violence and demeaning of women found in many secular rap songs. One of the first was the Crossover Community Church, Tampa, Florida.[38]

---

36 KRS-ONE, *Ruminations* (Welcome Rain Publishing, New York, 2005), pp. 179–80, cited in Efrem Smith and Phil Jackson, *The Hip-Hop Church: Connecting with the Movement Shaping Our Culture* (InterVarsity Press, Downers Grove IL, 2005), p. 63.
37 Smith and Jackson, *The Hip-Hop Church*, p. 154.
38 Smith and Jackson, *The Hip-Hop Church*, p. 181. See also Melva Wilson Costen, *In Spirit and in Truth: The Music of African American Worship* (Westminster John Knox Press, Louisville KY, 2004), pp. 92–3.

The focus here is the hip-hop Eucharist developed by Timothy Holder (Poppa T), when he was Rector of Trinity Episcopal Church of Morrisania. Timothy Holder explained its origin:

> HipHopEMass is the celebration of the wonder, love and beauty of God*HipHop*. Founded in the Episcopal (Anglican) tradition, HipHopEMass.org was created as an outreach to the children and young people of the South Bronx neighborhood of Trinity Episcopal Church of Morrisania in New York City. HipHopEMass today celebrates hip hop mission in New York, around the country and the world. Led by the rhyme and poetry of MC's and rappers, gospel, blues and soul have become hip hop, a liturgical anthem and backbeat . . . *Hip hop is a culture* that includes much of the culture and context of not only the South Bronx but of constituencies throughout America and the world of the 21st century.[39]

Holder and his team 'translated' the Episcopal eucharistic liturgy into hip-hop language, and celebrated it with rappers singing rap music. Here, then, is a blending of music and language. Recorded and live music began a half-hour before the service as a warm up. An MC and rapper greet the people with acclamations such as 'Amen! Word!' and 'Let us show God some love'. A Hip-hop soliloquy served as an Introit, and the MC proclaimed:

> Calling All the Rappers and Dancers of God!
> In the beginning was the Word
> And the Word was Hip Hop
> And the Word was God
> It don't quit
> And it don't stop.

Or:

> YO! Shout Out to All Peeps of God!
> God is in The House
> (or, 'God is in the Hood').[40]

---

39 Timothy Holder, *The Hip Hop Prayer Book with Holy Bible Stories* (Church Publishing, New York, 2006), pp. xi and xv.

40 Holder, *The Hip Hop Prayer Book*, p. 5.

The Sursum Corda is rendered:

> May the Lord be with you, Holla Back
> MC: Let the People say,
>   May the Spirit watch you and have your back.
>   (Repeat)
> Lift up your hearts to the sky
> MC: Let the People say,
>   We gonna lift them up to the Lord.
>   (Repeat)
> Lift 'em up high
> (Lift 'em up high).[41]

The Sanctus was rendered:

> GOD, You are Awesome
> GOD, You are Awesome
> GOD, You are awesome.
> The whole Universe is totally filled with your Awesomeness.
> HOSANNA! ALLELUIA![42]

A CD entitled *And the Word was HipHop* contains original music from the first two years of the HipHopEMass, with contributions from rappers and musicians from all over North America, for example, 'Unbelievable' by the Remnant, 'God is in the House' by D. Cross and Glory, and 'One Mic, One Life, One Love' by D. O.

The hip-hop Eucharist was designed for use in the heartland of the origin of hip-hop culture – the Bronx. It is certainly a 'blended' service, but is also an expression of a particular subculture. Whereas hip-hop itself has moved onto the global scene, it may be that the hip-hop Eucharist remains firmly a part of the subculture for which it was designed, and therefore it is rendered somewhat less marketable.

---

41 Holder, *The Hip Hop Prayer Book*, p. 9.
42 Holder, *The Hip Hop Prayer Book*, p. 9.

DANCING THE LITURGY: ST GREGORY OF NYSSA, SAN FRANCISCO, CALIFORNIA

An article in *Christian Century* entitled 'Back to the Future: Fourth-century style reaches Bay Area seekers', described the scene half an hour before a Sunday service at St Gregory of Nyssa Episcopal Church, San Francisco:

> In the domed entrance hall a choir is practicing motets. In the rectangular 'synagogue' area, where worshipers' chairs face each other across a long raised platform, the liturgist is rehearsing readers for the service. Worship leaders in brightly colored Liberian vestments hand out spiral-bound songbooks and welcome newcomers.
>
> Visitors are sure to be struck by the visual power of the scene as well. Circling the dome above the altar are vivid representations of saints, not all of them Christian. Gandhi, Malcolm X, Abraham Joshua Heschel, the Buddha and Muhammad are among the figures who form the two-tier line dance, along with Fyodor Dostoevsky and Ella Fitzgerald, Isaiah, Julian of Norwich, Martin Luther, Elizabeth I and Iqbal Hasih, a Pakistani murdered at age 13 for speaking out against child labor. Above the saints, who were painted by Mark Dukes, is a text from St. Gregory: 'The one thing truly worthwhile . . . is becoming God's friend'.
>
> On one wall, below the icon of a dancing Christ, is a framed rubbing of a tablet from a seventh-century Eastern, or Nestorian, church in western China. On the opposite wall, at the entrance to the synagogue area, the lectern is draped in African cloth and surrounded by Ethiopian ceremonial standards. Above the preacher's seat, which is a wide howdah from Thailand (a canopied seat for riding on an elephant), is a floor-to-ceiling icon depicting the marriage of the soul with Christ.[43]

---

43 Trudy Bush, 'Back to the Future: Fourth-century style reaches Bay Area seekers', *Christian Century*, vol. 119, no. 24 (20 November–3 December 2002), pp. 18–22, p. 18.

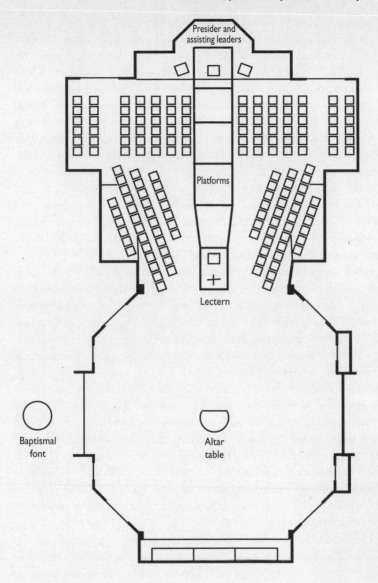

Figure 1: St Gregory's Episcopal Church present floor plan[44]

44 From John Runkle (ed.), *Searching for Sacred Space: Essays on Architecture and Liturgical Design in the Episcopal Church* (Church Publishing Inc., New York, 2002). Used with permission.

St Gregory of Nyssa Church in Woodland Road, San Francisco, is purpose-built (see Figure 1) to house the St Gregory of Nyssa eucharistic liturgy – a stational liturgy which was evolved and developed primarily by Richard Fabian and Donald Schell. Both are former chaplains at Yale University, and Fabian is a long-time member of Societas Liturgicae and the North American Academy of Liturgy. In a booklet on the rite, and dedicated to the memory of the British liturgical scholar Geoffrey Cuming, Rick Fabian has explained the rationale behind this rite. He has attempted to distil the insights from current liturgical scholarship concerning worship in the fourth century, and apply them to a rite that follows the Episcopal outline of worship, but that uses home-spun texts and music. Structurally, it is a traditional Western eucharistic liturgy, but overlaid with eclectic Eastern elements. The vestments worn by clergy and other liturgical ministers are made from material with African tie-dye colouring, and are suggestive of the Ethiopian Orthodox Church, as are the umbrellas and hats of the clergy. At the beginning of the service, congregation and newcomers are introduced to simple dance steps, and then in the processional hymn accompanied by tambourines, bells and cymbals, everyone takes a seat in the 'bema' area. The presiding clergy are seated at one end on a raised platform, and the congregation is seated collegiate style between the platform and the bema or ambo. The readings are followed by a period of silence, which is begun and ended by a gong. The brief sermon becomes a dialogue in which experiences are shared. Following the intercessions the congregation dances down to the entrance rotunda where a small square altar is located, and all stand around the altar for the Eucharistic Prayer and Communion. After the final hymn and blessing (with dance), a time of fellowship begins (coffee-hour). Fabian has explained: 'Our goal was not a "different" or "eastern" liturgy, but a liturgy embodying an authentic Anglican approach, gaining from modern scholarship, open to new material, and yielding experience to serve the whole church.'[45]

The worship is participatory, and inclusivity is important – indeed, the church invites all to communion, whether baptized or not, and hopes that those not baptized will move towards that commitment.[46]

---

45 Richard Fabian (comp.), pamphlet: 'The Book of Common Prayer at St. Gregory's' (1988), p. 2.
46 For communion as a converting ordinance at this church, see Sara Miles, *Take This Bread: A Radical Conversion* (Ballantine Books, New York, 2007). This secular intellectual, lesbian, left-wing journalist tells of her conversion at St Gregory's, and how she came to start the food pantry at this church.

The *Christian Century* article explained:

> For Fabian and Schell, however, St. Gregory is designed with
> American seekers in mind. But whereas most seeker churches
> work with the models of the shopping mall and the television
> audience in designing their space and worship service, Fabian
> likens worship at St. Gregory's to a rock concert, which he calls
> the modern secular experience that most closely resembles the
> divine liturgy. He seeks a worship that is an intense participatory
> experience of movement, singing, dancing and bonding. Schell
> adds another analogy: 'We also follow the model of a dinner party
> in how we welcome people. We ask, "How can we invite people
> in?"'[47]

How is the St Gregory of Nyssa rite to be assessed?[48] The building is
indeed purpose-built to house the choreography of the liturgy – built
with funds from the Fabian family fortune. Few congregations can have
a purpose-built church to house choreography, and few were built to
allow it even with drastic reordering. St Paul's Chapel, New York City,
certainly does not allow the full celebration style of St Gregory of
Nyssa.[49] This liturgy is definitely postmodern, but the claim by
Professor John Baldovin is perhaps a little over-optimistic: 'I have just
had the closest possible experience of what worship was like in the
fourth century.'[50] No fourth-century church would have icons of those
outside the Christian faith, and the Syrian church buildings may have
been modelled on the synagogue for the bema area, but also on an
understanding of the Temple for the sanctuary, with very strict rules of
who took communion. In other words, like all visions, it is highly
selective in what it takes from contemporary scholarship. Its icons of the
famous (who selected these, and excluded others?), its Shinto shrine for
the reserved sacrament, its use of Eastern gongs, its parody of Ethiopian
Orthodoxy, and its liberal West Coast inclusivity, all point to postmodern pastiche or bricolage culture, the 'pick-and-mix', and the religious
mall Eastern style is as much present as a rock concert. It certainly

---

47 Bush, 'Back to the Future', p. 19.
48 A video, 'Dancing with God', explaining the background, and with excerpts from
services, is available from the church.
49 See the photo in Donald Schell, '"Public Work" at Ground Zero', in *Open*, Associated Parishes for Liturgy and Mission (Spring 2008), pp. 3–4.
50 Bush, 'Back to the Future, p. 19.

engages in social justice, in particular through its food pantry, but its eclectic, predominantly white congregation seems to have little evangelistic effect on the nearby African American neighbourhood. The liturgy is, by most 'Anglican' standards, eccentric, and its style is so different from most Anglican worship that other parishes have found it difficult to take much from this rite. It is without doubt 'blended' – but it may be that the music, style of celebration and the texts make it difficult to move out of San Francisco – or, for that matter, out of St Gregory's.

BLENDED HIGH MASS, MARQUAND CHAPEL, YALE DIVINITY SCHOOL

Marquand Chapel at Yale Divinity School, which is an ecumenical divinity school, celebrates the Eucharist each Friday according to particular denominational forms, which vary from week to week, though remaining as ecumenical as possible. I have had the opportunity to celebrate a 'blended' High Mass in the Anglican tradition in Marquand Chapel on several occasions. The chapel itself has been reordered, and has movable chairs to allow complete flexibility. I have opted for a horseshoe shape for the chairs, which was also used in the chapel at Churchill College, before I was chaplain there, and long before Richard Giles made this format popular.[51] With a lectern and chairs for the assistants at one end, and the small square altar at the other, the centre was marked with the processional cross and the acolytes' candles. The cross provided the location for the chanting of the Gospel, as well as a communion station. The clergy and assistants moved from a lectern station to the altar during the offertory hymn. The blending was an attempt to do what Frank Senn has said of postmodern liturgy – that it should seek to enchant rather than entertain.[52] Traditional High Mass vestments were worn, and cross, candles and incense were used. The incense was blessed, and swung gently at the Gospel and during the Eucharistic Prayer, using a thurible of the Eastern Orthodox style –

---

51 Richard Giles, *Re-Pitching the Tent: Re-ordering the Church Building for Worship and Mission in the New Millennium* (Canterbury Press, Norwich, 1997). Churchill College Chapel had this arrangement from the late 1970s under Richard Cain, and then during my chaplaincy there – and it still continues. For the background of Churchill Chapel, see Mark Goldie, *God's Bordello: Storm over a Chapel* (Churchill College, Cambridge, 2007).
52 Frank C. Senn, *Christian Liturgy: Catholic and Evangelical* (Fortress Press, Minneapolis MN, 1997), p. 704.

short chains and bells. The texts were a blending from the Church of England's *Common Worship 2000* and *New Patterns for Worship*, both of which were unconsciously postmodern compilations with old and new, and attempting a richer language than the *Alternative Service Book 1980*. Other non-Anglican sources were also used. The ceremonial was thus a very simplified High Mass, but retaining enough ceremonial to suggest prayerfulness and a serious undertaking. The music was blended in a quite deliberate manner, to move from praise to a more contemplative mood. Thus a praise and worship rendering of 'Come Thou Fount of Every Blessing' was used on one occasion, and 'In Christ Alone' on another. On one occasion a verse from 'Be Still for the Presence of the Lord' was sung before and after the Scripture reading, and the full hymn was sung later, at the Offertory. On all occasions a setting of the Gospel has been used, sung by three women's voices. This particular chant was encountered during an Institute of Sacred Music study tour in Gotland, Sweden, and has been transcribed. My colleague, Professor Margot Fassler, has explained:

> [The] music is simply one way that settings were improvised for reading tones in the Middle Ages. You would have heard music like this, and many other styles of it as well, in any medieval church with two–three singers. It is easy to learn, wonderful for resonant spaces, and musically gorgeous. Of course, that just sounds like a definition of Gregorian chant, the oldest repertory of transcribable music in the entire world. This is one of the many ways that chant was decorated, in this case with polyphony, but they decorated with melismas, with tropes, with prosulae, you name it.[53]

This music is particularly powerful and haunting, as well as making sure women's voices are heard. It is also a reminder that melodic music from the enchanted medieval past can be surprisingly powerful in the re-enchanted postmodern world.

The Offertory has been a transition – on one occasion an *a cappella* solo by a Chinese student singing a haunting hymn from the Song of Songs composed by Xiao Min, a peasant woman from a house church in Henan, China.[54] A challah loaf was usually used, being one loaf, easy

---

53 Email reply to a request for a simple explanation, 2 July 2009.
54 Irene Ai-Ling Sun sang the song. See also Irene Ai-Ling Sun, 'Songs of Canaan: Hymnody of the house-church Christians in China', *Studia Liturgica* 37 (2007), pp. 98–116. A selection of this music is available on CD from <www.chinasoul.org>.

to break, and not leaving a mess. During communion the music has varied from Loreena McKennitt's rendering of the 'Dark Night of the Soul' from St John of the Cross,[55] to other contemplative/meditative music such as Arvo Pärt's 'Beatitudes', and Howells' 'O Pray for the Peace of Jerusalem'. Intentional use was made of short silences. The final hymn tended to be uplifting for the 'sending' back into the world.

In March of 2010 a blended service entitled West meets East was concelebrated.[56] This was a blend of old and new music, as well as Anglican/Western material, with Syrian Orthodox and Maronite elements. A horseshoe arrangement of chairs was combined with collegiate style layout, separated by a space with the cross in the middle, and flanked either side by an icon of the theotokos, and the lectern/pulpit, where the presbyters and deacons sat for the liturgy of the Word. The Introit was the contemporary song by Robert Prizeman, 'I am the Day', the notation reconstructed from the Libera CD with his permission. *Common Worship 2000* invitation to confession, confession and absolution included a ninefold Kyrie, recreated from memory from a setting for St Chad's College, Durham by Professor Arthur Hutchings. Music also included the Gotland Gospel setting, and Professor Elias Kesrouani's setting for the Fraction prayer used in the Maronite rite, of which Church he is a priest. Fr Kesrouani and Revd Care Goodstal-Spinks wore Syrian Orthodox vestments, and this author wore Maronite vestments. The anaphora of St James was used (Syriac version), part of which was chanted in Syriac. Two Anglican deacons quickly mastered the appropriate use of the metal fans or shakers (*marvahtho*) used during the Syrian Orthodox rite. The specially baked bread was stamped with the traditional Syrian Orthodox bread stamp. Again, the purpose was to use traditional and new elements in a service attempting to 'enchant'.

No doubt the examples under the heading 'Blended' could be multiplied many times over. The sampling here tries to explore a variety of ways to accomplish blending or fusion, beyond just the use of a different style of music. This form may be the most useful form for 'traditional' Western churches to develop, since it can be an organic or gradual change, leaving traditional structures and much traditional text in place.

---

55 Loreena McKennitt, 'Dark Night of the Soul', from the CD *The Mask and the Mirror* (Quinlan Road, 1994 and 2004).
56 DVD Yale Institute of Sacred Music, Marquand Eucharist, 26 March 2010.

APPENDIX:
CHANTING THE GOSPEL – THE GOTLAND *ORGANUM*

Gotland *Organum*
Matthew 9.9–13

The_____ ho - ly Gospel of our Lord Je - - -

sus___ Christ,___ ac - cord - ing to the___ E - van - ge - list

Mat - - - - - - thew: As Je - sus___ was walking along, he

saw a man called Matthew sitting at___ the___ tax booth;

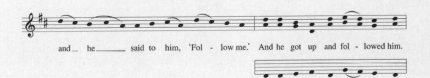

and___ he___ said to him, 'Fol - low me.' And he got up and fol - lowed him.

man - y tax -

And as he sat at din - ner in___ the house,

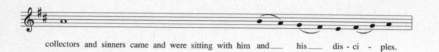

collectors and sinners came and were sitting with him and___ his___ dis - ci - ples.

When the Phar - i - sees saw this, they said to his dis - ci - ples,

Why does your teacher eat with tax-coll - ect - ors and sin - - - ners?'

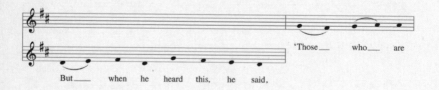

'Those___ who___ are

But___ when he heard this, he said,

Background

A May 2004 Institute of Sacred Music (ISM) study trip to Scandinavia included a memorable 24-hour diversion to Gotland, the Swedish island province best known for its 94 well-preserved medieval churches. The study group timed its arrival to include a visit to the splendid Visby Cathedral, inaugurated in 1225, for Sunday Mass. The cathedral choir sang several works by Swedish composers, none more striking than a simple three-voice *organum* chant setting of the day's Gospel. The chant, based on indigenous fourteenth-century sources, was sung *a cappella* by three choristers, all young women, who stood at the crossing. They were accompanied by a crucifer and torch-bearers. The cathedral choir's music director was kind enough to give the ISM a copy of the chant for use in worship at Yale's Marquand Chapel. ISM musicians have since set it many times for several distinct blended-worship settings and have found its effect undiminished in spite of significant variables such as space, acoustic and vocal resources.

Analysis

The chant's power derives from the clear contours of its tripartite structure and its seemingly ineluctable ascent, repeated *ad libitum*, from monody to three-part *organum*. The first phrase, sung by a mezzo-soprano, hovers around the tonic (D). A soprano begins the second phrase on the subdominant (G) but moves swiftly and insistently to the dominant (A). The third and final voice (a higher soprano) begins an octave higher than the first voice (on D) and then further intensifies the phrase by moving repeatedly both to the dominant (A) and its third degree (C#). All three voices then join for the luminous climactic phrase, sung in parallel, overlapping intervals (thirds, fourths and fifths) and moving decisively toward the affirmative final cadence.

Application

The setting above is the first sung at Marquand Chapel in the fall of 2004. It sets Matthew 9.9–13 to the Gotland chant. Setting the text to this chant tone involved an unusual challenge. The music's great and evident strength – its progressive move, in successive degrees of intensi-fication, toward a radiant finish – can seem, in service to a given Gospel text, overdeterminative or even dissonant. Does every Gospel passage move from timorous opening to decisive close? Of course not. (Consider, for example, the Beatitudes, which could well appear overinterpreted if set in degrees of intensity.) Yet the chant's strong trajectories cannot be ignored.

The first step involved identifying two or three legitimate focal points in the pericope:

(9) As Jesus was walking along, he saw a man called Matthew sitting at the tax booth; and he said to him, 'Follow me.' And he got up and followed him. (10) And as he sat at dinner in the house, many tax-collectors and sinners came and were sitting with him and his disciples. (11) When the Pharisees saw this, they said to his disciples, 'Why does your teacher eat with tax-collectors and sinners?' (12) But when he heard this, he said, 'Those who are well have no need of a physician, but those who are sick. (13) Go and learn what this means, "I desire mercy, not sacrifice." For I have come to call not the righteous but sinners.'

Verse 9 is a beautifully self-contained structure all on its own: Jesus walks along, sees Matthew and calls him; Matthew gets up and follows him. Matthew's bold and unlikely action stands out as a first focal point.

Verses 10–11 begin as scene-setting and intensify as they convey the potent and potentially explosive mix of people Jesus has attracted at dinner. The verses move organically toward a strong second focal point as the scene's radical social dynamic is underscored by the Pharisees' question.

Verses 12–13 lead to the pericope's final and strongest focal point as Jesus answers the Pharisees' question in unambiguous terms, challenging them to act in accordance with their own teachings. His language is deliberately provocative and ends with a bold claim to his own prophetic authority.

With three focal points as structural pillars, the Gospel passage can now be set. Arguing backwards, the *organum* passages are set first; the phrases that precede them are then set *ad libitum*, following the pericope's trajectories as discerned. It's important to note that the setting below reflects only one possible set of choices; a broad range of other choices and textual analyses could also be considered. A chant tone as beautiful and compelling as the Gotland *organum* carries exciting musical and liturgical possibility, as the act of setting passages to its strong contours is an exegetical act, and an act of worship that can bring vivid new dimension to the proclamation and amplification of sacred text.

Alan Murchie

Chapter 2

Consciously postmodern: alt., emerging and liquid worship

What is in a name? Though variously ascribed to Oscar Wilde, George Bernard Shaw and (usually) Winston Churchill, the adage 'Britain and America are two nations divided by a common language' takes on added dimensions with the terms 'alt.worship', 'emerging churches' and 'emerging worship', particularly when they are thrown into the mix with 'fresh expressions', 'deep church' and 'liquid worship'. They do overlap, and at times the boundaries are blurred. What they all have in common is that they are conscious postmodern expressions of Christian life and worship in a largely Western English-speaking culture, from North America and the UK to Australia and New Zealand. The <www.alternativeworship.org> website notes that when that site was first planned in 2001, the term 'emerging church' was not in widespread use. In the UK, Australia and New Zealand, the term 'alt.worship' had for some ten years been the generally recognized name for a consciously postmodern kind of church expression.[1] The website notes that currently, the two terms are used side by side, often interchangeably, to describe this kind of church expression, though it also points out that 'emerging church' at times also signifies a fundamental shift in church organization, and that not all 'emerging churches' will become what has for a decade or more been meant by the term 'alternative worship'.[2] In the USA, 'alternative worship' usually means a service that includes contemporary music – this is quite different from UK and Australian 'alt.worship'. The Emergent-UK website has now become 'Deep Church'.[3] 'Fresh Expressions' is a joint Church of England and

---

1 <http://www.alternativeworship.org/>.
2 For emergent churches in the USA, <http://www.emergentvillage.com/>.
3 <http://www.deepchurch.org.uk/about/>.

Methodist Church venture in the UK to develop new forms of being and doing church.[4] Whereas the more pioneering communities such as Sanctus1 and Moot are regarded as 'emerging churches', many operate out of traditional parishes and have a traditional ecclesiology and create 'emerging worship', and 'liquid worship' might also be found in some of these communities. For the sake of convenience, from this terminological cauldron we shall first discuss 'alt.worship', then 'emerging church' and 'emerging worship', and finally we will turn to 'fresh expressions' and 'liquid worship'. Given that much of this worship depends heavily on visual material, video projection and ambient music, the descriptions of the worship styles provided in this work are somewhat limited in what can be conveyed here.

ALT.WORSHIP: FIRST BEGINNINGS

Even if not the first alt.worship group, the origins of this postmodern expression of Christian faith are often traced to the Nine O'Clock Service (NOS), which itself began at St Thomas, Crookes, in Sheffield. This evangelical congregation, which already had charismatic worship services, had been influenced by the visit of John Wimber of the Vineyard Church in 1985. However, the vicar, Robert Warren, persuaded Chris Brain and some other members of the Nairn Street Community to attend one of Wimber's meetings. Chris Brain emerged as the leader of this community of about 30 people who lived a common life, sharing incomes and discussing religion and the Bible. A former Baptist, Brain began to attend St Luke's Church, Harrogate, which had charismatic worship, and he felt that God had called him to form a rock band, Candescence.[5] He was also influenced by David Watson of St Michael-le-Belfrey, York. Brain and his wife relocated in Crookes, Sheffield, and began attending St Thomas Church. Eventually the band was renamed 'Present Tense' (later just 'Tense') and became the centre and all-absorbing interest of the community, which had begun with Simon Towlson and the Brains in 1978. As it expanded, most of the community ended up working to allow the band to play in concerts, and then in the time-consuming and expensive preparations

---

4 <http://www.freshexpressions.org.uk/index.asp?id=1>.
5 Roland Howard, *The Rise and Fall of the Nine O'Clock Service: A Cult within the Church?* (Mowbray, London, 1996).

for NOS. Based on club culture,[6] and aimed at attracting those in the club culture age group (20s–30s), the Planetary Mass was developed and became popular. Many, including the then Bishop of Sheffield, thought that it might be the future of Church of England worship. Brain was ordained on a fast track, and the community became totally autonomous, with no real link to – and certainly no supervision from – its parent church. The collapse of NOS in a sex scandal in August 1995 led to its demise.

According to Roland Howard, Chris Brain came to reject the evangelical and charismatic styles of worship as being 'too matey' with God, and he wanted to stress the 'otherness' of God. He was reading postmodern texts, and wanted to develop worship that was visual and multimedia rather than centred on reason-based texts. 'Postmodernism was a significant subtext running through NOS's development.'[7] Brain became particularly interested in the theology of Jürgen Moltmann, and also the Catholic 'creation spirituality' exponent, Matthew Fox. NOS took place in the underground rotunda of Ponds Forge sports complex – leased for £35,000 per year. Roland Howard describes the atmosphere:

> A few steps further and into a different world, the world of primeval techno: darkness and druidic white-robed figures around an altar resembling a crescent moon coming out of partial eclipse with the sun, surrounded by a circle of pillars. When one's eyes have adjusted to the ultra violet light, hundreds of black clad figures peer out of the darkness swaying to the swirling, strangely ethereal breaths of ambient techno. The world outside has dissolved into synthesizer and computer-generated mysticism.
>
> A disembodied voice floats on undulating ambient waves of sound. The hypnotic aural ebb and flow carries the hesitant, ponderous amplified voice 'sample' of theologian Thomas Berry. He says: 'One of the issues that we face is understanding the order of magnitude of change that's taking place in our times . . . if we don't get the proper order of magnitude then everything misses the point . . . at this period of the senozoid, the human comes

---

6 See Sarah Thornton, *Club Cultures: Music, Media and Subcultural Capital* (Wesleyan University Press, Hanover and London, 1996).
7 Howard, *Rise and Fall*, p. 27.

after the long period of development, we come at the end, what is now turning out to be *the* end because shortly after humans come to exist on the planet humans begin to terminate the planet. Those waves upon waves of life expansion are now giving way to counterwaves of extinction, wave upon wave of extinction. The rainforests are being extinguished at an acre a second . . . and the rainforest may well be the most beautiful thing on the planet, it may be the most beautiful thing in the universe, and a person has to ask "What are we looking for in life?"' The voice is slowly extinguished and the tempo built up with synthetic snare and bass drum.

The crescendo builds, and the white-robed Revd Chris Brain, techno shaman, moves to the centre and says: 'Hello everyone, welcome to the Nine O'Clock Service at Ponds Forge in the Diocese of Sheffield, and to our Planetary Mass. The Planetary Mass is our weekly celebration of life and our joint ritual of celebration and repentance on behalf of our culture.[8]

The transcript of this service gives an outline of introduction, Thomas Berry quote, welcome (with extracts from Moltmann and Fox), a song ('Let your life come on, let your life come on through me', repeated 14 times), a body prayer with ambient music, and a reading from Deuteronomy announced with sleigh bells. Another song, 'Oh stay with me Jesus', is sung, and then a confession of sins, and song, 'To see what you see'. A very free 'eucharistic prayer' follows, recited by a number of voices over ambient music, and then a 'liturgical prayer'. Another song and a closing prayer with more words quoted from Matthew Fox conclude the service.[9] Chris Brain explained the Planetary Mass thus:

The service is an interpretative symbol for the reality of the worship already happening in creation. The whole universe is invited to an intimate event – the feasting on the cosmic Christ. In a sense, the church has no walls – we worship with and on behalf of plants, planets, animals and angels, celebrating Christ as

---

8 Howard, *Rise and Fall*, pp. 93–4.
9 <http://members.tripod.com/nineoclockservice/wrdser.htm>. This was a transcript from the 1993 BBC World Service broadcast, which I accessed on 11/29/2004; however, this text is no longer available online.

the origin, the Alpha, the source of all creation – the local community in the context of the great cosmic community. Creation, aware of its limitations, straining towards its fulfillment in Christ, sees in him the hope of wholeness and of freedom from sin and decay. Therefore, at the communion table we celebrate not only what is, and what is to come, but also becoming. As Christ is behind the creative explosion started at the Big Bang, and is the lifeforce of nature's continuing rebirth on its journey to fulfillment, we break the bread of the universe and drink the blood of the cosmos, a microcosm of the vast macrocosm.[10]

One attendee made these comments about the experience:

The pace of the music and images rose as attendants brought bread and wine to the table: they also brought money, and asked the courage to share: they brought soil, from which life comes, and they brought a Big Mac, pointedly praying for integrity. Having each taken wafers and wine they walked round the table and then round the circle of pillars increasing speed; some clockwise, some anti clockwise: this was meant to reflect the NOS view of the sacrament as being the epicenter of the big bang *'with ripples of life force spreading out like shock waves'*.[11]

The scandal of Chris Brain's life inside the community, and his sexual abuse of some of the devoted women, has led some to view alt.worship, and all experiments with postmodern worship, as potentially harmful. We should recall, however, that the worthiness of the minister does not affect the validity and efficacy of the worship, and the Sheffield hierarchy was far from blameless in allowing Brain so much autonomy, including his fast-track route to ordination. Many who attended the services found an intense experience of God. According to Paul Roberts,

---

10 Chris Brain, 'The Nine O'Clock Service' in David Gillett and Michael Scott-Joynt (eds), *Treasure in the Field: The Archbishop's Companion for the Decade of Evangelism* (Fount Paperbacks, London, 1993), pp. 163–75, p. 173.
11 <http://members.tripod.com/nineoclockservice/mortn.htm>. This article was accessed on 8/1/2002; however, it appears to be no longer available online.

the contribution of NOS was enormous, brilliant, seminal, God given. Shame it all went so badly wrong. If they had been non-cultic and more open to cooperation with others, alternative worship would be a serious missional force to be reckoned with in the church today.[12]

NOS can be criticized for espousing a questionable theology of Matthew Fox, who was forbidden to teach as a Catholic theologian, and expelled from the Dominicans (though found shelter in the Episcopal Church). However, the main criticism of this worship was the sheer amount of work and cost involved in presenting what is in essence a spectacular theatrical. Howard notes that there were about 15 teams of people working on each service, with some 70 people working from 5.00 a.m. on Sunday morning until 2.00 a.m. Monday morning. He commented:

> It is little wonder that each service cost thousands; what is more remarkable is that the costs were kept so low and that the funds to stage such an event continued for many years. But the costs were kept so low largely because congregation members were prepared to sacrifice massive amounts of time without recompense.[13]

The high cost raises the question of the use of technology in worship, since much consciously postmodern worship envisages the use of technology for visual and musical effect; it is multimedia based. The equipment required is far from cheap, and requires considerable expertise. But this form of worship also assumes a 'techno shaman' or a leadership group who 'plan' – although some might say impose and manipulate – worship for others, allowing the subjectivity of a few to easily dominate.

POST-NOS ALT. WORSHIP

If NOS made alt.worship notorious, Paul Roberts has conversely helped make it academically and pastorally respectable. Himself a

---

12 Cited in Eddie Gibbs and Ryan K. Bolger (eds), *Emerging Churches: Creating Christian Community in Postmodern Cultures* (Baker Academic, Grand Rapids MI, 2005), p. 86.
13 Howard, *Rise and Fall*, p. 96.

monthly practitioner of alt.worship at Trinity Church, Bristol, and a co-host of the <www.alternativeworship.org> website, Roberts has argued (rather like some of the critics of the post-Vatican II liturgies) that the new liturgies prepared in the late twentieth century are thoroughly modern, but inculturation demands developing worship suitable for a postmodern culture.[14] Noting that the cultural era often referred to as postmodern brings to the present generation the full range of fast-changing and radical influences, Roberts believes that the various alt. services offer the Church examples of Christianity inculturated to current technological society, or 'multimedia' society. He explains:

> On the first visit to a service, the main impression is visual. Screens and hanging fabrics, containing a multiplicity of colours, moving and static images continuously dominate the perceptions. There are other things: the type of music, often electronic, whose textures and range seem curiously attuned to the context of worship, smells, the postures adopted by the other worshippers, perhaps also their dress-style and hair. As the mental picture begins to fill up with detail, there is a growing appreciation that considerable technological complexity is sitting alongside simplicity and directness. The rituals – perhaps walking through patterns, tieing (*sic*) a knot, or having one's hands or feet anointed – are introduced with simple, non-fussy directions. The emphasis is on allowing people to do what will help, liberate, and encourage their worship rather than on the orchestration of a great event. The singing is normally simple, direct, chant-like. The structure of the event is not enormously complicated. When something is rather obscure, its purpose is to invite further reflection, perhaps teasing the worshippers to look deeper beyond the surface meaning. There is the occasional ritual joke. In many services, the steady, BPM-adjusted rhythm means that it would be possible on one level to participate merely by dancing. For many of those who stay, they have never before had an experience of Christian

---

14 For example, Paul Roberts, 'Thoroughly modern worship, thoroughly postmodern culture', a paper given at a conference at King's College, London, in December 1996. Also available at <http://alternativeworship.org/paulsblog/?page_id=153>.

worship like it. It is as though they have come to a new place which they instantly recognize as home.[15]

Roberts cites actual examples used:

- Two huge, colourful, slightly abstract banners, hanging from the roof, painted on fabric.
- The construction during the service of a 15-foot-high crucifix from junk taken from a skip . . .
- Slides of cityscapes projected on screens which enclosed the worship space entirely, giving a slightly agoraphobic sensation . . .
- A black and white Super-8 cine loop of cartoons of candles, dancing around the screen.
- An edited and 'looped' sequence of a swinging incense thurible.[16]

He explains that sometimes the music is there to be listened to, and sometimes it is merely for background effect. Alt.worship 'refuses to assign a single presidential role, but uses technology to allow a service to be "steered" using vocal instruction, prayers, slide/video announcements and the use of multiple voices'.[17] In 'congregations that have a connection to club culture, the DJ acts as both provider of music and also master of ceremonies'.[18] Services are normally home-grown, and can be over-didactic and chaotic, although compared to traditional (Anglican) worship, it is more holistic.

Roberts is not a lone voice in arguing for a new style of worship suitable for a postmodern culture. Pete Ward has edited two collections of short articles, with contributions from such exponents as Maggie Dawn, Mike Riddell and Graham Cray.[19] But in terms of practice, here we shall look at Jonny Baker at Grace, associated with St Mary's, Ealing;

15 Paul Roberts, 'Liturgy and Mission in Postmodern Culture: Some reflections arising from "Alternative" services and communities' (1995), <http://seaspray.trinity-bris.ac.uk/~robertsp/papers/lambeth.html>.

16 Paul Roberts, *Alternative Worship in the Church of England*, Grove Worship Book 155 (Grove Books, Cambridge, 1999), p. 5.

17 Roberts, *Alternative Worship*, p. 7.

18 Roberts, *Alternative Worship*, p. 7.

19 Pete Ward (ed.), *Mass Culture: Eucharist and Mission in a Post-modern World* (Bible Reading Fellowship, Oxford, 1999); *The Rite Stuff: Ritual in Contemporary Christian Worship and Mission* (Bible Reading Fellowship, Oxford, 1999). See also Brian and Kevin Draper, *Refreshing Worship* (Bible Reading Fellowship, Oxford, 2000).

Doug Gay, founder of the Late, Late Service of Glasgow, and Simon Rundell, vicar at Gosport and host of Blesséd.

Initiated by Mike Starkey, curate of St Mary's, Ealing, and Mike Rose in 1993, Grace was joined by Jonny Baker and his wife Jenny, and has been a leading UK alt.worship group.[20] Baker, whose experience has been in youth ministry, argues that alt.worship is more than a cosmetic change to the style of church, but really has a different plausibility structure with its own authenticity, since it resonates with both the curators of worship and with the culture outside the church.[21] He notes that popular culture features in a myriad of ways in alternative worship:

> The space itself is likely to be marked out by televisions with looped images and screens with projected still images. These might well include traditional icons but are usually interspersed with images from contemporary culture – for example, a McDonald's sign juxtaposed with a slogan 'fast food' for lent (*sic*); or a looped image of a sped up tube journey to convey the busyness of urban life.[22]

Doing such things reframes the tradition and contextualizes the gospel. Coming out of a more evangelical background, he stresses that alt.worship is both post-charismatic and post-evangelical.[23] Sample services from Grace are available on the website, and the service of November 2007 for example, entitled 'Hospitality Communion', outlined the following: entry into the church where the Grace people are in a circle reciting a mock formal liturgy (a parody about exclusion); the welcome, with the dismantling of the circle, and large bean bags being hurled for sitting in comfort; discussion groups' hospitality sound-bites; song ('Toilet song'!); introduction of visitors from the Netherlands; hospitality soundbites; group discussion; hospitality soundbites; reading/meditation; confession; song ('Table of Christ'); eucharistic prayer; and blessing.

---

20 For the history, see the Grace website, <http://www.freshworship.org/node/424>.
21 Jonny Baker, 'Alternative Worship and the Significance of Popular Culture', <http://www.freshworship.org/node/94>.
22 Baker, 'Alternative Worship'.
23 Jonny Baker and Doug Gay with Jenny Brown, *Alternative Worship: Resources from and for the Emerging Church* (Baker Books, Grand Rapids MI, 2003), pp. 22–3. See also *Grace*, Pocket Liturgies, Proost, <www.proost.co.uk> (2007).

The February 2009 service, 'The Gift', required that the central space be filled with bean bags, and big gift boxes. A cat's cradle of strings ran across columns towards the chancel, and tangled in these were small gifts. The altar had an old-fashioned balance-type scale on it. The theme was introduced, followed by stories about gifts given and received. Good intentions about gifts were examined, followed by a talk about gifts with strings attached. This led into a talk about how God gives, with verses of Scripture being read while rice was poured onto the scales, and a response was said. Then Psalm 50 was read, followed by the Grace remix of Psalm 50. After further clarification on God's gifts, each person came to the table and rice was poured over their hands as a sign of God's generosity. A grain or so was put back into the empty side of the scales as a token of relationship. After the service the rice could be taken away to cook and eat.[24]

The Late, Late Service was a Glasgow enterprise with Doug Gay and Andrew Thornton, which represented a Church of Scotland approach to alt.worship. Music was recorded on the Sticky Music label, and the words of many of the services are still available on Andrew Thornton's website. Gay, now teaching pastoral theology at Trinity College, Glasgow, co-authored a book with Jonny Baker and, one may presume, shares the views expressed there. Of the services online, two have been selected for discussion here. 'Celebrating the Feast' (A Quiet Service) began with 'Holy Space', and had a reading from Isaiah 55.1–2, followed by a responsorial confession. Readings from John 2.1–11 and Luke 14.12–23 were listed, although it is unclear when they were read or how. The service 'A Ritual of Reflection' involved stations with visual images and objects, including some for tasting, while quiet instrumental music played – this was to last 15–20 minutes. An invitation to the Feast centred on four areas where food was set up, and included a meditation lasting 15 minutes. Prayers of intercession were followed by the song 'Our God in Heaven', and a rubric 'We Share the Gifts'.

The Communion Service of 1995 seems to have been designed to follow the postmodern equivalent of a 'Word' service. It opened with a confession of sin, a prayer for new life (followed by 'Bells'), an extended explanation for the sharing of peace, and a eucharistic prayer of the classical shape, with all participating in the reading of the epiclesis which was displayed on the screen. 'Bells' ended this portion of the

---

24 See also *Grace*. Pocket Liturgies.

service, which was followed by rubrical instruction for serving communion.

Simon Rundell comes from the more Catholic wing of the Church of England. Blesséd is the website that describes alt.worship, and explains that it is a travelling service – held from time to time at certain churches. The service is a Eucharist, and its format is perhaps nearer that of 'blended' worship – indicating how much overlap there can be. The Blesséd Liturgy for St John the Baptist, 24 June 2009, was held at St John the Baptist, Winchester. The Gathering and Entrance featured YouTube clips,[25] and then after the trinitarian greeting and salutation, the Opening Introduction of Explanation and Invitation to Metanoia were shown on the screen. A Penitential Rite included a Blesséd video and an activity, which were followed by an absolution. A Gloria, Collect and Word (with more YouTube), the Renewal of Baptismal Vows and a video of a ritual followed, and then the Creed with a 'God Waits' video was shown. There were visual intercessions, followed by the Peace and another video. The offertory was a Litany of Saints, and a Eucharistic Prayer from *Common Worship 2000*. Video clips accompanied the Lord's Prayer, Agnus Dei and distribution of communion. After the Post-communion prayer, another YouTube clip accompanied the Blessing and Dismissal. The end music was 'Polyphonic Spree'.[26]

Simon Rundell kindly supplied me with a DVD of the Blesséd 'In the Light' Eucharist celebrated at St John's, Peckham, on 4 February 2006. In a large hall, with traditionally furnished altar, and many candles, the service used video clips along with special music and lighting in an otherwise dark room. There were many young people present. It was an imaginative Church of England sung Eucharist, though the voice of the celebrating bishop was somewhat more conducive to sleep than to meditation and devotion. Simon Rundell has explained the intention as follows:

Blesséd took something well loved and cherished and gave it a new slant. Nothing within the mass is there without purpose or significance, so a fresh, youth-oriented approach afforded new ways of communicating ancient truths. By maintaining the shape of the liturgy as described by Dom Gregory Dix . . . and at times

---

25 <http://www.youtube.com/watch?v=KFOGeOcgVCs> and <http://www.youtube.com/watch?v=AndLNmeBlrI>.
26 All of the video websites and YouTube clips are printed on the pdf service.

radically reinterpreting it, the whole encounter with God is re-explored, and new nuances and themes develop: eucharistic prayers are mimed, creeds are given a rave feel in a language not spoken by anyone in the audience, the Gloria is tap-danced and the liturgy is shared by all as dough is kneaded, baked and broken across a single act of worship. The end result is something that is at once both familiar and yet very challenging.[27]

Here alt.worship is more integrated with the traditional liturgy than the examples from Grace and the Late, Late Service. However, together these examples illustrate the wide understanding of alt.worship, and the subtitle of Baker and Gay's book illustrates how 'alt.' and 'emerging', for some, become interchangeable terms. This is further illustrated by the most thorough survey and study of 'emerging' churches published so far, namely the work of Gibbs and Bolger.[28] Their study covers alt.worship communities in the UK, as well as consciously emerging churches in the USA. Although the style and type of worship is similar, one particular difference, as noted by Paul Roberts, is that emerging churches are conscious of their ecclesiology, and most have no denominational affiliation, while many UK alt.worship congregations are within a particular denomination (often the Church of England), and exist as a congregation within a congregation.

EMERGING CHURCH AND EMERGING WORSHIP

One of the 'emerging' church pioneers has commented that 'The emergent church defies simple explanation and categorization. It is pluriform and multivocal.'[29] He goes on to say that 'emergent Christians do not have membership or doctrine to hold them together. The glue is the relationship.'[30] According to the survey of Gibbs and Bolger,

---

27 Simon Rundell, 'Blesséd: A sacramental perspective of alternative worship with young people' in Stephen Croft and Ian Mobsby (eds), *Fresh Expressions in the Sacramental Tradition* (Canterbury Press, Norwich, 2009), pp. 132–9, p. 136.

28 Gibbs and Bolger, *Emerging Churches*. See also Frank Emanuel, 'An Incarnational Theology of the Emerging Church', a research paper towards the degree of MTh, Saint Paul University, Ottawa, 2008.

29 Tony Jones, *The New Christians: Dispatches from the Emergent Frontier* (Jossey-Bass, San Francisco CA, 2008), p. 40.

30 Jones, *The New Christians*, p. 56.

'emerging churches' are communities that 'practice the way of Jesus' and encompass three core practices which combine to create six other practices. The three core practices are:

1 Identifying with the life of Jesus.
2 Transforming secular space.
3 Living as community.[31]

Because of these activities the communities:

1 Welcome strangers.
2 Serve with generosity.
3 Participate as producers.
4 Create as created beings.
5 Lead as a body.
6 Take part in spiritual activities.[32]

By this definition, Gen X megachurches and Gen X young adult services do not qualify, nor do purpose-driven churches or Vineyard churches, since they lack some of these nine practices. Inspirations for emerging churches have been the work of N. T. Wright on Jesus; John Howard Yoder on the Church and ethics; and missiologists David Bosch and Lesslie Newbigin. A major catalyst has been the books of emerging church pioneer Brian McLaren (pastor of Cedar Ridge Community Church, Maryland, until 2006). Other influential pioneers include Doug Pagitt (Solomon's Porch, Minneapolis), Tony Jones (national co-ordinator of Emergent Village, a website for emergent churches), Dan Kimball (Vintage Faith Church, Santa Cruz), and, in New Zealand, Mark Pierson (Cityside Baptist, Auckland) and Steve Taylor (Graceway Baptist Church, Ellerslie).[33]

Many of the leading exponents (predominantly white, male Gen Xers) are originally from an evangelical background and, like the history

---

31 Gibbs and Bolger, *Emerging Churches*, p. 43.
32 Gibbs and Bolger, *Emerging Churches*, p. 45.
33 For a recent overview by US emerging church leaders, see Doug Pagitt and Tony Jones (eds), *An Emergent Manifesto of Hope* (Baker Books, Grand Rapids MI, 2007). For a New Zealand and Australian contribution, see Mike Riddell, Mark Pierson and Cathy Kirkpatrick, *The Prodigal Project: Journey into the Emerging Church* (SPCK, London, 2000).

of that movement, continue a quest for cultural relevance. In this case, it is to be relevant to a postmodern culture, and particularly Gen X, the generation to which many belong. This involves an emphasis on an incarnational theology, and encountering God in and through the local secular world – the postmodern world. Having left the purely literary world of modernity, this requires encountering the Holy through the symbolic, iconic and sacramental.[34] Emerging churches are communal churches, not consumer churches – they are local and relational, and as such are usually small. They may meet weekly and during the week, often at different venues, and sometimes they meet for worship once a month. They are a community of welcome, of mutual accountability, and their spirituality is eclectic and corporate. Leadership is open and decentralized – in theory at least. Members may make use of spiritual practices adapted from monasticism – 'walking the labyrinth' is a common devotion. These churches tend to be small communities in which the community plans its own rituals which make sense to its members in the locality in which they are found geographically, as well as in the place the community occupies in its current spiritual pilgrimage. A member of Graceway, New Zealand, explained that she had experienced the community as 'a listening church; a personal church; a relational church; a deep-thinking church; a multimedia church; a living, breathing church; an inclusive, accepting church; an honest, real church'.[35] Although its pioneers believe that this is the form of the future Church, its ecclesiology and theological emphases have not gone unchallenged.[36]

According to Dan Kimball, emerging worship has a number of important elements. There is a move from a spectator type of gathering to community participation; it has an organic design, an organic flow; it is highly visual, making use of home-grown art work, often created as part of the worship service itself. It makes use of older rituals, and therefore uses candles and incense, but uses them in new ways, and creates new rituals. It makes use of videos, projection screens and appro-

---

34 Gibbs and Bolger, *Emerging Churches*, p. 73.

35 Steve Taylor, *The Out of Bounds Church? Learning to Create a Community of Faith in a Culture of Change* (Zondervan, Grand Rapids MI, 2005), p. 85.

36 For example, D. A. Carson, *Becoming Conversant with the Emerging Church: Understanding a Movement and Its Implications* (Zondervan, Grand Rapids MI, 2005); R. Scott Smith, *Truth and the New Kind of Christian: The Emerging Effects of Postmodernism in the Church* (Crossway Books, Wheaton IL, 2005).

priate music.[37] Riddell, Pierson and Kirkpatrick argue that the motifs, symbols, music and language will be meaningful to those worshipping, although they may not be as meaningful for, or understood by, those outside that subculture.[38] Emerging worship is eclectic – all of life and history and experience are in the grab bag; all forms of media are available in worship, which includes slide and video projectors, and all forms of art – visual, fine and performing. 'Everything is considered for possible use in new worship.'[39] How, then, does this work out in practice? Here we will consider accounts of worship from Doug Pagitt's Solomon's Porch Community; Karen Ward's Church of the Apostles, Seattle; and Mark Pierson's Cityside Church, New Zealand.

The Solomon's Porch Community originated in January 2000 in a small second-floor loft space in Linden Hills, Minneapolis. This emerging church was fuelled by a desire to find a new way of life with Jesus, in community with others, that honoured Pagitt's past (youth pastor of a megachurch) and that boldly moved to the future.[40] Pagitt describes what a visitor would encounter having ascended the stairs (the lower level has a lobby, kitchen and art gallery space):

> The door is on the long end of the 4,000-square-foot rectangular room. The walls are multicolored and decorated with paintings, photographs, and sculpture. Tables are covered with candles and communion elements. People expecting rows of folding chairs find instead groupings of couches, chairs, end tables, recliners, and the like arranged in the round with an open center area. The musicians are located across from the door, but not in the center. Projector screens adorn the corners of both long ends of the room so people can see a screen no matter which direction they face. Because we meet in the round, some people are facing the door, and others are looking away from it.[41]

According to Pagitt, the worship is not meant to be a show or a concert, but is designed as an interactive experience. For example, music is a

---

37 Dan Kimball, *Emerging Worship: Creating Worship Gatherings for New Generations* (Zondervan, Grand Rapids MI, 2004), pp. 76ff.
38 Riddell et al., *The Prodigal Project*, p. 79.
39 Riddell et al., *The Prodigal Project*, p. 70.
40 Doug Pagitt and the Solomon's Porch Community, *Reimagining Spiritual Formation: A Week in the Life of an Experimental Church* (Zondervan, Grand Rapids MI, 2003); see also <www.dougpagitt.com>.
41 Pagitt, *Reimagining Spiritual Formation*, p. 49.

distinctive element (they write their own), and people's stories take the place of the old evangelical testimony. Holy Communion is an important practice as well – the elements are set around the room, and the community serves one another. Rejecting modernity's dualism, the community is concerned with body as well as soul, and thus symbolism plays an important part in the community, from making the sign of the cross, to anointing with oil, and even massage as both meditation and prayer.[42]

A service in March 2007 was attended and recorded by Yale Institute of Sacred Music research student, the Revd Lucas Grubbs.[43] The music instrumentation consisted of electric guitars, a drum set, a wide array of percussion instruments, keyboards, microphones and many other instruments. The worship area was strewn with Bibles and theological books, and space was made for children's art. Also spread throughout the worship space were tables set with an abundance of fresh baked bread, ceramic and glass pitchers of wine, and dishes with foods – which served as communion stations. Doug Pagitt spoke about Lent and preparing for Easter, but in very classic evangelical style. The sermon was taken over by a covenant partner (congregant), who was also a massage therapist, and members lined up for a massage and prayer over them during the sermon. Talking seemed to take a great deal of the worship time. Grubbs noted that technology also played a huge part in Solomon's Porch.

Karen Ward is a Lutheran pastor who serves an emerging community, Church of the Apostles (COTA), in a Lutheran and Episcopal partnership. Ward says, 'It was to be a sort of "mission lab", a small, local, fresh expression of church "communitas", grounded in a theology of the Holy Trinity.'[44] It began in 2002 as a house church and morphed into a shop-front mission, operating a non-profit coffee shop, tea bar and performance gallery called 'The Living Room'. When still in that space, Ward described COTA worship as being 'ancient and future.'

---

42 Pagitt, *Reimagining Spiritual Formation*, pp. 79–81.

43 Lucas Michael Grubbs, 'Emerging Church Liturgy: Three examples of postmodern worship', an extended paper (with CD recording) towards the degree of STM, Yale University, March 2008.

44 Karen Ward, 'A Story of Anglimergence: Community, covenant, Eucharist and mission at Church of the Apostles' in Croft and Mobsby (eds), *Fresh Expressions*, pp. 156–61, p. 157.

We Bach and rock. We chant and spin. We emo and alt. We are a CCM-free zone.'[45] She continues:

> We write our own church music and incorporate mainstream music as well – everything from Rachel's to U2, Björk to Moby, Dave Matthews to Coldplay. We have no need to 'Christianize' music. God is sovereign, and the whole world is God's, so any music that is good already belongs to God.
>
> We have DJs and turntables, taggers and spray paint, emcees and poets. We have our own icnonographers. We have a ministry of making our own Anglican prayer beads and cards. We are nu (*sic*) monastics – urban, postmodern monks. Our community is our priory. And since most monasteries have guesthouses as an open door to the world, our store-front is our guesthouse.[46]

In 2006 the community moved across the street into a disused church, now called 'Fremont Abbey'. It is a co-op in that it houses a community arts centre, a community café and a church community (Church of the Apostles). It functions as an anchorite community, and Ward sees it as 'a postmodern, emerging, Anglo-Catholic new monastic community'.[47] The Eucharist is celebrated at 5.00 p.m. on Saturday.

Lucas Grubbs visited and recorded the service on 10 March 2007. The narthex was filled with tables, chairs and couches, and items for sale included rosaries and CDs. During the liturgy a young woman was stationed in the corner of the church painting her own works of art, which she saw as her form of Christian ministry. Of the liturgy planning group, Grubbs comments:

> The Eucharistic portion of the liturgy was presided over by Ward, but the liturgy as a whole was executed by close to a dozen different ministers, each with his or her own job. This was the group that gathered in the sacristy for last minute preparations before the service. All of the liturgical leaders appeared to be in

45 Jennifer Ashley with Mike Bickle, Mark Driscoll, Mike Howerton (eds), *The Relevant Church: A New Vision for Communities of Faith* (Relevant Books, Lake Mary FL, 2004), p. 85.
46 Ashley et al., *The Relevant Church*, p. 85.
47 Croft and Mobsby (eds), *Fresh Expressions*, p. 160; Grubbs, 'Emerging Church Liturgy', p. 24.

their 20s or 30s. All of them had the distinct appearance of being pop-culture savvy and influenced by urban fashion trends, from tattoos to piercings, to thrift store clothing. Clearly, this was no ordinary liturgical planning team.[48]

The theme or title of the service was 'The Midst of Suffering', which focused on the victims of Hurricane Katrina. Music for a prelude came from an MP3, a digital format sound recording, and lent itself to meditation. During this time the community was invited to participate in 'open space', which are areas in the worship space for one's own personal spiritual devotion – akin to 'liquid' worship. Among the various areas provided were space where images were projected on hanging sheets, and an area where participants could write concerns on pieces of paper and post them on a large board. Musical instruments included electric guitars, drums, keyboards, hand instruments and laptop computers. After opening words, the song 'Since I Am So Sick' was sung, and Psalm 63.1–8 was recited by Ward while a group of hand drummers made intense percussion to carry the text. The Gospel was narrated by a community member against background music. Two more songs were followed by the Metalentenstoryverb (= homily!). More 'open space' time and background music followed prior to 'Family Biz' (= notices). An offering was taken, and then a eucharistic prayer (written in house, and rather short as in some Lutheran traditions), and distribution of the elements was accompanied by MP3 music. After an 'Invitation to Community', the benediction was given, followed by a song and the dismissal, though conversation and fellowship continued.

A fuller eucharistic rite is posted on the Anglimergence website, to accompany Ward's recent essay in a collection on UK Fresh Expressions.[49] Based around the structure of Gathering, Open Space, Eucharist and Sending, this rite begins with the YouTube video 'GOOD'; the UN Millennium Declaration, with a narrator giving an explanation; a chant of lament (Psalm 10A) and further narration. The Open Space included a video or photograph montage featuring people in need, with background music. There are eight prayer stations. A bell is rung and people are invited to rinse their hands in the water bowls provided and return to their seats. After more narration (explanation) an extended confession with song is followed by an absolution, 'Psalm

---

48 Grubbs, 'Emerging Church Liturgy', p. 28.
49 Croft and Mobsby (eds), *Fresh Expressions*; see also <www.canterburypress.co.uk>.

drumming' (Psalm 10B), Gospel, prayers of the people introduced with song, and with sung responses, concluding collect and Peace. The offering is followed by the eucharistic prayer – mainly from Prayer B of the ECUSA Book of Common Prayer (1979) (itself a classic expression of modernity and glaringly out of place in a postmodern Eucharist!). Songs, 'Oh Let All Who Thirst, Let Them Come to the Table' and 'You are the Bread of Life', are sung. Sending has a threefold blessing, a closing song and closing words.

Cityside Baptist Church in Auckland, New Zealand, has an older Baptist history, but evolved into an emerging church under Mark Pierson who came as missioner/pastor in 1993, and then pastor in 1995. In the book Pierson co-authored, some idea is given of the use of art, symbols and ritual in this worship. Instead of being a worship leader or planner, the emerging 'leader' becomes 'an artist, a framer, a reframer, a recontextor, a curator of worship'.[50] A context for worship is provided that allows open-endedness, so that the main outcome is that the worshippers have met with God. Here Pierson describes an example of 'good' emerging worship that was prepared for a chapel service in a theological college:

> [W]e chose to empty the chapel of all furniture, black out the windows and line the floor with black polythene. Two tonnes of sand was trucked in and spread over the floor, candles in paper bags set up around the walls and eerie desert-wind sound effects played through the sound system.
>
> People took off their shoes and socks and stood or sat in the 'desert'. The service consisted of four Bible stories of desert experiences, each followed by silence, a repeated a cappella solo and a one-minute 'rant'. As punters left they took phials filled with sand as ongoing reminders of the experience.[51]

Everything is considered for possible use in worship, and multimedia images may be juxtaposed with ancient chants and techno music. The question is raised as to whether or not bread and wine are the only elements acceptable for communion: 'In services I've been involved with we've variously used hamburger buns and large bottles of coke in a

---

50 Riddell et al., *The Prodigal Project*, p. 63.
51 Riddell et al., *The Prodigal Project*, p. 67.

festival setting . . . and New Zealand Chardonnay and Pavlova (a sweet eggs and sugar dessert) during services with a New Zealand theme.'[52] And perhaps most extraordinary for many:

> I took part in a worship service that had road kill (dead opossums and ferrets) on the floor, and where we 'anointed' each other on the forehead with used engine oil. For the rural farming community people who prepared the worship this was entirely appropriate (as were the country and western style songs we sang!).[53]

The website of Mark Pierson's church explains the worship thus:

> We are committed to maximum participation and to the develop-ment of the creativity, gifts and relationship among the community that is Cityside church, so our services generally involve a number of different people leading us in different ways.
>
> Our worship follows a monthly rotating cycle of services, with a theme-based communion service on the first Sunday of the month, and a sequence of service formats on the 2nd, 3rd, and 4th Sundays. Alongside a few repeated liturgical segments, some of the rostered elements in these services include: prayers, confes-sion, singing, meditative worship, storytelling, hot text (biblical, contemporary, or original composition), sermon, and morning tea – but not all of them every week. Where a month has five Sundays, the fifth service will involve some alternative form of gathering – either a free-form service, or an activity outside the building. This will be advertised in advance.
>
> Each person leading a particular segment of worship can do so in whatever form, style, medium, level of creativity that s/he wishes to. Variety is encouraged.[54]

Mark Pierson is no longer at Cityside, but a tradition of emergent worship is continued by Pastor Brenda Rockell, though now more family-oriented. The service on Sunday 16 August 2009 (Brenda

---

52 Riddell et al., *The Prodigal Project*, p. 73.
53 Riddell et al., *The Prodigal Project*, p. 75.
54 See 'services' at <http://www.cityside.org.nz/>. (Note: the wording on the website has since been changed.)

Rockell was away) began with the Aaronic Blessing being beamed on an overhead projector, and the congregation listening to a recording of a sung setting of the text. Psalm 104 was read, and then the words of 'It is Well with My Soul' were projected, and a special recording of the music was listened to, after which all joined in. Then came a period where people could move to various stations to write about affliction on a glass mirror, or participate in centring prayer, or rewrite the hymn 'It is Well', or simply meditate while quiet music played. A male member of the congregation then spoke about a book he had read, and several people gave a testimony about their life that week. After the notices were given, a sermon was offered by a male member of the congregation about loving people, and how to implement various listening techniques so that people feel they've truly been heard. Prayers followed and then a benediction was said by all.

These worship forms and ideas from three 'emergent' churches raise some interesting questions. Karen Ward is an African American pastor in a community sponsored by two mainline denominations. The worship service is a Eucharist of the classical shape and, like Blesséd, is more akin to 'blended' or 'fusion' worship. What is new requires a narrator – an explanation – which raises questions about who has decided and chosen the theme and its interpretation. In other words, conscious didactic elements are thinly disguised as worship. With Doug Pagitt and Mark Pierson (as indeed with Jonny Baker's 'alt.worship') we have two leaders who are Gen Xers and who seem to have been dissatisfied with their evangelical background. They have discovered ritual and symbol, but lacking a deep tradition, they invent new and varied rituals. Of course this is thoroughly postmodern, but it seems to reflect a very superficial understanding of ritual. Anthropological and ritual studies tend to stress the deep structures of rituals. It is not that rituals do not change, but they do so gradually. Serious rituals and symbols do not change every week, nor do they require lengthy explanation. In fact, explanations (narrations) are a hallmark of the very modernity that these services claim to supersede.

FRESH EXPRESSIONS AND EMERGING WORSHIP

The term 'fresh expressions' is used in a Church of England report entitled *Mission-Shaped Church*. Chaired by Bishop Graham Cray, who had long championed the need for ecclesiological and liturgical responses to postmodernism, the report noted 12 kinds of development in terms of new outreach and mission. The report explained the phrase 'fresh expressions' thus:

> It suggests something new or enlivened is happening, but also suggests connection to history and the developing story of God's work in the Church. The phrase also embraces two realities: existing churches that are seeking to renew or redirect what they already have, and others who are intentionally sending out planting groups to discover what will emerge when the gospel is immersed in the mission context.[55]

It was later explained as follows:

> A fresh expression is a form of church for our changing culture established primarily for the benefit of people who are not yet members of any church.
> - It will come into being through principles of listening, service, incarnational mission and making disciples.
> - It will have the potential to become a mature expression of church shaped by the gospel and the enduring marks of the church and for its cultural context.[56]

As with the consciously emerging churches in the USA, these newer ecclesial groups are keen on enculturating the gospel, or producing what is often termed an 'incarnational theology'. The culture is that of postmodern Britain, existing alongside the extant Church of England parish model, and is often connected in some way to a parish or cathedral. This co-existence has been described by some as a mixed-economy church. Not everyone is convinced of the usefulness and long-term future of the new models, including Martyn Percy who has contrasted the bourgeois nature of many of the groups, which are concerned with art galleries, journeys, stones, rivers, sunsets, sky and young people, and are silent on old people, death, images of decay or

---

55 Graham Cray (chair), *Mission-Shaped Church: Church Planting and Fresh Expressions of Church in a Changing Context* (Church House Publishing, London, 2004), p. 34.
56 Steven Croft, 'What Counts as a Fresh Expression of Church and Who Decides?' in Louise Nelstrop and Martyn Percy (eds), *Evaluating Fresh Expressions: Explorations in Emerging Church* (Canterbury Press, Norwich, 2008), pp. 3–14, p. 10.

hardship.[57] Some of the pioneers in these new missionary enterprises view the traditional church model as tired, worn out and irrelevant, and so there is tension in some quarters between the constituents of this 'mixed economy'.[58] It is also unclear how many of the members of the 'fresh expressions' churches really are the unchurched, and how many are simply bored members of the traditional church seeking something different. Since these communities are consciously engaging postmodern culture, the worship is also postmodern; yet along with David Male we ask, 'Are fresh expressions of church being created, or is what is really happening simply developments of fresh expressions of worship?'[59] Our concern here is neither to reflect upon the nature nor to speculate on the long-term success of these communities, but rather to present some of the worship forms that they have developed.

'Visions' was a 'fresh expressions' community long before fresh expressions was established. Based in York, it began in 1989 when a group met together to plan a Christian arts and music nightclub that would be using a disused warehouse for a month as part of a series of events surrounding a mission in York Minster.[60] Following the completion of this project, a number of the group continued to meet and develop multimedia services. They attached themselves to St Michael-le-Belfrey, York, and were also influenced by NOS. Calling themselves 'Warehouse', the original services were begun in 1992, and centred on dance (club culture), including the use of video and word loops. Long-time member Sue Wallace explains:

> A couple of years after we began our dance service, we started our Communion service. The Communion now takes place on the first Sunday of the month and the dance service on the third Sunday of the month. The Communion was more meditative in style, using gentle ambient synthesizer music throughout. This was where we began our first experiments in integrating more experimental and practical forms of prayer. We soon discovered

57 Martyn Percy, 'Old Tricks for New Dogs? A critique of fresh expressions' in Nelstrop and Percy (eds), *Evaluating Fresh Expressions*, pp. 27–39.
58 See Robin Gamble, 'Mixed Economy: Nice slogan or working reality?' in Nelstrop and Percy (eds), *Evaluating Fresh Expressions*, pp. 15–23.
59 David Male, 'Who Are Fresh Expressions Really For? Do they really reach the unchurched?' in Nelstrop and Percy (eds), *Evaluating Fresh Expressions*, pp. 148–60.
60 Sue Wallace, *Multi-Sensory Prayer* (Scripture Union, Bletchley, 2000, 2005 edn), p. 58. See <www.visions-york.org>.

just how powerful these were, both as a way of communicating with God and as a way of discovering more about ourselves. We were inspired by other groups doing similar things with their worship throughout the country and integrated some of their ideas into our worship. We also changed our name from *Warehouse* to *Visions*, to reflect our multimedia nature and also our desire to have dreams and visions about the shape of the church of the future.[61]

Some of the alt.worship used in Visions is reproduced in Sue Wallace's *Multi-Sensory Prayer*, which also gives advice for preparing a suitable worship space, including the use of prayer stools, comfortable chairs, rugs and floor cushions. Gentle music – from ambient synthesizer music to plainchant – provides helpful back-sounds to prayer; and incense or fragrant oil, and gentle light from candles is urged. Banners, icons or other images are helpful as well. Posture and breathing are also important. Among the many rituals for inclusion in such services is 'Fruit', which was used as a meditation on Pentecost. In this service, a bowl of different fruits, side plates and knives are required. While the community passes the bowl, people select a fruit for themselves. A script for the meditation is provided. The ritual ends with eating some of one's fruit, and passing it around for others to share.[62]

Visions, which now meets in St Cuthbert's Church, York, has started a new project at York Minster, in the crypt. It is called 'Transcendence: An Ancient-Future Mass', and is celebrated on the second Sunday of every month at 7.30 p.m. In a recent essay Sue Wallace has written:

It was to be a genuine piece of teamwork between Visions and the Minster. Transcendence is very formal and traditional in some ways: we use Common Worship Order 1, we wear robes, we have processions complete with thurifer and crucifer, we sing hymns, and all is generally set to a Latin Mass, sometimes sung by the amazing Minster song men. On the other hand, the hymns are sung to trip hop, or ambient dance backings, and the building is dark and candlelit, with moving images on every available space. The congregation can sit on chairs or, if they wish, they can lie

---

61 Wallace, *Multi-Sensory Prayer*, pp. 58–9.
62 Wallace, *Multi-Sensory Prayer*, p. 42.

down and relax on rugs and cushions. One of the most popular elements of the service is the chance to move around the building, normally to visit prayer stations set up in different chapels during a time of creative prayer. We started Transcendence with two trial services in October and November 2007, inviting people to tell us if they thought we were on the right track. We were completely blown away by the warmth and enthusiasm of the responses![63]

These services, which are available as video podcasts,[64] fall more into the category of a 'blended' or 'integrated' service (indeed, the term 'Ancient-Future' was one of Robert Webber's key terms).

Sanctus1 is a 'fresh expressions' community in Manchester. The website explains that this fluid, organic community believes the creative spirit of God is active and moving in culture.[65] It meets for tea or coffee at 7.30 p.m., and then an evening event follows, which may be a walk, or a discussion, or small group activity. A small group also gathers every Sunday at 7.00 p.m. in Sacred Trinity Church for a short liturgical service. It regards itself as an 'emerging church'. Some of the liturgies are published in the Proost Pocket Liturgies series.[66] The introductory section states:

We aim for our worship to be holistic and to allow the freedom to explore new ways in which to wonder at God. We draw from the vast resource of the Christian spiritual journey. Sanctus1 is an ancient-future church, drawing from the past to resource the present and into the future.[67]

Worship is described as the work of the people, and central to what the community does. The liturgy booklet continues:

Sometimes themes are generated in response to a current issue or topic, and sometimes in response to a cultural, faith or life experience. Sometimes worship is created and/or led by just one person,

---

63 Sue Wallace, 'Alternative Worship and the Story of Visions in York' in Croft and Mobsby (eds), *Fresh Expressions*, pp. 9–15, p. 14.
64 <http://web.mac.com/malcolm.wallace/iWeb/Transcendence/Video%20Podcasts.html>.
65 <http://www.sanctus1.co.uk/sanctus1home.htm>.
66 *Sanctus1*, Pocket Liturgies, Proost, <www.proost.co.uk> (2008).
67 *Sanctus1*, p. 9.

and sometimes by a group of people or the whole community. Sometimes the worship is planned and prepared to the nth degree; sometimes it is created on the spot to be used then and there by all. Sometimes it is a high-tech, multi-sensory affair; sometimes there is just space and a few words and time for reflection. Sometimes we 'magpie' ideas, actions, words, clips and more; sometimes we start from scratch and make things for and from ourselves.[68]

Ingredients of worship include candle-lighting, call to worship, confession and absolution, ritual, reading, sharing bread and wine, prayers, blessing, and candle dispersal. Visual elements may include film clips, TV clips, adverts, music videos and 'actions', such as writing something, holding something, making something, or discussion, or even games and quizzes. Sample words from the ingredients include a 'Mancunian Call to Worship' – the following excerpt illustrates the style of language used:

> We call to you and you answer us, for you are already here in the city and we merely meet you where you are:
> flashing up on a screen,
> underlying the bass line,
> concealed in a tattoo,
> glimpsed in a familiar stranger,
> scrawled on a wall,
> woven into the fabric of our lives,
> ritualizing our routine.
> We call to you and you answer us in mysterious ways. We remain patiently expectant that we will meet you at work, rest and play in the urban environment. The city is emphatically if unconventionally beautiful, but in common with all beautiful human constructs, it is fundamentally flawed. Our structures and routes imperfectly but sincerely reflect the Creator's original plan and intent. But we seek you with heart, soul, mind and strength, acknowledging that you are already in the world and working in the world.[69]

---

68 *Sanctus1*, pp. 12–13.
69 *Sanctus1*, p. 34.

The response throughout this quite lengthy explicatory call to worship is 'We call to you and you answer us'.

A section entitled 'Bread and Wine' explains that these elements are shared 'in some way' every week – sometimes the Bible is read; sometimes 'it is consecrated by a minister or priest'; and sometimes it is simply laid out for people to help themselves or share in small groups. The exact nature of the elements varies from baked in the microwave, to naan or soda bread, and the 'wine' from grape juice to an Australian Shiraz. An outline of a Eucharist celebrated at Greenbelt 2007 entitled 'Heaven in ordinary' is given, though a fuller (and rather different) text of this is available on the web, and it is the latter that is considered here.[70] After a 'trinitarian' blessing of three candles, the opening song was 'Come All You People'. Working in small groups, the gathered community was given a 'worship bag' containing paper to make a paper chain with everyone's name on it. The reading was the wedding in Cana of Galilee, followed by the song 'Let Us Build a House Where Love Can Dwell and All Can Safely Live'. The talk was given by Ann Morisy, Commission Officer for the Commission on Urban Life and Faith. Intercessions were offered, with a response. A biodegradable balloon was provided on which to write a prayer, word or symbol before releasing it. An envelope was also provided for an offering. The song 'Jesus, You Are the Living Bread' was sung, a prayer of thanks was given for the offering, and then a confession with responses, concluding with a short prayer for forgiveness. Bread, wine, cup and napkin were also in the worship bag, and were to be placed within the paper-chain circle. An extended communion invitation was spoken: 'Welcome, Welcome to this meal, A meal where heaven becomes ordinary . . .'[71] While elements were blessed on stage, one person from each of the various groups held up the bread and wine to be blessed. The eucharistic prayer was prayed by Bishop Nelson from Uganda. No opening dialogue was given in the text, and it began 'God our mother and father', with short paragraphs addressed to each member of the Trinity. It is best described as a typical Protestant eucharistic prayer, centring on consecration and 'us' now. It lacked any eschatological dimension, or sense of a church outside this gathering, which was probably a lost opportunity. A short post communion prayer was followed by the hymn 'O Lord My God! When I in Awesome Wonder'. Those aware of the history of Christian

---

70 *Sanctus1*, pp. 41–6; <http://benedson.blogs.com/GBservice.pdf>.
71 <http://benedson.blogs.com/GBservice.pdf>.

liturgy will probably find it difficult to see where the 'ancient' was in this rite; my own knowledge of that history would see it as more an expression of evangelical modernity. The Pocket Liturgies from Sanctus1 indicate that candle-lighting is an extremely important and invariable opening ritual for the community. There is even a litany for a wedding candle (why this rite of modernity, and not a rich blessing of the wedding cup?), where apparently God speaks and affirms that he is more than a candle. This is perhaps not the most felicitous apophatic language.

The third community being considered here is Moot, which meets in the heart of the City of London under the leadership of Ian Mobsby, author of *Emerging and Fresh Expressions of Church* (Moot Community Publishing, London, 2007). Services commenced in 2003, and have been held weekly since 2005.[72] The monthly pattern of worship is as follows: first Sunday, Little Service; second Sunday, Creative Eucharist; third Sunday, Alt.service or Big Service; fourth Sunday, Scream Service (for families with children); and on any fifth Sunday, Compline or Agape Service. The community sees itself as a postmodern monastic community. Only the Little Service is readily available, and has the structure of Invocation, Welcome, Introduction, Confession, Meditation/Reflection, Scripture or other reading, Homily/Storytelling, Reflective Activity, Prayer and Intercession, End Liturgy and Blessing. Songs from COTA, Seattle, are sometimes used, and the sign of the cross is encouraged, as is physical movement. The sample services have a 'neo-Celtic' feel to them, and although trinitarian, the epithets 'Creator, Redeemer and Companion' are the preferred terms. A sample blessing from Little Service on the theme of 'Balance' reads:

> The God of hope and balance,
> fill us with joy, peace and love
> And the blessing of God be upon all of us
> Now and always.
> And now may the Creator
> who balances the universe
> in the palm of God's hand,
> the Redeemer who died for you,

---

72   <http://www.moot.uk.net/SitePage/spaceapart.htm>.

and the Companion who cares for you
walk with you in the week to come.[73]

Eucharistic liturgies are promised for publication in 2010.

LIQUID WORSHIP

Liquid Modernity was the title of a study by Zygmunt Bauman, in
which he argued that solid modernity – the triumph of modernity over
nomadic culture – was now beginning to liquefy.[74] Changes in technology mean that one's identity is no longer located in a particular
company or trade. This in turn inspired the title of Pete Ward's study,
Liquid Church.[75] Ward explained:

> [W]e need to shift from seeing church as a gathering of people
> meeting in one place at one time – that is, a congregation – to a
> notion of church as a series of relationships and communications.
> This image implies something like a network or a web rather than
> an assembly of people.[76]

According to Ward, 'liquid church' is essential because it takes the
present culture seriously and seeks to express the fullness of the
Christian gospel within the culture. The 'mixed economy' of 'fresh
expressions' would seem to be precisely an example of this liquidity, as
are the 'emerging' churches of the USA. Ward's book, in turn, inspired
Tim Lomax and Michael Moynagh to develop samples of 'liquid'
worship.[77] In brief, 'liquid' worship is where there are worship zones in
one building or location, and people move from zone to zone as they
wish. If Lomax and Moynagh invented the term, they did not invent
the actual phenomena. The Thomas Finnish Mass allows for writing

---

73 Ian Mobsby, Mark Mcleary, Carey Radcliffe and Michael L. Radcliffe (comp.), *Moot
Community, Little and Compline Services*, Pocket Liturgies, Proost <www.proost.co.uk>
(2009), p. 41.

74 Zygmunt Bauman, *Liquid Modernity* (Polity Press, Malden MA, 2000).

75 Pete Ward, *Liquid Church* (Paternoster Press, Carlisle, 2002). See also Ian Mobsby,
'Liquid Modernity and the Need for Transcendent Encounter', paper, 3 February 2003,
<http://www.moot.uk.net/docs/fluid.pdf>.

76 Ward, *Liquid Church*, p. 2.

77 Tim Lomax and Michael Moynagh, *Liquid Worship*, Grove Worship Book 181
(Grove Books, Cambridge, 2004).

intercessions at side altars, private meditation or laying on of hands, all going on at the same time. We have also already encountered descriptions of 'emergent' worship where, at places in the service, a number of activities are offered at a particular point during the worship.

According to Lomax and Moynagh, 'liquid' worship is 'a flexible form of worship in which individuals are free to combine the different elements of worship into their own preferred journeys'.[78] They further qualify the service in terms of 'full liquid' every Sunday, 'group liquid' (a particular group), an 'occasional liquid' worship, and 'partial liquid' worship (meeting together for the Word, and then moving to different stations or zones). The dangers, as they admit, are that some will stay away from worship altogether, or that people will select some zones and keep away from others. Examples of 'liquefying' are given, for instance, the Peace – conventional, a chanted Peace, or a party-game Peace. 'Liquid' responses to a sermon include prayer ministry, meditation, a ritual response, writing one's own affirmation of faith, writing a poem, painting a picture, sharing the Peace with extended conversation, writing one's own communion preface, or saying the creed with pauses for reflection, all of which would be parallel activities. Further examples are provided for download on the web, such as the service used at St Mary's, Luton, on Good Friday 2003, and an outline for a Mothering (= Mid-Lent or Rose) Sunday Service. The former, rather like 'Stations of the Cross', had 15 stations. The first station, entitled 'Dying and Living', was near the font area, and invited participants to reflect on the truth that baptism is dying to sin and rising with Christ. They signed themselves with the sign of the cross, and said a prayer. Technical requirements included halogen lights, water, glitter ball, baptistery blacked out to represent the tomb, and blue tea light candles on the baptistery. People entered the 'tomb' one at a time. The second station was entitled 'Surrender', and included a song, paper chains, and the reading of a prayer. Technical requirements for this station included a large chain around the north transept, and fencing around the worship zone with a 'keep out' road works sign.[79] Many ideas for such simultaneous events are found in Andy Flannagan's *Distinctive Worship*.[80]

---

78 Lomax and Moynagh, *Liquid Worship*, p. 3.
79 <http://www.grovebooks.co.uk/resources/worship/W181/W181holyspace2004.html>.
80 Andy Flannagan, *Distinctive Worship: How a New Generation Connects with God* (Authentic Media, Carlisle, 2004).

CONCLUDING REMARKS

Given the plethora of communities doing alt.worship, emerging worship, fresh expressions worship and/or liquid worship, only a small sampling has been considered here. The services are often new creations each time, and are extremely varied and variable, thus only a few tentative observations are offered here.

Christian worship is at once an incarnational, or incultured, ritual, and a transcendent/eschatological or counter-cultural ritual. A conscious wish to enculturate liturgy always runs the risk of embracing the culture so fully that for all its apparent transcendence/eschatology, the result is simply a cultural incantation.[81] In a cultural climate that values creativity, it is all too tempting to be ever creating 'meaningful' rituals, but in the end these often have meaning primarily for the individuals who created them, and, like parables, have to be explained to those outside. The result is that a huge amount of explicatory material factors into these attempts at postmodern worship, and explication (even when disguised in prayer) is very much a symptom of modernity. Much of what is written for a particular community is so local as to become narcissistic, and although conscious of culture and the city, seems oblivious to entering a tradition of the saints, with little expression that this worship joins with that of the rest of the Church and the heavenly host. Perhaps the main question that needs to be posed is whether or not much of this is genuinely postmodern worship. It certainly takes place in a postmodern culture and is created by those who consciously wish to engage with this culture. However, much of the 'creativity' is already found in the late 1960s and throughout the 1970s – a period during which John Killinger's *Leave It to the Spirit* promoted much of the same:

> Each person is handed a scrap of colored paper as he enters, and must find a seat where there is a matching piece of colored paper. Traditional church music emerges from a speaker in one section of the room, and instrumental rock music from a speaker in an opposite section. Strobe lights rake the dimly lit room, illuminating various objects such as a garden rake, a bird bath, a crucifix, a

---

81 Bryan D. Spinks, 'Christian Worship or Cultural Incantations?', *Studia Liturgica* 12 (1977), pp. 1–19.

pot of flowers, and sometimes remaining momentarily focused on someone's head and face.[82]

But that was in 1971 at a time when the arts, audio-visual effects and a direct style of address in prayer were all urged by the Fisherfolk Community.[83] Additionally, more intimate and direct prayer was being encouraged by the translation of the prayers of Michel Quoist and the younger English Congregational ministers in the late 1960s.[84] I recall attending 'experimental worship' in a London church in late 1975, which included contemporary music, banners, candles and balloons. Were these postmodern *avant la lettre*? Or is it the case that much of what passes for postmodern worship is in fact 'retro' – worship of the 1970s, but remixed and reframed with current video, computer and music synthesizer technology? Retrophiliacs may indeed be postmodern, but retro remains merely retro.

---

82 John Killinger, *Leave It to the Spirit: A Handbook for Experimental Worship* (SCM Press, London, 1971), p. 97.

83 Patricia Beall and Martha Keys Barker, *The Folk Arts in Renewal: Creativity in Worship, Teaching and Festivity as Developed by the Fisherfolk* (Hodder & Stoughton, London, 1980).

84 Michel Quoist, *Prayers of Life* (Gill & Macmillan Ltd, London, 1965); Caryl Micklem et al., *Contemporary Prayers for Public Worship* (SCM Press, London, 1967); Caryl Micklem et al., *More Contemporary Prayers* (SCM Press, London, 1970).

Chapter 3

Entertaining worship or worship as entertainment? Megachurch seeker services and multi-sensory worship

According to the important recent study by Scott Thumma and Dave Travis, a megachurch is simply a Protestant church that averages at least 2,000 attendees in its weekend services.[1] The authors observe:

> In 2007, there were 1,250 megachurches out of a total of 335,000 U.S. congregations of all religious traditions. This relatively small number of very large Protestant Christian churches has the same number of attendees at weekly services (roughly 4.5 million) as the smallest 35 percent of churches in the country. The pastors of these churches wield tremendous power within their denominational groups, in the larger Christian world, and even in the public and political realms. The ministry activities and worship styles of the megachurches affect tens of thousands of smaller churches in the country and, thanks to the Internet, literally millions of pastors around the world.[2]

Although megachurches do have precursors (Henry Ward Beecher's Plymouth Church and Aimee Semple McPherson's Angelus Temple are examples from the nineteenth and early twentieth centuries), most writers see them as something new, dating from the 1970s. The name comes from the obvious feature of the buildings – their size. Describing

---

1 Scott Thumma and Dave Travis, *Beyond Megachurch Myths: What We Can Learn from America's Largest Churches* (Jossey-Bass, San Francisco CA, 2007), p. xviii.
2 Thumma and Travis, *Beyond Megachurch Myths*, p. 1.

the 2002 Grace Church in Eden Prairie, Minnesota, Jeanne Halgren Kilde makes this point:

> The new building, consisting of a worship auditorium seating some 4,500 people and containing state-of-the-art audio and video projection technology, backstage and rehearsal spaces for musical and dramatic performances, cafeteria, coffee shop, bookstore, and accompanying Sunday school wing with graded classrooms, constitutes the first building phase of what is projected to be close to a $100 million campus, which will eventually include a new recreation building and seniors' wing as well.[3]

Many of the megachurches have denominational ties; however, few give such ties any prominence, and instead tend to function as though they were non-denominational churches. For example, Robert H. Schuller of the Crystal Cathedral was ordained in the Reformed Church of America (Dutch), and Rick Warren of Saddleback Church has a Southern Baptist background, but their churches neither claim nor champion those denominations. Closely connected with this is what Wilmer Macnair has called 'celebrity culture': 'the preaching, music, and all aspects of the worship events resemble the performances in which one or a few people are on stage and hold forth in front of vast seas of adoring fans.'[4] Denomination is replaced by the mega-pastor. Macnair explains:

> Distinctive about the mega-church is that it exists as a church that is *of* and *by* a certain pastor. The personality and the *charisma* of a person are at the center of the church's life. In many cases, the current pastor of the church is also the founder.[5]

In some cases the megachurch takes the form of a family business, with a hereditary succession. Joel Osteen, with no seminary training, succeeded his father John Osteen as Senior Pastor at Lakewood, and the

---

3 Jeanne Halgren Kilde, 'Reading Megachurches: Investigating the religious and cultural work of church architecture' in Louis P. Nelson (ed.), *American Sanctuary: Understanding Sacred Spaces* (Indiana University Press, Bloomington and Indianapolis, 2006), pp. 225–49, p. 225.

4 Wilmer E. Macnair, *Unraveling the Mega-Church: True Faith or False Promises?* (Praeger, Westport CT, 2009), p. 7.

5 Macnair, *Unraveling*, p. 12.

Crystal Cathedral is run by the Schuller family, with Robert junior succeeding his father, only later to be fired by the 'retired' Robert senior. The membership (and there are always more attenders than members) has little say in removing a pastor or running the 'business'.

As might be expected, not all megachurches have exactly the same style of worship. Thumma and Travis divide the worship styles into four categories:

1 Old Line/Program-Based
2 Seeker
3 Charismatic/Pastor-Focused
4 New Wave/Re-Envisioned.[6]

Mars Hill Church, Seattle, led by Mark Driscoll, would fit their category 4, though the worship of this church is more commonly termed 'emergent', whereas Joel Osteen and Lakewood fall into category 3. Thumma and Travis discovered that the vast majority of megachurches are characterized by contemporary praise music, led by a worship team, accompanied by orchestra, drums and electric guitars, and augmented by state-of-the-art sound systems and huge projection screens.[7] A quarter of megachurches have multiple services, catering to different styles and different audiences.

The concern of this chapter is with selected megachurches whose worship style, or styles, have been characterized as driven by concern for church growth, and whose worship is of the 'seeker' type. Promoted particularly by Bill Hybels at Willow Creek, a 'seeker' service is aimed at the unchurched, and tailored to fit the culture of the unchurched – in particular, the Boomer generation.

This type of worship has been emulated by a number of smaller mainline Protestant churches of various denominations in the hope of reversing decline in membership. In a recent study of nine Lutheran congregations in the Greater Bay area of California, Stephen Ellingson has catalogued the move away from the traditional Lutheran liturgy and the designation 'Lutheran' to espouse a megachurch seeker style service, in which doctrinal language is replaced with therapeutic language of self-fulfilment, which itself is an accusation made against some of the

---

6 Thumma and Travis, *Beyond Megachurch Myths*, p. 31.
7 Thumma and Travis, *Beyond Megachurch Myths*, p. 27.

megachurches. In Ellingson's opinion, it rests on a theology in which the individual replaces God and church as the primary religious actor, and in which growth is elevated to the highest organizational and religious value. Choice, innovation and experimentation come to be prized as the means to achieve growth, while preserving tradition is devalued because it cannot accomplish the work of conversion.[8] The resulting market-driven forms of worship are seen by critics as providing entertainment rather than worship, and of dumbing down the gospel. However, as Lester Ruth has shown, churches using seeker services themselves fall into two groups. There are those which, like Willow Creek, have worship services at a different time for the committed or core congregation, whereas others have only 'seeker' services as the main diet of worship.[9]

THE ROOTS OF WORSHIP AS ENTERTAINMENT?

A number of writers have argued that though the actual presentation of 'seeker' services might be new – in the use of modern technology – their basis is not new at all, and can be traced back to the revival camp meetings of the so-called frontier tradition at the end of the eighteenth century, and to the 'new measures' of Charles Finney in the nineteenth century.[10]

One of the first frontier camp meetings was organized by a Presbyterian minister, James McGready, in 1800, and was derived from the Scottish Presbyterian open-air communion seasons in which the meeting ended with an altar call – to communion.[11] Barton Warren Stone was impressed by the meeting, and himself arranged for a camp meeting at Cane Ridge, Kentucky, in 1801. The event lasted six or seven days, and included not only Presbyterian ministers, but also

8 Stephen Ellingson, *The Megachurch and the Mainline: Remaking Religious Tradition in the Twenty-First Century* (University of Chicago Press, Chicago IL, 2007), p. 184.

9 Lester Ruth, 'Lex Agendi, Lex Orandi: Toward an understanding of seeker services as a new kind of liturgy', *Worship* 70 (1996), pp. 386–405.

10 Lester Ruth has rightly questioned the accuracy of the use of 'frontier', especially when used in a negative manner as regards this worship tradition. Lester Ruth, 'Reconsidering the Emergence of the Second Great Awakening and Camp Meetings among Early Methodists', *Worship* 75 (2001), pp. 334–55; see also Lester Ruth, *A Little Heaven Below: Worship at Early Methodist Quarterly Meetings* (Abingdon Press, Nashville TN, 2000).

11 See Leigh Eric Schmidt, *Holy Fairs: Scotland and the Making of American Revivalism*, second edn (Eerdmans, Grand Rapids MI, 2001).

Baptists and Methodists. This event is noted for its 'signs of the Spirit', including bodily agitation and exercise, as well as the barking exercise. It was also marked by the large attendance of strangers, tent preaching to convert the strangers, and side-show entertainment. Alongside the older communion preparation and admission to communion, as a side event, were the singing of spiritual songs, preaching and conversion. The latter has been seen as the basic 'ordo' of the evangelical revivalist worship service.[12] But this basic pattern was brought to perfection in an indoor theatre setting by Charles G. Finney. A lawyer by training, Finney was 'converted' in 1821, and began a preaching ministry even though he had no formal theological education and wasn't ordained until 1824. He used his lawyer's skills in rhetoric in the pulpit – though, in fact, he substituted a lectern for a pulpit. His 'new measures' entailed being free of any inherited liturgical pattern to do whatever was needed. He wrote:

> Their commission was, 'Go and preach the gospel, and disciple all nations.' It did not prescribe any forms . . . Do it – the best way you can – ask wisdom from God – use the faculties he has given you – seek the direction of the Holy Ghost – go forward and do it. This was their commission. And their object was to make known the gospel in the *most effectual* way . . . No person can find any *form* of doing this laid down in the Bible. It is *preaching the gospel* that stands out as prominent there as the great thing. The form is left out of the question.[13]

Finney developed the camp meeting format, with singing, preaching, and an altar call – though not to communion, but to the anxious bench (where converts come forward to a bench to confess and weep for their sins in front of the congregation) as a mark of conversion and repentance. Finney was appointed minister of Chatham Street Chapel, New York, which in fact was a refurbishing of the Chatham Theatre, but one which kept much of the theatre space intact. Here, quite literally, church became theatre. Jeanne Halgren Kilde has observed:

---

12 Gordon W. Lathrop, 'New Pentecost or Joseph's Britches? Reflections on the history and meaning of the worship ordo in the megachurches', *Worship* 72 (1998), pp. 521–38, p. 531. Though see also Melanie Ross, 'Joseph's Britches Revisited: Reflections on method in liturgical theology', *Worship* 80 (2006), pp. 528–50.
13 Charles Grandison Finney, *Lectures on Revivals of Religion*, ed. William G. McLoughlin (The Belknap Press of Harvard University Press, Cambridge MA, 1960), p. 251.

This decision resulted in a significant alteration of relationships between minister and congregation within this building. For services, a portable lectern most likely was placed in the middle of the stage for preaching purposes, and Finney's trademark anxious bench was set below the stage. The result, of course, was that perhaps for the first time in U.S. religious architecture, the preacher was fully released from the cage of the elevated pulpit and given the physical performance space that a secular orator commanded. Although the visual link to a higher authority was severed, the preacher now had access to the performative authority of the actor . . . Released from the confines of a pulpit, a preacher could pace the width of the room and use expressive physical gestures to communicate with the audience, thus creating a far more dramatic presentation than was possible in a traditional church.[14]

In 1836 the Broadway Tabernacle replaced the Chatham Street Chapel. This was purpose-built for Finney (though he moved shortly afterwards), and was based on the advantages observed of a theatre space. Halgren Kilde notes:

As had the chapel, the tabernacle also enhanced the performance of the stage speaker and the ability of talented preachers to establish and maintain charismatic power over the audience. Rather than framing the performance with a proscenium as had the chapel, the tabernacle intensified the visual and aural elements of the service – the spectacle – and thus made the stage a more compelling place to look. While the chapel organizers placed the choir on the stage behind the pulpit, a strategy unprecedented in ecclesiastical settings, the tabernacle placed the organ pipes on the back wall behind the pulpit, creating a highly dramatic visual background for the speaker. Organ pipes towered above the stage, rising behind five rows of choir desks at the rear of the stage. The thrust stage itself jutted out almost midway into the room, and on it stood an assemblage of chairs accommodating various individuals. And, of course, the preacher himself, whether standing above

---

14 Jeanne Halgren Kilde, *When Church Became Theatre: The Transformation of Evangelical Architecture and Worship in Nineteenth-Century America* (Oxford University Press, New York, 2002), pp. 34–5.

the stage on the pulpit dais or walking on the lower apron, provided the most interesting spectacle of all.[15]

Finney was not the only preacher of his day to use democratic pragmatism in worship, but he has become the prime example. Finney's basic 'ordo', of a song service as a preliminary, leading to the sermon or message, followed by a 'harvest of converts', has become the foundational pattern of many evangelical churches, and the megachurches, with nineteenth-century theatre techniques and designs being replaced by late twentieth-century television chat-show models, and marketing techniques. In the Tabernacle, Finney preached to the converted, but a good number of megachurch pastors have been more concerned with the type of audience first attracted to Finney's Chatham Street Chapel – the unconverted, or unchurched.

MEGACHURCH STARS: ROBERT SCHULLER AND JOEL OSTEEN

Robert H. Schuller was ordained in the Reformed Church of America, the roots of which were the Dutch Reformed Church. Schuller made a special study of Calvin's use of Scripture, and excelled at preaching the classic sermon of this tradition. His reading of Dale Carnegie's *How to Win Friends and Influence People*, and Norman Vincent Peale's *The Power of Positive Thinking*, resulted in a shift in his style, and after pastoring a church in Chicago, he moved to California to begin a new missionary church. It first met in the Orange Drive-in Theatre in Orange County in 1961. Later there would be a purpose-built Reformed church, the Tower of Hope, and then in 1980 the famous Crystal Cathedral. In his California ministry, Schuller adopted and developed marketing and church-growth techniques, and although his services are not designated 'seeker' services, they are certainly geared to the unchurched. Schuller himself writes:

A small church is great if your mission is to serve only the indoctrinated members of your sectarian denomination – Lutheran, Dutch Reformed, Presbyterian, Episcopalian, or whatever. But if you want to win unchurched people, drop the label from your

---

15 Halgren Kilde, *When Church Became Theatre*, p. 45.

name. Call it a community church. And program your church services and your sermons and your activities to appeal to the spiritual needs of the unchurched.[16]

Although much more concerned with preaching style and vision for growth, Schuller has also advised: 'Let your Sunday morning services aim at inspiration, entertainment and a basic commitment to Jesus Christ. Then get them into a small classroom setting where they will be more receptive to the deeper doctrines of your church.'[17]

Schuller was one of the first to capitalize on TV broadcasting, and so the techniques and requirements of TV entertainment became a crucial ingredient in the presentation of his services. The *Hour of Power* is broadcast every week, and Schuller usually takes the role of the chat-show host, introducing a guest and the visiting preacher. The setting is the star-shaped building with over 10,000 panes of glass, fountains in the middle of the worship hall, and a door which opens onto fountains and a backdrop of the California hills. The orchestra and Crystal Cathedral Choir give professional and polished performances, as do guest choirs and individual singers. Indeed, music plays a major role, with each service normally having two congregational hymns, two choir anthems and two pieces sung or played by guest musicians. The conclusion of each is greeted with applause. The guest is usually a celebrity guest, and may be a movie or music personality, a sports hero or a business entrepreneur.[18] This is indeed an entertainment-based church, complete with commercial breaks advertising the latest gift for those who send in donations. Critics question whether there is any depth to the worship, and whether entertainment has actually supplanted worship. Schuller's own 'new Reformation' theology has been criticized for using self-help and positive-thinking concepts in place of biblical ideas. For example, Schuller's contemporary understanding of sin as 'a lack of self-esteem' is regarded by many as not being a proper dynamic equivalent.[19]

---

16 Robert H. Schuller, *My Journey: From an Iowa Farm to a Cathedral of Dreams* (HarperOne, San Francisco CA, 2001), p. 291.
17 Robert H. Schuller, *Your Church Has Real Possibilities* (Regal Books, Glendale CA, 1976), p. 135.
18 See also Dennis Voskuil, *Mountains into Goldmines: Robert Schuller and the Gospel of Success* (Eerdmans, Grand Rapids MI, 1983).
19 Robert H. Schuller, *Self-Esteem: The New Reformation* (W Publishing Group, Nashville TN, 1982).

Lakewood Church in Houston, Texas, is the largest megachurch con-gregation/audience. The church was founded by John Osteen. John was an ordained Southern Baptist minister who, in the late 1950s, was one of those who experienced gifts of the Spirit in the wave of charismatic renewals that had begun at that time. A good half of his congregation, and most of his denomination, disapproved of this charismatic shift, and in 1959 he left and began his own charismatic church in an old feed store. The church would gradually experience an increase in the number of attenders and move to a new purpose-built complex – Lakewood Church. John died in 1997, and was succeeded as senior pastor by one of his sons, Joel, who had dropped out of Oral Roberts University. Joel had skills in marketing and TV production, and had taken charge of Lakewood TV broadcasts, but had never preached until the Sunday before his father's death. He became interim pastor, and was then appointed senior pastor. Richard Young has written:

> As a television producer and marketing director for the church, he knew what kinds of things would get the attention of people and create a response to the gospel. In television, you must grab the attention of people in the first few moments or they will change the channel. Joel knew that in a church service the same principle would apply. What happens in the first few minutes of the service must grab the attention of people and then prepare them for what is ahead.[20]

Under Joel's leadership, the congregation leased the Compaq Center, the former stadium of the Houston Rockets basketball team. It was leased from the city for 30 years, and renovated to make it suitable for Lakewood worship services, which are also televised. It seats 16,000 and Joel's message is broadcast to 150 countries. He has been described as one of America's premier 'pastorpreneurs'.[21] Lee and Sinitiere comment:

> [His] carefully crafted messages along with media acumen make the Houston pastor a rising star in the evangelical world. Osteen's

---

20 Richard Young, *The Rise of Lakewood Church and Joel Osteen* (Whitaker House, New Kensington PA, 2007), pp. 141–2.
21 William Martin, 'Prime Minister', *Texas Monthly*, August 2005, at <http://www.texasmonthly.com/cms/printthis.php?file=feature.php8issue=2005-D8-01> (accessed 27/8/2009).

story, like those of other evangelical innovators, reveals much about the interplay between religion, media, capitalism, and consumer habits in American culture.[22]

Lakewood Church is run as a family business, with Joel's mother Dodie, his wife Victoria, his brother and sister and their spouses all having key roles and forming the board at Lakewood. From the early days the church has been multiracial, and still is. In late 1999 Cindy Cruse-Ratcliffe, who was already an established name in the contemporary Christian music world, joined the staff. She, along with Israel Houghton, an African American leader in praise and worship music, composes most of the songs used at Lakewood. Lee and Sinitiere have commented:

> Cruse-Ratcliffe and Houghton, along with choir director Dakri Brown, help Lakewood's ten-piece orchestra and large choir generate the energy of a rock concert. They blend an array of contemporary gospel music styles to create a worship experience that appeals to the tastes of its diverse audience.[23]

And, since there are many Spanish speakers, Marcos Witt was hired to lead worship for the Hispanic community.

There are five giant screens and many small monitors spaced throughout the auditorium. The symbolism is limited to a giant globe of the world, which is a symbol of the world Christ died for, though this symbolism is far from obvious. The service at 11 a.m. on Sunday 27 September 2009 began with music by the singers and orchestra, 'We are overcome by your Word'.[24] Then Joel and Victoria Osteen walked onto the stage, and Joel gave a welcome, and asked who could say that God had been good to them. The audience was invited to celebrate God's good news so the week would go better, and they should know that God was smiling down on them, and they should shake off any guilt. Visitors were invited to raise their hands, and were welcomed. Victoria also welcomed everyone, saying how good it was to be in the

---

22 Shayne Lee and Phillip Luke Sinitiere, *Holy Mavericks: Evangelical Innovators and the Spiritual Marketplace* (New York University Press, New York and London, 2009), p. 26.
23 Lee and Sinitiere, *Holy Mavericks*, p. 34.
24 Accessed on the Lakewood Church website, <http://www.lakewood.cc/pages/home.aspx?gclid=CIzj3k-ErkACFZdM5QodXysNaA7>.

house of God and that God would teach us to see wonderful things. After she offered a prayer to God, a time of praise and worship commenced, led by Houghton first, and then Cruse-Ratcliffe. The songs included 'Giver of Every Breath I Breathe', 'Where would I Be Without Grace?', 'Grace that Bought Me', 'Our God, who Reigns Forever', 'My Savior Lives' (this was repeated many times), 'He Arose over Death and the Grave' (sung first as a solo by Cruse-Ratcliffe, and then became congregational), and 'You Ask Me how I Know He Lives?', and with the lights turned down, 'Indescribable'. Some of these are parts and extracts from longer Praise and Worship songs.

Joel then led a prayer of praise and thanks for God in our lives, saying that we are like the one leper who returned to God to give thanks. God is healing us, and we are not going to focus on what is wrong with us, but what is right. God is the one who guides us and opens doors to us. Our best days are still ahead of us. Thanks were given that we are strong, healthy and redeemed, and request made that we should go into the week ahead not with guilt and depression, but in faith. The prayer posture is an interesting variant on the orantes position, with index fingers pointing and gesticulating upwards.

A brief talk followed promising that God would make the audience healthier, have better finances and a better career. God is still on the throne, and God will reward them because he runs over with goodness. They will be stronger, healthier and more prosperous, and God wants them to be great. Then followed the time of ministry with people coming down to a team, which included Joel, for prayer. Background music was 'Worthy is the Lamb who was Slain' and 'Oh Lord You've Searched Me, You Know My Way'. During this time wafers and small cups of wine were passed out, and Victoria gave an explication, explaining that today's theme was about the Body of Christ. We celebrate God's life in us. We do this in remembrance, because Jesus said, 'This wafer (*sic*) represented his body, and the cup his blood. We are going to release his power in us by taking communion.' Then all consumed the elements. A thanksgiving followed with the song 'You Tore the Veil'. Victoria thanked everyone for coming, and Steve Austin, Director of Pastoral Care, announced the ministries that Lakewood offers. Then came the tithes and offering, and a youth group performed 'Believe in what you are told'. Joel thanked the children, welcomed visitors again, and gave his message, beginning with Hebrews 4.16 ('Let us therefore approach the throne of grace with boldness, so that we may receive mercy and find grace to help in time of need'). The talk ended with an altar call, for people to receive the Lord Jesus. He offered another prayer of thanks, and the service concluded with the song 'I am Saved by Grace'.[25]

Schuller and Osteen are two stars of the megachurch phenomenon. The 'ordo' of their respective churches has strong continuity in kind with that developed by Finney. The concern for the professional techniques of TV entertainment, together with concern for the unchurched and a user-friendly understated religious message, place them as close associates of the 'seeker' service.

SEEKER SERVICES: WILLOW CREEK

The Willow Creek Community Church was the blossoming of what was originally a youth group called Son City, which was started by Dave Holmbo and Bill Hybels at South Park Church, Park Ridge, Illinois in 1974. Hybels had been raised in the Christian Reformed Church (Dutch), and was destined to be part of the family business. He left the family business and took a job in the shipping department of a Christian organization in the Chicago area. Holmbo was the leader of the South Park Church youth music group, and had asked Hybels to lead the Bible study there. The youth group wished to reach out to non-believers, and felt that something more than meeting in a church basement, singing 'Kumbaya' and listening to long Scripture sermons was needed. Pritchard notes that in order to attract the attention of high school students, the topics and activities of Son City (like many evangelical youth groups) naturally drifted toward high school level entertainment which often included the use of A\V screens and drama.[26] Son City also developed teams led by a group leader in an effort to achieve their goals. The success of Son City and its principles of organization would be adopted at Willow Creek. Kimon Sargeant writes: 'The first was the importance of a separate service for seekers that featured contemporary music, lots of creative entertainment, and relevant messages.'[27] Holmbo and Hybels left their positions at South

---

25 See also the account of a service in Martin, 'Prime Minister'.

26 G. A. Pritchard, *Willow Creek Seeker Services: Evaluating a New Way of Doing Church* (Baker Books, Grand Rapids MI, 1996), p. 35.

27 Kimon Howland Sargeant, *Seeker Churches: Promoting Traditional Religion in a Non-traditional Way* (Rutgers University Press, New Brunswick NJ, 2000), p. 193.

Park, and in the autumn of 1975 began their ministry in Willow Creek Community Church.[28]

Hybels was influenced by the example of Robert Schuller who had gone knocking on doors asking people, if they didn't go to church, why, and what they would like to see happen in church. Hybels did the same, since Willow Creek was designed to cater to the unchurched and attract them to become church. It was the lapsed or unchurched Boomer generation that was targeted, spoken of as 'unchurched Harry and Mary'. They needed to hear music of a similar style to what they listened to on radio or TV; they needed anonymity and informality; they needed to hear a message with something for them in it. Money was raised to build a church complex at South Barrington emulating 'the best of corporate America in quality, design, and style'.[29] This meant that Willow Creek's complex would make a visual appeal as a corporate office or a mall, rather than looking like a church, or even a crystal cathedral. As Sargeant observes, 'seeker church experts often proclaim the shopping mall, Disney, and other customer-sensitive companies as models for the twenty-first-century church'.[30]

The Sunday 'seeker' service at Willow Creek is a well-rehearsed (down to the minute) professional production. The themes change, and the content varies slightly, but generally it follows the Finney 'ordo', with even less explicit reference to the Christian faith. Nancy Beach, director of programming at Willow Creek, explains: 'The seeker service was designed to do two things: communicate the basic truths of Christianity in relevant ways our nonchurched friends could understand; and provide believers with a meaningful experience.'[31] According to Sargeant, the aim is

> to surprise, to move, and eventually to captivate the hearts of their attenders. Furthermore, the claim is made that 'by mirroring the forms of contemporary culture and by deemphasizing the outdated traditions of church services they have found a new way to cultivate more genuine, less ritualistic worship'.[32]

---

28 The story is told in detail in both Pritchard, *Willow Creek Seeker Services*, and Sargeant, *Seeker Churches*.

29 Sargeant, *Seeker Churches*, p. 19.

30 Sargeant, *Seeker Churches*, p. 8.

31 Nancy Beach, *An Hour on Sunday: Creating Moments of Transformation and Wonder* (Zondervan, Grand Rapids MI, 2004), p. 43.

32 Sargeant, *Seeker Churches*, p. 56.

Taped instrumental music is played over the sound system while the audience arrives, since unchurched 'Harrys' find silence a threat. A prelude of live music begins immediately before the service, and it is usually an instrumental piece, though the type of music and instruments vary. Then a singer with a microphone walks onto the stage and gives a welcome. A song, which the audience/congregation is asked to join in, follows. Then an invitation to greet someone next to each attender (a user-friendly version of the Peace/right hand of fellowship) is given. Several pieces of vocal music may follow. Then, a short talk with a message and a drama presentation are usually featured. Comments/announcements and the collection of offerings (but guests are asked *not* to give) conclude the service, along with a closing song.

An outline of a service by Bill Hybels for 6–7 August 2009, which was designed for the Willow Creek church's 'Summit Sunday', and entitled 'Holy Discontent', included the following five segments:

1 Worship, with a song (Up energy congregational seems to be a type rather than a title); video, 'My King is . . .', and song 'How Great is Our God' (15 minutes).
2 Comments/service set up/speaker intro (5 minutes).
3 Video message: Bill Hybels (41 minutes).
4 Comments/announcements/offering (5 minutes).
5 Closing song with video: 'God of this City' (5 minutes).[33]

There is no liturgical calendar, though the themes of the services do follow the 'Hallmark' card chronology. It is certainly not the case that Bill Hybels and the Willow Creek staff do not share and hold main orthodox Christian beliefs – they simply do not believe that the 'seeker' service is the right place for them. However, reflecting on the messages of Willow Creek, Kim Sargeant was of the opinion that through their own psychological make-up, each person has a window into God's character. Apparently God is now so immanent as to be affected by our psychological states, and our feelings, which is evidence of how a therapeutic sensibility is influencing the theological discourse of 'seeker' church pastors.

---

33 <http://www.willowcreek.com/Events/Leadership/2009/summitsunday.asp>.

SEEKER SERVICES: THE SADDLEBACK PHILOSOPHY

The author of best-sellers *The Purpose-Driven Church* and *The Purpose-Driven Life*, Rick Warren is the founder and pastor of Saddleback Community Church, Saddleback Valley, California. Warren attended California Baptist College in Riverside, California, and after a 'prophetic word' spoken to him in 1973 by preacher W. A. Criswell was ordained by the Southern Baptist Convention in 1975. He later studied at Southwestern Baptist Theological Seminary in Forth Worth, Texas. When he left seminary in 1979, he rejected offers of pastoral assignments in favour of founding his own 'missionary' church. Taking note of Robert Schuller's door-to-door visitations, Warren, too, asked those who belonged to no church what they would like to have in a church. As a result, on Easter Sunday 1980, 205 people – many of them unchurched – attended the first Saddleback Community Church service, held at Laguna Hills High School. Warren writes:

> Having so many unchurched people at the service actually made it quite comical. When I asked people to open their Bibles, nobody had one. When we tried to sing some songs, no one sang because they didn't know the tunes. When I said, 'Let's pray', some of the people just looked around. I felt as if I was standing before a Kiwanis or Rotary meeting.[34]

That church grew over the next ten years, holding services in a variety of venues, from high schools to theatres. In 1995 the present complex was opened, on a 120-acre hilltop, having been designed by theme park experts, with various buildings, a large parking lot, and Bible story re-enactments. By 2006 the megachurch boasted attenders numbering 25,000. Lee and Sinitiere comment:

> Like Disney World, Saddleback is a large and beautifully designed campus that inundates people with options. Seven different worship services take place every weekend, and people can choose from ten different venues depending on their music and worship style preferences (everything from jazz and reggae to punk rock)

---

34 Rick Warren, *The Purpose-Driven Church: Growth without Compromising Your Message and Mission* (Zondervan, Grand Rapids MI, 1995), p. 44.

and then watch a videocast of Warren's sermon. Some members like to sit outside and listen to the service broadcast on one of many outdoor speakers while enjoying the picturesque, mountainous Southern Californian backdrop. Others choose to watch a videocast of the service while sipping iced coffee or munching on a bagel in Saddleback's Terrace Café. This restaurant overlooks the entire campus and sits less than a hundred feet from the Worship Center. Attendees also mingle through an outdoor bookstore stocked with purpose-driven study materials and a variety of Bibles and other books, along with plenty of Warren's trademark preaching attire, a short-sleeve Hawaiian shirt.[35]

The worship space centres on a raised stage, and thus resembles a concert theatre.

As with Willow Creek, Saddleback has been concerned with the 'seeker-sensitive' approach to worship in order to attract the unchurched and make them feel comfortable – even to the point of them being able to watch on a screen rather than having to experience any physical participation. According to Warren, a service should be provided where members can bring their unsaved friends 'without embarrassment'.[36] The targets of their outreach are Saddleback Sam and his wife Samantha – the targets determine the components of the services: 'music style, message topics, testimonies, creative arts and much more'.[37] The entire service, not just the invitation, must be planned with the unchurched in mind. This includes pace and flow, since the unchurched (and the churched?) get bored very quickly. The unchurched, in Warren's view, cannot handle long prayers.

At Saddleback, 'IMPACT' is the acronym used in the design and planning for the flow desired during worship. The opening song must **I**nspire **M**ovement – it must be upbeat and bright, to make attenders dance, clap or smile, and loosen up their muscles. The songs then move to **P**raise – songs about God; then to **A**doration – intimate songs to God at a slower pace; then **C**ommitment – usually first person singular, allowing a personal commitment to God. It is all **T**ied together by the final song, which should be short and upbeat.[38] Of considerable impor-

---

35 Lee and Sinitiere, *Holy Mavericks*, p. 143.
36 Warren, *The Purpose-Driven Church*, p. 48.
37 Warren, *The Purpose-Driven Church*, pp. 253–4.
38 Warren, *The Purpose-Driven Church*, p. 256.

tance, too, are information tables, directional signs, and taped background music, just as in retail stores, because music relaxes people. The very last thing wanted in a 'seeker' service is silence.[39] Visitors (guests) should be allowed to remain anonymous. The first spoken words of the service should be a welcome: 'Welcome to Sunday at Saddleback! We are glad you're here. If you're here for the first time, we want you to sit back, relax, and enjoy the service we've planned for you.'[40]

Warren explains that at Saddleback the mood wanted in the 'seeker' service is one of celebration. Everything must be well maintained – attention is given to plants, lighting and seating. A church should invest in the best sound system it can afford, and seating needs to be comfortable. A printed order of service is helpful for the unchurched so that there are no surprises for them; but it must be in non-technical terms. A wide range of contemporary music styles should be offered – 'we use the style of music the majority of people in our church listen to on the radio'.[41] A MIDI keyboard and some MIDI discs are important acquisitions, especially since the MIDI technology can add tracks to the music provided by the 'live' musicians, and because much of the music will be for listening, since the unchurched feel uncomfortable with congregational singing. In preaching, the common ground with unbelievers is not the Bible, but our common needs, hurts and interests as human beings. Warren, in fact, is less nervous about preaching doctrine and using Christian symbols than Hybels, but he keeps the service and the message 'user-friendly', always with the unchurched in mind as his target audience.

SEEKER SERVICES: COMMUNITY CHURCH OF JOY, PHOENIX, ARIZONA

In his book entitled *Entertainment Evangelism: Taking the Church Public*, Walt Kallestad, Senior Pastor of Community Church of Joy, writes that for his church, 'focusing on entertainment means connecting with people by showing hospitality, receiving and caring for guests, as well as capturing and holding people's attention'.[42]

39 Warren, *The Purpose-Driven Church*, p. 259.
40 Warren, *The Purpose-Driven Church*, p. 262.
41 Warren, *The Purpose-Driven Church*, p. 285.
42 Walt Kallestad, *Entertainment Evangelism: Taking the Church Public* (Abingdon Press, Nashville TN, 1996), p. 24.

Kallestad's book is primarily concerned with strategy for church growth and the need for change. According to Kallestad, the aspect of church life most challenged by change is worship, because worship is the heartbeat of the Christian Church.[43] Once the evangelistic vision found its place, it was obvious that worship had to change. Citing George Hunter's book *How to Reach Secular People* (Abingdon Press, Nashville TN, 1992), he argued that if secular people do not understand the jargon, relate to the music, know when to stand or sit, then they conclude that the Church is not for them. Churches, therefore, have had to remove cultural barriers that kept people from further considering their faith. After 17 years of living the vision, the result has been the Community Church of Joy, which is affiliated with the Evangelical Lutheran Church of America, and offers five different styles of worship each weekend. Saturday evening worship is the 'Contemporary Country', with a Call to Worship, Welcome, Opening Song, Special Feature, Gifts, Message and Closing. Sunday morning worship includes an 8.30 'Spirited Traditional' service, which attracts lifelong Christians; a 9.30 'Contemporary Blend', which attracts members and longtime visitors; a 10.30 'New Contemporary' service designed for the unchurched, visitors and younger people; and an 11.30 'Modern Contemporary' service intended to reach secular people – particularly the Baby Boomers.[44] In fact, the website accessed in August 2009 offers three services, all on Sunday: a traditional service at 8.15, and contemporary services at 9.35 and 11.15. Lester Ruth has called this the 'Spectrum Model', where there is a choice of styles on a Sunday, over against the Willow Creek model, where on Sundays only the 'seeker' service is offered.[45] Ruth notes of The Community of Joy:

[A]fter the more traditional service – the early service on Sunday morning – the altar is moved out of the chancel, which is transformed into a stage. In like manner, the use of traditional hymns decreases throughout the morning, participation levels go down, use of drama increases, and the music styles become more related to the culture of the different target audiences. Generally, seeker service characteristics become more evident as the morning pro-

---

43 Kallestad, *Entertainment Evangelism*, p. 59.
44 Kallestad, *Entertainment Evangelism*, pp. 71–3.
45 Ruth, 'Lex Agendi, Lex Orandi', p. 391.

gresses. The bottom line in all of these services is choosing the most effective means of communication for those in attendance.[46]

It was the former associate pastor, Timothy Wright (currently of Community of Grace, Arizona) who gave clear recommendations for designing a seeker service in his 1994 publication *A Community of Joy*. After listing six negative drawbacks to 'liturgical' worship, Wright outlined the necessary ingredients to make the 'campus' visitor-friendly, invoking a philosophy reminiscent of Rick Warren's: directional signs are important; the opening welcome and music are crucial – a dynamic choir anthem creates a climate of expectancy; name tags should be used for visitors (and everyone) since these are non-threatening; to make the 'liturgical' worship more visitor-friendly, the entire service should be printed in the bulletin; and musicians should be positioned at the front of the worship space.[47] However, it is 'contemporary' worship that is the main focus of Wright's book. Adding a new style of worship to the Sunday 'menu' offers consumers a choice, and the result is new members. A visitor-oriented service stresses presentation over participation, celebration over the cerebral, and intimacy over awe.[48] Such a service uses contemporary music that 'resembles the music played on "secular" radio stations',[49] 'Contemporary' services set a relaxed and accepting environment, which means, for example, that 'liturgical garments do not mix well with contemporary services'.[50] A 'contemporary' service should be held at a later time because guests often do not decide to attend until late in the morning. High-quality music should be used, and requires a superior sound system. The service must be kept moving, and the 'audience' may applaud or say thanks at certain points during worship. Each service is typically built around a theme, and sermons should give need-meeting messages.[51]

Wright also offered several variations of a visitor-oriented service, though the ingredients remain the same, even though they are shuffled differently. Format 1 recommends the following:

---

46 Ruth, 'Lex Agendi, Lex Orandi', p. 399.
47 Timothy Wright, *A Community of Joy: How to Create Contemporary Worship* (Abingdon Press, Nashville TN, 1994), pp. 41–8.
48 Wright, *A Community of Joy*, pp. 56–61.
49 Wright, *A Community of Joy*, p. 68.
50 Wright, *A Community of Joy*, p. 69.
51 Wright, *A Community of Joy*, pp. 70–4.

Call to worship

Welcome

Worship Chorus

Bible Reading and Prayer

Special Feature (minidrama, skit, or guest interview)

Special Music (band, soloist, or choir)

Gifts (a second welcome, invitation to come again, brief announcements, and 'nonthreatening' introduction to the offering)

Special Music

The Message

Closing[52]

MULTI-SENSORY WORSHIP:
GINGHAMSBURG CHURCH, TIPP CITY, OHIO

Bill Hybels and Rick Warren have been concerned with the unchurched, and both conducted surveys of what would bring some of those people to church. However, unchurched 'Harry and Mary' and 'Saddleback Sam and Samantha' all seem to have been of the Boomer generation, so the 'seeker' service has been inadvertently tailored for this audience. Nancy Beach of Willow Creek noted that she had to bite her tongue when a few representatives from Gen X had the audacity to tell the leadership that Willow Creek 'music was not optimal for reaching them and their friends, and that our overall style of communication needed adjustments for their age group'.[53] The initial response seems to have been to cater to younger people, hoping that on maturity they would make the transition to the Boomer-designed services. More recently, Willow Creek has undertaken a self-assessment, which was published in 2007 as *Reveal: Where Are You?* It revealed a high percentage of persons who were dissatisfied with spiritual growth, and as a result the report commented: 'Much like parents, the church may need to shift its relationship with its maturing disciples into something quite different in order to maintain an appropriate level of influence and provide the support they need.'[54]

---

52 Wright, *A Community of Joy*, pp. 131–3.
53 Beach, *An Hour on Sunday*, p. 48.
54 I recall this from a conversation with Sally Morgenthaler, who had been called in as a consultant.

In comparison to Willow Creek, Mike Slaughter, Lead Pastor of Ginghamsburg Church – a United Methodist megachurch – seems to be more consciously focused on Gen X and postmodernism, and has written about the 'emerging' church.[55] Whether a megachurch can claim to be emergent is a moot point, but it is probably fair to say that the multi-sensory high-tech worship here is inspired as much by 'seeker' services as by forms of 'emergent' and 'alt.worship'.

This church traces its foundation to 1863 and the evangelist B. W. Day.[56] In 1979, when Dr Mike Slaughter arrived, it had a membership of 118, with worship attendance hovering around 90. By 1994 the church had moved to a new campus, and became host to 4,500 people each week. In 2005 and 2006, Ginghamsburg was listed as one of the top 50 churches in the USA, and its Lead Pastor was noted as one of the top 50 most influential Christians in America. Worship services at Ginghamsburg are held on Saturdays at 5.00 p.m. and Sunday mornings at 10.15 and 11.45.

Ginghamburg's approach to worship, and examples of it, can be found in the publications of Mike Slaughter, and of the church's Creative Director, Kim Miller. Slaughter's book, *Out on the Edge*, argues that most people can make no sense of the Church today, and part of the reason is the shift in culture to a post-literate age. The Church has been left behind in the pre-electronic media age.

> People aren't coming to our churches because all they expect to hear is information and reasoned correction. Post-moderns are not looking for information *about* God. We are suffering from an information overload, which creates a muggy and clammy feeling that we have 'been there, done that.' This saturation of information contributes to the sense of ambiguity about Christian truth. This generation is looking for an experience of God, and they don't expect to find God in church.[57]

He notes that Ginghamsburg got interested in Gen X in 1995 – but prior to that the same contemporary worship style that was effective for

---

55 Michael Slaughter with Warren Bird, *Unlearning Church: Just When You Thought You Had Leadership All Figured Out* (Group Publishing Inc., Loveland CO, 2002).

56 See the website, <http://ginghamsburg.org/> (accessed 1/9/2009).

57 Michael Slaughter, *Out on the Edge: A Wake-Up Call for Church Leaders on the Edge of the Media Reformation* (Abingdon Press, Nashville TN, 1998), p. 38.

unchurched Boomers was deemed effective for Gen X.[58] But of course, Gen X is also unchurched, and for them Slaughter advocates a strategy that is beyond the abstract, cerebral models of the literate age, and that bridges the truth of God's gospel with the 'felt needs in people's lives'.[59] This suggests a 'seeker' service for Gen X, so Slaughter explains that since December 1994, the church has used multi-sensory worship, and almost half of those who have attended have been the unchurched. He writes:

> We use electronic media in an interactive form with music, litera-ture, painting, drama, dance, writing, filmmaking, poetry and movie clips. We borrow ideas from David Letterman's 'almost live' spots, in which he appears to leave the studio by playing clips that are really produced earlier. With this tactic I am able to go 'on location' in the middle of my sermon. Electronic media open the door to unlimited creative possibilities.[60]

Planning for the weekly services begins on Wednesday at 8.00 a.m., with a meeting of the Creative Coordinator (Kim Miller), the Technical Coordinator, the Communications Director, the Multi-Media Director, the Band Leader, the Lead Pastor and the Support Pastor. They consider these six elements of worship design: Word (Scripture), Felt Need, Desired Outcome, Theme, Metaphor and Structure.[61] A sample structure provides the following order for worship:

> **Opening Music**. *Band*: Instrumental, 'Somewhere Over the Rainbow'
>
> **Opening Video Clip**. *Multi-media Coordinator: The Wizard of Oz (two-minute segment, which includes Dorothy agreeing to go forward with her 3 new companions; encountering dangers)*
>
> **Call to Worship**. *Creative Coordinator: (from centre platform; based on the idea of not traveling alone)*
>
> **Song Celebration**. *Band*: 'Love is What We've Come Here For'

---

58 Slaughter, *Out on the Edge*, p. 39.
59 Slaughter, *Out on the Edge*, p. 69.
60 Slaughter, *Out on the Edge*, p. 76.
61 Slaughter, *Out on the Edge*, pp. 77–9.

'We've Come to Praise You' *(congregational songs led by the band, with words projected on the screen)*

Prayer. *Creative Coordinator: (soft music underscores a prayer which gives us the opportunity to pray for others who will journey with us)*

Brief Reprise. *Band*: 'Surely the Presence of the Lord'

Bridge/Offering. *Creative Coordinator: (a connecting piece which calls the ushers and affirms community)*

Featured Music. *Band*: 'I'll be There for You' *(as the theme song for the TV show 'Friends,' this The Rembrandts' tune reaches out to younger people in the congregation, as well as carrying the theme for the weekend forward)*

Drama. *Troupe: Four 'Buster-type' [Gen X] persons who resemble (in both looks and mannerisms) the characters of the Wizard of Oz wrestle with the challenges of community in a coffee-house setting.*

Message. *Lead Pastor*: 'Traveling Companions'

Closing Words. *Creative Coordinator*

Send Out. *Band*: 'I'll be There for You'.[62]

Both Slaughter and Kim Miller describe the time consumed from Wednesday to Sunday in planning, rehearsing and performing such worship services. For Miller the main ingredients are Word (the chosen Scripture text), Felt Need (the human issues we bring to the theme), Desired Outcome (goal of the service); Theme (the title of the service); and 'Look' (the objects, images, processes or experiences that support the message visually).[63] An example of 'Look' for the theme of 'resurrection' is 'Butterflies and orange flowers'.[64] Miller writes:

> In our postmodern age, Jesus' words challenge us to lose the performance and replace it with participation, to lose the talking heads and replace them with pictures and stories, to lose the emphasis on numbers of pew-sitters and replace it with numbers of life-losers.

---

62 Slaughter, *Out on the Edge*, p. 82; Kim Miller, *Designing Worship: Creating and Integrating Powerful God Experiences* (Group Publishing, Loveland CO, 2004), pp. 51–65.
63 Miller, *Designing Worship*, p. 47.
64 Miller, *Designing Worship*, p. 48.

We haven't changed the message here at Ginghamsburg; the message has changed us. Worship celebrations have become the launching pad, the mission control tower for all other ministries. Because even in postmodernity, worship is still the place where the greatest number of real followers check in once a week to refocus, refuel, and refresh their spirits. As the worship team, we're responsible to make sure it happens. But it's never really about us or our ideas.[65]

Kim Miller has provided outlines of many of the services that have been planned for Ginghamsburg as resources for other churches.[66]

Given the thematic nature of these services, and the apparent lack of any use of the United Methodist Service Book, it would seem that the worship is akin to Willow Creek and Saddleback, but simply prides itself on being more multi-sensory. The use of video clips and drama seem to place it within Willow Creek's origin, namely, evangelical youth ministry events. It makes no pretence about using entertainment TV as a model and an inspiration. The cost in time is comparable to the Sheffield Nine O'Clock Service, but the decidedly American Protestant background of the church means that it is unable to draw on the more mystical and enchanting aspects of worship. That does not make it inferior, but it does make it just what it is: a Gen X 'seeker' service.

MODERN ENTERTAINMENT WITH POSTMODERN TECHNOLOGY?

In liturgical circles the term 'entertainment' generally has a highly negative connotation. In its essence, worship is entering into the fellowship of the divine Trinity, and this necessarily has an awesome side to it. However, although the word 'entertainment' is often understood as something that is superficial and amusing, it can also mean 'hosting or being hospitable', as well as an 'eye- and ear-catching spectacle'. The medieval High Mass was both eye- and ear-catching, and thus could be explained as entertainment, as well as being the liturgical drama that welcomed and embraced the Church as the body of Christ. The fact

---

65 Miller, *Designing Worship*, p. 50.
66 In addition to *Designing Worship*, see Kim Miller and the Ginghamsburg Church Worship Team, *Handbook for Multi-Sensory Worship* (Abingdon Press, Nashville TN, 1999); vol. 2, 2001).

that megachurch worship and 'seeker' services attempt to entertain does not necessarily mean that such worship is a priori inferior to other styles. It is the model and level of the entertaining that perhaps is the more important aspect. A number of writers from this tradition openly admit to being influenced by the world of TV, particularly chat shows, as well as the worlds of pop music and marketing. Popular media entertainment is often superficial and ephemeral. Given that worship has a serious or deep side, it may be questioned whether adopting such models results in a trivial presentation of the gospel, and a dumbing down of its message. The verses from 1 Corinthians 9.20–22 become an important text for the entrepreneurs of this worship style. However, even for Paul this had limits – witness what else he says in 1 Corinthians, as well as in Galatians. Michael Horton has been very critical of Joel Osteen's sermons, which he feels represent a variety of moralistic, therapeutic deisms. They have a basic message that 'God is there for you and your happiness. He has some rules and principles for getting what you want out of life, and if you follow them, you can have just what you want.'[67] Robert Schuller avoids too much God-talk and keeps off any controversial issues. Many of the 'seeker' services use contemporary Christian music, the words of which often are very superficial and do not often tell the Christian story in the depth found in hymnody. The use of so much secular material for the 'themes' of worship may also be problematic. The questions have to do with whether or not this is an appropriate cultural model, and whether or not the culture has intruded too far and muted the gospel and the (theo)logic of Christian worship.

The parallels and affinities with Finney have been noted. However, important studies by Todd Johnson and Pete Ward have drawn attention to the influence of youth ministry in the form of the worship service that is found in many contemporary evangelical churches, and in the megachurches.[68] Johnson argues that the tendency has been to try to reach youth with the same techniques used by Madison Avenue on the Pepsi generation – a confluence of message with media, in which the two have become indistinguishable. The market-driven rituals of

---

67 Michael Horton, *Christless Christianity: The Alternative Gospel of the American Church* (Baker Books, Grand Rapids MI, 2008), p. 68.
68 Todd E. Johnson, 'Disconnected Rituals: The origins of the seeker service movement' in Todd E. Johnson (ed.), *The Conviction of Things Not Seen: Worship and Ministry in the 21st Century* (Brazos Press, Grand Rapids MI, 2002), pp. 53–66; Pete Ward, *Growing Up Evangelical: Youthwork and the Making of a Subculture* (SPCK, London, 1996).

evangelism and catechesis have provided an entire generation with a new language of God that had not previously been used in worship. Those who have never experienced youth ministry find 'seeker' services accessible because they use the 'religious' language of our society – advertising. Johnson observes:

> In a culture saturated by consumerism, no translation to the mythic language of the 'seeker service' is necessary. It has already translated the gospel into the categories of self-improvement and entertainment and has explicitly created a ritual setting that reflects the business and consumer world of middle-class suburbia.[69]

The link with youth ministry is clearly discernible in the story of Willow Creek and Son City. The Willow Creek services were adapted by Boomers for Boomers, and were as much an expression of modernity as were the liturgical rites of Vatican II. They are modern worship forms using postmodern technology. The congregations are large, and consist mainly of Boomers. Willow Creek's self-study has identified a cultural or generational gap. Postmodern seekers of spirituality tend to prefer something deeper, something smaller, and more local. Eddie Gibbs warns that the

> current expansion of megachurches should not lead them to a sense of false security. In the long term, they will not be immune to the downturn looming over denominations in general, and will have to face consequences similar to those that lead to the demise of struggling smaller churches.[70]

It may be that big is no longer beautiful, and those seeking a deeper spirituality will require a deeper encounter in worship than the marketing/chat-show/rock concert style of worship provides, which is still, for all the technology, the mainstay of megachurches.

Another factor in question is, 'Who plans these services?' As with many of the 'emergent' and 'alt.worship' churches, the worship seems to be chosen by a small group who market it to their consumers. At one

---

69 Johnson, *Conviction*, p. 63.
70 Eddie Gibbs, *Churchmorph: How Megatrends are Reshaping Christian Communities* (Baker Academic, Grand Rapids MI, 2009), p. 108.

level all liturgy is planned and performed by a small group on behalf of others. However, official denominational liturgical forms at least have a wider genesis than one small group of worship-planners, as in the megachurch paradigm. The wider denomination acts as a control, and allows for a certain commonality, and thus communal worship. Most megachurch worship and seeker services seem to be planned by a small group, and the audience is just that – an audience. This leads to questions about ecclesiology and the understanding of the Church as the body of Christ.

Further questions stem from the fact that, like a TV chat show or a rock concert, a large financial investment in modern audio and video technology is required, and the church becomes a techno-church. What happens when the technology fails? And is it the case that in this post-modern era, good Christian worship can only take place with such technology? Quentin J. Schultze has pointed out that often little thought is given by many of the churches that use this technology, though usually the megachurches are able to fund truly high-end equipment and engage professionally trained people to work it. Additionally, the technology is often placed ahead of the questions concerning the heart and purpose of worship. Schultze writes that a colleague attended a media-saturated service and commented that 'the service was largely a show – a multimedia extravaganza, with no time for silence and contemplation'.[71] In postmodernity there seems to be a true longing for a place in worship that allows room for silence, but megachurches and 'seeker' services seem to abhor silence. Perhaps the main question, however, is 'Does this thoroughly modern "ordo" become postmodern simply by using the latest technology and contemporary music styles?'

---

71 Quentin J. Schultze, *High-Tech Worship? Using Presentational Technologies Wisely* (Baker Books, Grand Rapids MI, 2004), p. 57. See also LaMar Boschman, *Future Worship: How a Changing World Can Enter God's Presence in the New Millennium* (Renew Books, Ventura CA), 1999.

Chapter 4

Praise and Worship songs and worship in the charismatic churches

Praise and Worship music (P&W) has been mentioned in passing in earlier chapters. It was this type of Christian music that Robert Webber had in mind when arguing for 'blended worship', and it is the music often found in emergent worship, and in megachurches such as Lakewood and Saddleback. The music style is that of popular culture and mainly soft rock. Rather like U2, many of these artists have become names in their own right, have received awards for their music, and often market their music on secular as well as religious labels. Thus some of the more famous songs and albums have become part of the contemporary Christian music (CCM) scene and industry. Howard and Streck write:

> While contemporary Christian music began in the late sixties and early seventies with a relatively homogeneous folk-pop sound (think James Taylor), today one can find the adjective 'Christian' applied to most styles of contemporary popular music. Christian heavy metal ('heavenly metal' as some have dubbed it), Christian industrial, Christian punk, Christian blues, Christian folk, Christian rap, Christian new age, Christian Celtic, Christian alternative rock, Christian electronica – all of these and still others not listed can be found on the shelves of the Christian bookstores where the music is generally sold. All are identified as CCM.[1]

According to the *Encyclopedia of Contemporary Christian Music*, CCM first came into existence as a 'recognizable entity during the Jesus

---

1 Jay R. Howard and John M. Streck, *Apostles of Rock: The Splintered World of Contemporary Christian Music* (University of Kentucky Press, Lexington, 1999), p. 8.

movement revival of the late 60s and early 70s', and included artists such as Children of the Day, Love Song and Barry McGuire.[2] It developed out of rock and roll, as this was the only musical idiom available to these artists. In 1969 a newly formed organization, The Gospel Music Association, began giving 'Dove' awards to honour CCM artists. However, prior to the Jesus movement, the music designed and developed for Christian youth groups also fed into this new genre. In the USA Robb Redman lists groups such as Youth for Christ, and the 'youth musicals' such as *Tell It Like It Is* (1969).[3] Pete Ward traces the development in England from the evangelical youth movements to the emergence of *Youth Praise* in 1966, published by Falcon Books for The Church Pastoral Aid Society. He observes that the collection 'reflects the way that evangelical youth work was characterized by the steady adoption of this 1960s youth culture. The Christian youth work scene had started to spawn its own version of "beat music".'[4] Two of the groups that contributed material were the Venturers and the Followers. Ward traces the growth of this industry through MGO (Musical Gospel Outreach) and the magazine *Buzz*; through the influence of the Jesus movement in England and the Festival of Light; through the initial charismatic renewal associated with Graham and Betty Pulkingham and the publication of *Sound of Living Waters* in 1974. The 'folksy' sound of the Fisherfolk would give way to the Third Wave charismatic movement and soft rock, with Graham Kendrick representing this shift in music. Newer collections included *Songs of Fellowship* in 1979, and the albums *City of God* and *Mission Praise*, with companies such as Kingsway Music and Thankyou Music. As a safeguard for songwriters and music publishers, the Christian Copyright Licensing Scheme (CCLS) was launched in 1985.[5] Robb Redman has traced the development in the USA through Maranatha! Music, which was born out of Calvary Chapel, Costa Mesa, California, with an album released in 1974, to the

---

2 Mark Allen Powell, *Encyclopedia of Contemporary Christian Music* (Hendrickson, Peabody MA, 2002), p. 10.
3 Robb Redman, *The Great Worship Awakening: Singing a New Song in the Postmodern Church* (Jossey-Bass, San Francisco CA, 2002).
4 Pete Ward, *Selling Worship: How What We Sing Has Changed the Church* (Paternoster Press, Bletchley, 2005), p. 27.
5 The story is told in detail by Pete Ward in *Selling Worship*, and also in his book *Growing Up Evangelical: Youthwork and the Making of a Subculture* (SPCK, London, 1996). For CCLS, see Ward, *Selling Worship*, p. 85, and for Christian Copyright Licensing, Inc. (CCLI) in the USA, see Redman, *The Great Worship Awakening*, p. 62.

founding of Integrity Music in 1987, and the EMI Christian Music Group and its label Worship Together, as well as a host of minor labels.[6] Trade publications include *Contemporary Christian Music*, *CCM Update* and *Cross Rhythms*. By the 1980s the special-interest network that this early music had spawned had developed into a multimillion-dollar industry, and by the late 1990s it generated nearly US$1 billion in yearly revenues. Ward observes that, 'What began as a theological and evangelistic imperative was to result in an economic reality. The worship scene was to be increasingly made up of these various interconnecting media and business relationships.'[7] Popular music and the marketing culture were influencing worship. However, as Powell has explained, the roots of the words of these songs lie within groups representing Christianity's more conservative factions, with the result that the image of Christianity expressed in most contemporary Christian music has 'an emphasis on a personalized, private relationship with Jesus as opposed to a concept of incorporation into a community that relates to Christ corporately'.[8] Personal holiness and the belief that God is speaking directly to the individual, and a focus on sentiment and piety, take precedence over social justice and a traditional sacramental experience.[9] What is more, the appetite for such music seems insatiable, with constant publication of new songs. Prolific songwriter Graham Kendrick summarizes thus:

> Publishing contemporary praise and worship songs, which really only got under way in the 1980s, has become very influential, and new songs, recordings, songbooks and computer resources proliferate. In many churches, platform performance – assisted by related technology from public address systems to digital projection – has displaced pulpit-centred services. The microphone has profoundly affected church worship culture. 'Personality' worship leaders and songwriters have arisen and become figureheads, and the influence of churches or movements that have pioneered a new sound or style goes round the world at an unprecedented speed. Some worship bands have set their sights on invading popular culture with music that carries the spirit and motive of

---

6 Redman, *The Great Worship Awakening*, pp. 55–71.
7 Ward, *Selling Worship*, p. 95.
8 Powell, *Encyclopedia*, p. 17.
9 Powell, *Encyclopedia*, p. 17.

worship but with a more subtle content designed to relate to the nonbeliever searching for spiritual answers to their felt needs.[10]

Howard and Streck find three strands in the world of CCM. The first is Separational CCM, typified by Rebecca St James, where the music is a religious tool for evangelism, exhortation and worship, though often it is music for the already converted. Second is Integrational CCM, with such artists as Amy Grant, which sees Christian music much like other music, namely for entertainment. What makes it Christian is that it is by a believer, and imparts a message that is often implicit rather than explicit. The third strand is Transformational CCM, represented by Mike Heard, Charlie Peacock and the Choir, which believes its music is created in the name of artistic expression and carries the values of truth and honesty. A crucial cultural context is pinpointed by Allan Bloom's comment:

> [N]othing is more singular about this generation than its addiction to music . . . Today, a very large proportion of young people between the age of ten and twenty live for music. It is their passion; nothing else excites them as it does; they cannot take seriously anything alien to music.[11]

The intention here is not to rehearse the development of this industry, or to discuss the appropriateness of the music.[12] Instead the focus will be on some of the P&W songs that have been generated by the Third Wave neo-charismatic movement.

---

10 Graham Kendrick, 'Worship in Spirit and in Truth' in Stephen Darlington and Alan Kreider (eds), *Composing Music for Worship* (Canterbury Press, Norwich, 2003), pp. 86–103, pp. 91–2.

11 Allan Bloom, *The Closing of the American Mind* (Simon & Schuster, New York, 1987); Howard and Streck, *Apostles of Rock*, p. 4.

12 For fuller discussion, see Don Cusic, *The Sound of Light: A History of Gospel and Christian Music* (Hal Leonard, Milwaukee WI, 2002); Howard and Streck, *Apostles of Rock*; Charlie Peacock with Molly Nicholas, *At the Crossroads: Inside the Past, Present, and Future of Contemporary Christian Music* (Shaw Books, Colorado Springs, 1998, 2004); John M. Frame, *Contemporary Worship Music: A Biblical Defense* (P & R Publishing, Phillipsburg NJ, 1997); Steve Miller, *The Contemporary Christian Music Debate: Worldly Compromise or Agent of Renewal?* (OM Literature, Waynesboro GA, 1993).

THE THIRD WAVE

Whether or not Peter Wagner was the first to coin this term, his book *The Third Wave of the Holy Spirit* gave it currency.[13] It describes the charismatic/Pentecostal revival that began in the late 1970s and early 1980s. The 'first wave' is usually associated with the event of speaking in tongues which was linked with the preaching of Charles Parham in 1900, and then subsequently with Parham's disciple William Seymour and the latter's revival at Azusa Street in Los Angeles in 1906. It grew out of the holiness movement. Cecil Robeck describes an early meeting at 312 Azusa Street:

> Services were long, and on the whole they were spontaneous. In its early days music was *a cappella*, although one or two instruments were included at times. There were songs, testimonies given by visitors or read from those who wrote in, prayer, altar calls for salvation or sanctification or for baptism in the Holy Spirit. And there was preaching. Sermons were generally not prepared in advance but were typically spontaneous. W. J. Seymour was clearly in charge, but much freedom was given to visiting preachers. There was also prayer for the sick. Many shouted. Others were 'slain in the Spirit' or 'fell under the power.' There were periods of extended silence and of singing in tongues. No offerings were collected, but there was a receptacle near the door for gifts.[14]

The revival spread, and among the many Pentecostal churches that emerged at this time were the Assemblies of God, and then Aimee Semple McPherson's International Church of the Foursquare Gospel.

The 'second wave' in Wagner's thought was the revival of the late 1950s and early 1960s, though it can also be linked with the Latter Rain revival in the late 1940s. This second wave would include John Osteen, but, more importantly, certain figures in the historic denominations such as Fr Dennis Bennett of St Mark's Episcopal Church, Van Nuys, California; and the revival would also impact the Roman Catholic

---

13 C. Peter Wagner, *The Third Wave of the Holy Spirit: Encountering the Power of Signs and Wonders* (Vine Books, Ann Arbor MI, 1988).

14 Cited in Daniel E. Albrecht, *Rites in the Spirit: A Ritual Approach to Pentecostal/Charismatic Spirituality* (Sheffield Academic Press, Sheffield, 1999), p. 33. See also Cecil M. Robeck, Jr, *The Azusa Street Mission & Revival: The Birth of the Global Pentecostal Movement* (Nelson Reference & Electronic, Nashville TN, 2006).

Church, with such exponents as Fr Francis MacNutt. The charismatic communities that Episcopal priest Graham Pulkingham founded in the USA and the UK, the Fisherfolk, and Noel Stanton's Jesus Fellowship and the Jesus Army also had their origins in this second wave.

Wagner's 'Third Wave' is the 1980s neo-charismatic revival, which he associated with John Wimber and the Vineyard Church, and which spread to other evangelical churches, including a number of evangelical Church of England congregations. The 'Toronto Blessing' was also part of this movement, but both the Jesus movement and the Restoration movement were part of what fed the Third Wave. The latter was particularly important in the United Kingdom. Inspired by the writings and teaching of Arthur Wallis, notable leaders and groups included Barney Coombs's Salt and Light, Gerald Coates's Pioneer Trust, and Roger Forster's Ichthus Fellowship.[15] There has also been a neo-charismatic revival amongst some of the older established Pentecostal churches, for example, leading to the founding of Hillsong, which had its roots in the Assemblies of God. One of the hallmarks of most Third Wave worship has been the use of P&W. However, since singing P&W is certainly not the preserve of charismatic and neo-charismatic churches, the songs that have been generated from this Third Wave have been extremely influential among churches and congregations attempting to give a modern feel to their worship services. James Steven comments:

> The publication of *Songs of Fellowship* by Kingsway has put a large selection of Restoration songs in the hands and on the lips of many Christian worshippers. The annual gathering of Spring Harvest introduces many people of all denominations to this music.[16]

'PRAISE AND WORSHIP' AS LITURGICAL FLOW

Among many musical lovers of classical hymns and conservatory music, P&W has received considerable criticism, and some of it is probably well deserved. Nick Page, for example, illustrates the banality of many

15 Andrew Walker, *Restoring the Kingdom: The Radical Christianity of the House Church Movement*, rev. edn (Eagle, Guildford, 1998); Nigel Wright, 'The Nature and Variety of Restorationism and the "House Church" Movement' in Stephen Hunt, Malcolm Hamilton and Tony Walter (eds), *Charismatic Christianity: Sociological Perspectives* (St Martin's Press, New York, 1997), pp. 60–76.
16 James Steven, *Worship in the Restoration Movement*, Grove Worship Series 110 (Grove Books, Bramcote, 1989), p. 4.

of the lyrics of earlier P&W, as well as the poor quality of much of the music.[17] That is not true of all of this genre, and whatever criticisms may be made, it is popular and influential, spilling out into many churches, particularly in what are termed 'contemporary services'. The latter are frequently like Webber's 'blended worship' – the normal worship service, but with some P&W songs and choruses inserted in place of traditional hymns. However, in the charismatic Praise and Worship service, there is a particular movement of mood and tempo, and quite deliberately so. Judson Cornwall (d. 2005) was from the Assemblies of God tradition, and in his book *Let Us Worship* he made a careful distinction between 'Praise' and 'Worship', and likened the flow of the service to a journey into the Holy of Holies in the Temple. Praise is fast and upbeat, and it progresses to a slower, quieter and more intimate mood.[18] Cornwall suggested a five-stage movement through the worship:

1 Songs of Personal Testimony in the Camp
2 Through the Gates with Thanksgiving
3 Into His Courts with Praise
4 Solemn Worship inside the Holy Place
5 In the Holy of Holies.

Cornwall suggests two possible options for rounding off – either a quiet time sitting in the presence of the Lord, or back to the outer court with a celebratory song. This is followed by preaching, altar call or time of ministry, and then the dismissal. This means a careful selection of the songs, and not simply a random selection – which is frequently the case in many 'contemporary services'. Thus, for example, the service at Lakewood (Chapter 5) had songs move from upbeat praise to slower more meditative worship.

---

17 Nick Page, *And Now Let's Move into a Time of Nonsense . . . Why Worship Songs are Failing the Church* (Authentic Media, Bletchley, 2004). Page comments: 'You'd be forgiven for thinking that the most important ability in writing worship songs is the ability to cut and paste verses from the Bible – simply rip out a chunk of Scripture and glue it into place. Never mind if the words don't fit, or the isolated verse doesn't make sense' (p. 87).

18 Judson Cornwall, *Let Us Worship* (Bridge Publishing Inc., Plainfield NJ, 1983), pp. 155–8.

A very similar outline is given by James Steven in relation to the Restoration churches:

1 15–45 minutes of songs and hymns
2 Notices and hymns
3 Scripture passage and sermon – at least 45 minutes
4 Prayer and music as response.[19]

Steven notes that the music tends to fall into three categories. A fast tempo is used with songs expressing joy, a mid-tempo for those that express God's majesty, and a slow tempo for intimacy and closeness.[20] The Old Testament Temple and David as the ideal worshipper are important models.[21] Sarah Koenig has persuasively argued that the P&W time does not simply fill the liturgical gap which in other churches is filled by the Eucharist:

> Praise and Worship time is a means of coming into close contact with the mercy and love of the Divine – one might even consider it a means of grace. It not only replaces the service of the Table as a primary ordering liturgical element, it also in some sense functions eucharistically for its participants.[22]

She points out that P&W songs express 'encounter with God in highly tangible terms, describing seeing, touching, and even tasting' and ingesting the Divine.[23] Christ is made present in the congregation by the Spirit, whose presence is invoked in the songs, and instead of ingesting elements of bread and wine, the congregation asks God to dwell in their hearts. In addition, the songs serve an anamnetic purpose, allowing the congregation to revisit the paschal event and the event becomes current again as its effects spill over into the present.[24]

---

19 Steven, *Worship in the Restoration Movement*, p. 6.
20 Steven, *Worship in the Restoration Movement*, p. 8.
21 Steven, *Worship in the Restoration Movement*, pp. 12–13.
22 Sarah Koenig, 'This Is My Daily Bread: Toward a sacramental theology of evangelical praise and worship', *Worship* 82 (2008), pp. 141–61, p. 147.
23 Koenig, 'This Is My Daily Bread', p. 149, with reference to Matt Redman's 'Better Is One Day' and Marie Barnett's 'Breathe'.
24 Koenig, 'This Is My Daily Bread', pp. 150–2.

JOHN WIMBER, THE VINEYARD CHURCHES AND VINEYARD MUSIC

In the early 1960s John Wimber brought together a music group that called itself the Righteous Brothers, and they reached the top of the charts a couple of times. During their marriage difficulties, his wife Carol found solace in prayer and searching out belief – John would later join her in that quest. He left the Righteous Brothers, and became a member of the Yorba Linda Friends Church, an evangelical Quaker church. In the late 1970s he and Carol started a house church in their home, which was originally affiliated with the Calvary Chapel fellowship of churches begun by Chuck Smith at Costa Mesa. Calvary Chapel had grown to large numbers with many converts from the hippie movement, who brought a rock music tradition with them. Smith, who was originally from the Foursquare Gospel Pentecostal tradition, recognized gifts of the Spirit, but Calvary Chapel did not make them a prominent part of evangelistic ministry, though it did promote CCM. The Vineyard, a house church branch of Calvary, had already been pioneered by Kenn and Joanie Gulliksen. As Wimber's church began to put greater emphasis on gifts of the Spirit, the Calvary leadership suggested he move over to Gullicksen's Vineyard. Ultimately Wimber was recognized as the leader of the Vineyard, and it separated from the Calvary Chapel fellowship.[25] Thus came about the Vineyard Christian Fellowship in Anaheim, California. David Pytches explains that the Californian style was laid back, and casual:

> This approach was carried over also into the conduct of worship. The music leader, in tee-shirt, shorts and trainers, would stand up with his guitar before the mike on a raised platform, and invite folks to sing along and worship the Lord. And there was John Wimber on the synthesizer and Dick Heying, now on the drums behind him! . . . The music that followed matched their culture and was, in spite of all appearances, superbly professional.[26]

---

25 For the background, see Bill Jackson, *The Quest for the Radical Middle: A History of the Vineyard* (Vineyard International Publishing, Cape Town, 1999).

26 David Pytches, 'A Man Called John' in David Pytches (ed.), *John Wimber: His Influence and Legacy* (Eagle, Guildford, 1996), pp. 9–39, p. 29.

In early 1980 the Vineyard had an experience of the Holy Spirit, and in his books and teaching Wimber particularly emphasized a power evangelism with prophetic words, miracles of healing and intimacy in worship. As a musician who had had a recording in the secular charts, it is perhaps no surprise that Wimber founded Mercy Publishing to promote the music the Vineyard produced, with an album called *Hosanna* released in 1984. Wimber visited the UK in 1981, and influenced a number of leading Church of England evangelical leaders such as Sandy Millar, David Watson and David Pytches. The prolific CCM writer and composer Matt Redman[27] was originally associated with David Pytches' church at St Andrews, Chorleywood, and Vineyard-style worship has supplanted official Church of England liturgical formularies in many of the charismatic evangelical Anglican churches.[28] In 1983 Vineyard Ministries International was founded, and in 1986 the Association of Vineyard Churches was established.

Wimber set out a fivefold flow for worship, designed to move worshippers towards intimacy with God:

1 Call to Worship. This may be through a song such as 'Come, Let Us Worship and Bow Down', or it may be a jubilant song such as 'Don't You Know It's Time to Praise the Lord?'
2 Engagement. This is 'the electrifying dynamic of connection to God and to each other. Expressions of love, adoration, praise, jubilation, intercession, petition.'
3 Expression. This is praise from the heart.
4 Visitation from God.
5 Giving of substance.[29]

Matt Redman has expressed the Vineyard stages a little differently:

---

27 For his ideas on worship, see Matt Redman, *The Unquenchable Worshipper: Coming Back to the Heart of Worship* (Regal, Ventura CA, 2001), and as compiler, *The Heart of Worship Files* (Regal, Ventura CA, 2003). Recent albums include *Beautiful News* (2006) and *We Shall Not Be Shaken* (2009).

28 For example, St Aldate's Church, Oxford, though the writer's experience of worship there on Trinity Sunday 2004 suggested that there was not a clear idea about the intended progression of P&W. It may have been an off day.

29 John Wimber (ed.), *Thoughts on Worship* (Vineyard Music Group, Anaheim CA, 1996), pp. 4–6.

1 Call to Worship.
2 Engagement.
3 Exaltation.
4 Adoration – bringing love songs before the throne of God.
5 Intimacy – a visitation from God.[30]

In both cases, Bible reading and/or preaching and a dismissal with song follow. Wimber also emphasized that worship not only involves our thoughts and intellect, but also our body, and in Scripture this takes the form of singing, playing musical instruments, dancing, kneeling, bowing down and lifting hands.[31] These, too, have become characteristic among charismatic congregations. The publication *Let Your Glory Fall* contained songs and a number of essays on worship.[32] The collection of songs is grouped into seven sections suggested by the Lord's Prayer:

I 'Our Father in Heaven' – Celebrating His Goodness

The 16 songs include Andy Park's 'The River is Here' and 'Yahweh' (1994), as well as songs by Carl Tuttle ('All the Earth Shall Worship', 1982), and David Ruis ('You are Worthy of My Praise', 1993).[33] The chorus of Kevin Prosch's 'His Banner Over Me' (a song inspired by Song of Songs 2.4) is:

> And his banner over me is love
> Yes, his banner over me is love.

2 'Let Your Kingdom Come' – Longing for His Presence

The 18 songs include some by Brian Doerksen ('Come and Fill Me Up', 'Light the Fire Again'), as well as some by Park and Ruis. The chorus of Ruis's 'Let Your Glory Fall' makes the following invitation:

---

30 Matt Redman, 'Worshipper and Musician' in Pytches (ed.), *John Wimber*, pp. 62–70, pp. 65–6.
31 Wimber, *Thoughts on Worship*, p. 3.
32 Vineyard Music Group, *Let Your Glory Fall: Songs and Essays* (Mercy/Vineyard Publishing, Anaheim CA, nd, *c*. 1994). My thanks to Justus Ghormley for furnishing me with a copy of this publication.
33 For Tuttle, see <www.carltuttle.com>; and for Ruis, see Powell, *Encyclopedia*; for Park, see below.

Let your glory fall in this room
Let it go forth from here to the nations
Let your fragrance rest in this place
As we gather to seek your face.

3 'Your Will Be Done' – Passion for His Righteousness

The 16 songs include Park's 'We Will Ride', Scott Brenner's 'Draw Near
to Me', and Craig Musseau's 'Pour Out My Heart'. A contribution by
Brian Doerksen and Cindy Rethmeier, 'I Want to Know You', has these
lyrics:

I want to know you
Lord I must know you
I want to be found in you
I want to be clothed in your truth.

So I fix my eyes on you
Lord I must see you
I put my faith in you
I spend my life on you

I want to know you,
I want to love you
I want to know you more
Jesus, Jesus (2×).

4 'Give Us Our Bread' – Hunger for His Passion

The 14 songs include Craig Musseau's 'Arms of Love', Kelly Carpenter's
'Draw Me Close', and songs by Doerksen and Scott Brenner. John
Barnett's 'Holy and Anointed One' has the following lyrics:

Jesus, Jesus
Holy and Anointed One
Jesus

Jesus, Jesus
Risen and Exalted One
Jesus

(chorus)
Your name is like honey on my lips
Your Spirit like water to my soul
Your word is a lamp unto my fee (*sic*)
Jesus I love You, I love You.

5 'Forgive Us as We Forgive' – Receiving His Mercy and His Compassion

The 13 songs include Andy Park's 'Soften My Heart with Oil', Brian Doerksen's 'Refiner's Fire', and Carl Tuttle's 'Oh Lord Have Mercy'. Also included is Randy and Terry Butler's 'At the Cross':

I know a place, a wonderful place
Where accused and condemned
Find mercy and grace
Where the wrongs we have done
And the wrongs done to us
Were nailed there with him
There on the cross

(1st chorus)
At the cross, (at the cross)
He died for our sin
At the cross, (at the cross)
He gave us life again

(2nd chorus)
At the cross, (at the cross)
You died for our sin
At the cross, (at the cross)
You gave us life again.

6 'Deliver Us From Evil' – Walking in His Freedom

The nine songs include Brian Doerksen's 'Remember Mercy':

Lord, I have heard of your fame
I stand in awe of your deeds, oh Lord

I have heard of your fame
I stand in awe of your deeds, oh Lord.

(chorus)
Renew them. Renew them
In our day, and in our time, make them known
Renew them. Renew them
In our day, and in our time, make them known
In wrath, remember mercy
In wrath, remember mercy.

7 'Yours Is the Glory' – Declaring His Power and Greatness

The 13 songs include Linda Barnhill's 'Glorify', Joey Holder's 'Unto the King', Terry and Randy Butler's 'You Oh Lord are a Great God', as well as David Ruis's 'We will Dance', which has the following lyrics:

Sing a song of celebration
Lift up a shout of praise
For the Bridegroom will come, the glorious One
And oh, we will look on his face
We'll go to a much better place

Dance with all your might
Lift up your hands and clap for joy
The time's drawing near, when he will appear
And oh, we will stand by his side
A strong, pure, spotless bride

(chorus)
We will dance on the streets that are golden
The glorious pride at the great Son of man
From every tongue and tribe and nation
Will join in the song of the Lamb

Sing aloud for the time of rejoicing is near
Sing aloud for the time of rejoicing is near
The risen King, our groom, is soon to appear
The risen King, our groom, is soon to appear
The wedding feast to come is now near at hand

The wedding feast to come is now near at hand
Lift up your voice, proclaim the coming Lamb
Lift up your voice, proclaim the coming Lamb.

Songs such as these are at the heart of this type of worship, and not mere ornamentation. The Vineyard has many artists and bands that have produced albums, and it would be difficult to overestimate their influence. One of the most recent in the UK is from the Burn Band with an album entitled *All from You* (2006), which includes these selections: 'All from You', 'King Forever', 'Son Shining', 'Thank You', 'So Near', 'I Love You', 'How could I Live without You', 'Come to Me', 'You're the Love', 'Have Mercy', 'Joy' and 'More than a Friend'. Two of the most prolific composers have been Brian Doerksen and Andy Park. Doerksen featured as a worship leader on some 25 albums under the Vineyard label, but since 2002 he has recorded solo albums under Integrity's Hosanna Music label. Andy Park is a worship leader at the Vineyard in North Langley, British Columbia, though was originally based in California and worked with John Wimber. Like Doerksen, he has a number of Vineyard albums, and more recently has solo albums – *I Saw Heaven* (1990), *Night and Day* (2001), *In the Secret* (2004), *Unshakeable* (2006), and *Wonder Working God* (2009). The latter features the songs 'Our God Reigns', 'Wonder Working God', 'New Day', 'How Priceless', 'Help Somebody', 'Friend of the Poor', 'Messiah', 'One Thing I Ask', 'Like a Lily', 'Fleece of White' and 'Your Grace is Sufficient'. In his book *To Know You More*, Park sets out a biblical basis for worship and gives advice for worship leaders.[34] According to Park, worship music came out of him 'because I dove headlong into the wonderful, all-consuming pursuit of the greatest treasure in the universe – Jesus'.[35] He made his first musical recording in 1980, and shortly afterwards wrote another song based on Psalm 67. In 1985 he wrote 'Precious Child', which begins, 'Show me, dear Lord, how you see me through your eyes'.

Park explains the importance to him (and the Vineyard) of expressing intimacy with God in song and music. He is also well aware that people remember songs better than sermons, and that 'if we are worship leaders, we *are* theologians, so we'd better be singing the real truth'.[36]

---

34 Andy Park, *To Know You More: Cultivating the Heart of the Worship Leader* (InterVarsity Press, Downers Grove IL, 2002).
35 Park, *To Know You More*, p. 15.
36 Park, *To Know You More*, p. 90.

Park is also appreciative of older hymns (with more contemporary renditions) because they are well known and tell the story of salvation in a manner that many P&W songs do not. He writes:

> Regarding song selection, I use mostly modern worship songs and a few hymns. I mostly use an acoustic rock band, but sometimes I don't use bass and drums. I sing gentle songs and high energy songs. I sing songs that proclaim the attributes of God and his saving work on the cross, and also simple songs of love and devotion.
>
> But everything I do is within a narrow range of instrumentation – guitars, keyboards, drums and bass, with the occasional acoustic instrument, such as flute, penny whistle or saxophone. I don't use a choir (though I did occasionally in Anaheim), and I don't use hymn-books.[37]

He also advises on how to select a 'Worship Set', and presents three main models according to the beats per minute (bpm) of the songs. Beats per minute are an important factor in song selection since 'praise' is more vigorous and 'worship' is slower and more intimate. The first example is the 'Classic progression', complete with a graph showing a sloping curve downwards. This example begins with 'We Want to See Jesus Lifted' (132 bpm), 'Lord I Lift Your Name on High' (88 bpm), 'In the Secret' (126 bpm), 'Who is Like Our God' (82 bpm), 'How Great Thou Art' (80 bpm), 'Holy and Anointed One' (70 bpm) and 'This is Love' (66 bpm).[38] The second model is 'the Earthquake progression', depicting a graph with dips. Sample songs are, 'I Could Sing Your Love Forever' (86 bpm), 'Shout to the Lord ' (74 bpm), 'Unto the King' (126 bpm), 'Isn't He' (68 bpm), 'More Love More Power' (69 bpm), 'We will Dance' (132 bpm), 'Undignified' (114 bpm) and 'The River is Here' (116 bpm).[39] A third model is 'Mild progression', which has a sharp initial dip, but progresses with more gentle rises and dips after that. Examples are, 'All Who are Thirsty' (156 bpm), 'Hungry' (70 bpm), 'Blessed be the Name' (70 bpm), 'The Lord is Gracious and Compassionate' (69 bpm), 'Once Again' (60 bpm), 'There is a Redeemer' (80 bpm) and 'Yet I will Praise' (67 bpm).[40] Park also notes: 'I still copy a lot

---

37 Park, *To Know You More*, pp. 118–19.
38 Park, *To Know You More*, p. 164.
39 Park, *To Know You More*, p. 165.
40 Park, *To Know You More*, p. 166.

of arrangements from worship CDs, using what I like, throwing out what I don't like and the things my band isn't equipped to do. Then I add my own ideas.'[41]

HILLSONG AND DARLENE ZSCHECH

Hillsong was started in 1983 at Baulkham Hills, a suburb of Sydney, Australia, by Brian and Bobbie Houston. The Houstons had moved from New Zealand to assist with Brian's father, Frank Houston's, Sydney Christian Life Centre in 1978. The church plant Brian and Bobbie founded at Baulkham Hills was originally called Hills Christian Life Centre. It later merged with Sydney Christian Life Centre at Waterloo to form Hillsong Church, which is affiliated with the Assemblies of God. There are currently four campuses across Sydney, and fifteen extension services. Additionally, it has churches in London, Kiev, Cape Town and Stockholm. Hillsong services are also held in Paris, Berlin and Moscow. Like many neo-charismatic churches, there is an emphasis on baptism in the Spirit and gifts of the Spirit. The original Baulkham Hills building, which opened in 1997, is now mainly used for administration, and in 2002 a much larger convention centre, which houses a vast worship space and mall-like shops selling books, music and soft beverages, was opened adjacent to the original building. Hillsong congregations are large, and also of a lower average age than most churches.

Hillsong UK holds its services at the Dominion Theatre, Tottenham Court Road, London. At the 10.30 service on Sunday 25 October 2009, displayed on the screen on the stage were the words 'Jesus' and 'Welcome Home', along with a cross. The service began with loud instrumental music and blue stage lights. After playing a few video clips the music became louder. The congregation clapped as the band came on stage, and the songs 'One Hope for All' and 'We've Got New Life' were sung, followed by the quieter 'I will Lift Up My Eyes'. Following a soft instrumental interlude, another loud song was played, and then the quieter 'For Eternity'. Big-screen projections during the service included depictions of the band. The pastor Gary Clarke came to the centre of the stage and asked for prayer requests, which included prayers for unemployed members to get jobs. This was followed by the children's choir singing, and then the dedication of babies, with a charge to parents to be models for their children by putting God first. The pastor's wife Cathy, who serves as co-pastor, led prayer for the babies and their parents, using the classic evangelical phraseology of 'Lord, we *just* pray for . . . , and we *just* pray that'. After applause for parents and babies, the offertory was taken, and the associate pastor spoke about faith in Hebrews 11.5. Displayed on the projection screen was an advertisement about how to belong to Hillsong, and then, following a prayer for tithing, CDs and books being offered for sale were also advertised. The band then played 'In a World that's Lost', and after a brief prayer a lectern was placed centre-stage for Gary Clarke to preach. A 45-minute sermon on Colossians 3 followed, with the pastor walking up and down on the stage, his figure being projected on the large screen. The message was 'If you believe right, you will live right'. It concluded with quiet music and an altar call. The congregation then repeated a prayer for Jesus to come into their lives. New converts were given Bibles. After introducing the pastoral leader, there was another prayer, and then the band sang a final loud song. A brief prayer and the dismissal 'Take care' concluded the worship.

Since the 1990s Hillsong has released about forty P&W albums. Hillsong United, its youth ministry and band, has sold recordings by the millions in the USA.[42] This younger generation of musicians at Hillsong includes Joel Houston, Marty Sampson and Reuben Morgan. However, the church's best-known musicians and worship pastors are Geoffrey Bulloch and Darlene Zschech, though neither of them are now with the Baulkham Hills church. Zschech, famous for the song 'Shout to the Lord', has featured with Hillsong's worship band on many CDs, and has two solo albums.[43] She has been involved with music from childhood, and had been involved with Christian worship bands before joining the Hills Christian Life Centre in 1990. Zschech has written some devotional reflections on her faith and vocation as a worship pastor, having become a Christian at the age of fifteen through the Royal Ranger youth programme.[44] According to her, praise and worship are prayer – and prayer is intimate, intercessory and powerful.[45]

---

42 Cassandra Zinchini, 'Taking Revival to the World', *Christianity Today* (October 2007), p. 35.
43 See <http://darlenezschech.homestead.com/Discography.html>.
44 Darlene Zschech, *Extravagant Worship* (Bethany House, Minneapolis MN, 2001), p. 111.
45 Zschech, *Extravagant Worship*, p. 61.

Praise is not a 'happy-clappy' song; rather it is a declaration, a victory cry, proclaiming faith to stand firm in the place God has given us.[46] 'Praise and worship is active, not passive. It is a decision of the heart, the mind, and the will to enter His gates into God's presence. We don't worship to feel good; worship declares God's reigning power into our lives.'[47] The heart of worship, she believes, is to allow us to bring an offering of the heart, lifting our voices, and it releases what we have to give; it leads to service in the world.[48] Of Hillsong she writes:

> [E]ven with all the recording projects we do and new songs we bring to record, I always encourage our writers to never become project-based writers. We must always be heaven-based writers whose hearts are desperate to catch the 'new song' in everything we write. A passion for our songs to be pure in spirit and truth must remain whether a song is to be sung to thousands or to a divine audience of One. I don't want to write songs that sound like songs we've already heard or songs that sound like the latest hit on the radio. I search for songs that bring a prophetically fresh sound, something straight from the Father's heart.[49]

With sincere belief that the words and music are a gift of the Spirit, she writes:

> In my experience the worship of this generation seems simply to serve as many denominations as is possible – could this be part of the new song? We have been questioned about our approach, condemned for it, but I say we have never claimed to be experts; it has never been 'out with the old, in with the new.' Just 'Lord, this is my heart song.' As we risk looking foolish and comical to some, our music continues to be a lifeline to so many. Every one of our writers receives many letters from people saying 'the songs cause what in my heart is in the distance . . . to become close by way of songs that are slightly more intimate in content.' Changing a song

---

46 Zschech, *Extravagant Worship*, p. 52.
47 Darlene Zschech, *The Kiss of Heaven: God's Favor to Empower Your Life Dream* (Bethany House, Minneapolis MN, 2003), p. 149.
48 Zschech, *The Kiss of Heaven*, pp. 142ff.
49 Zschech *Extravagant Worship*, p. 193.

from 'We love you' to 'I love you' is, for many, a powerful and confronting journey.[50]

Zschech's album *Kiss of Heaven* contains 14 songs, all of which she has composed herself or jointly, other than the last track, which is 'Walk On' by U2. It has the songs 'Pray' (based on the Lord's Prayer), 'Heaven on Earth', 'Faithful', 'Beautiful Saviour', 'Everything about You', 'Promise', 'Irresistible', 'Kiss of Heaven', 'Everlasting', 'Shout to the Lord', 'Dreams', 'Wonderful You', 'Thankful' and 'Walk On'. The lyrics of 'Dreams' give some idea of the intimacy of many songs of the P&W genre:

> Take this heart of mine. You've captured me. I'm so in love with
>   You.
> My destiny defined is spending every moment just to know You.
> I need to know You more.
> You're my world, You're my heart's desire.
> Faithful love takes me higher. I found more than I ever dared
>   imagine. Love has found a way, love has found a way.
> I've opened my heart to You, You've taken what was broken, made
>   me new. And all that I need to find are ways to let You know
>   how much I love You.
> I want to love You more.
> Angels are gathering to bow and sing an anthem to Your Name.
>   Lifted on Heaven's wings. This song in my heart needs to say,
>   Oh, how I love You Lord.
> You're my world, You're my heart's desire.
> Faithful love takes me higher. I found more than I ever dreamed
>   or imagined.
> Love has found a way, love has found a way.[51]

The intimacy here is reminiscent in part of Donne's poem 'Batter my heart Three Personed God', but the words also echo the intimacy of

---

50 Darlene Zschech, 'The Role of the Holy Spirit in Worship: An introduction to the Hillsong Church, Sydney, Australia' in Teresa Berger and Bryan D. Spinks (eds), *The Spirit in Worship – Worship in the Spirit* (Liturgical Press, Collegeville MN, 2009), pp. 285–92, pp. 290–1.
51 Darlene Zschech, 'Dreams', from the CD *Kiss of Heaven* (Extravagant Worship, 2003).

many secular soft rock songs. God as lover is a common theme in the intimate P&W songs.

THE ICHTHUS FELLOWSHIP AND
THE SONGS OF GRAHAM KENDRICK

The Ichthus Fellowship was founded by Roger Forster, who has been associated with a number of evangelical associations and missions, and had an experience of being baptized in the Holy Spirit. He founded Ichthus in 1974 with 14 people meeting in a front room, and by 1992 it had 47 congregations. Its theology has been of a more open kind than many Restorationist groups, and has been characterized by social and racial inclusiveness, with concentration on mission and practical Christianity. Graham Kendrick was formerly a member of this fellowship, though now he is associated with Compassion International, a foundation he established to combat poverty among children. The son of a Baptist minister, at college Kendrick was baptized by the Spirit, and through this was exposed to the first wave of simple songs that came out of the charismatic revival. While with Ichthus, Kendrick was involved with Roger Forster, and Gerald Coates of Pioneer, in founding the March for Jesus (1987–2000), which made Christians visible on the streets, witnessing to a secular world. He is probably the most published and most well known of British P&W composers, and his songs are sung across the denominations. His best-known song is 'Shine, Jesus, Shine'.

Kendrick outlined his views on worship in a book of the same title.[52] True worship involves knowing God as our Father, and looking with unveiled faces into the Lord's face.[53] It is also a political act, for if Jesus is Lord, all other 'lords' are excluded. Worship includes being reconciled to others, and as we meet

> we should find ourselves in a kind of invisible triangle, joined by the Spirit and relating together in a common experience of worship yet focused upon the Lord. As we move from the horizontal plane closer to the apex of the triangle, we find ourselves moving closer together.[54]

---

52 Graham Kendrick, *Worship* (Kingsway Publications, Eastbourne, 1984).
53 Kendrick, *Worship*, p. 35.
54 Kendrick, *Worship*, p. 49.

Kendrick also stressed the picture of God revealed by Jesus – 'a God with a heart just like the heart of a father, when it is at its most tender, its most sensitive, its most generous, its most protective and its most forgiving'.[55] In his chapters on leading worship, Kendrick uses the model of the Temple, and writes that in worship we are changed because we look into the gaze of God. What emerges in this work is the importance of intimacy with God.

Elsewhere he has suggested that P&W springs from recovery of a number of emphases – the priesthood of all believers (songs become the property of all), evangelism and mission, importance of the Scriptures, fellowship, and baptism in the Spirit.[56] The resulting music has been dubbed 'baptized rock and roll' because the 'domination of the three-and-a-half minute radio pop song in popular culture has largely shaped the genre of the worship chorus – rhythmic, instant, strong on emotion, light in content'.[57] His own concerns when writing a song are sincerity and theological content. In his view, the qualities of a good congregational song are accessibility, simplicity and theological integrity, and it must carry conviction.[58]

As far as his own needs as a songwriter are concerned, Kendrick has said that he needs 'musical creativity, to innovate, to break redundant musical habits, and to find musical stimulation'.[59] Albums have appeared regularly since 1971.[60] The inspiration and circumstances of some of his compositions are described by Kendrick in *Behind the Songs*.[61] Thus the song 'Fighter' reflects a time when he was 'beginning to recognize (*sic*) the importance of a more radical and visionary Christian faith', and how he was looking at the world as a battle for the souls of men and women, bringing a challenge to the churches – 'Where have all the Christian soldiers gone?'[62] 'No Need to Fear' was composed after losing his sister Gillian to cancer, and inspired by Psalm

55 Kendrick, *Worship*, p. 73.
56 Kendrick, 'Worship in Spirit and Truth', pp. 86–103.
57 Kendrick, 'Worship in Spirit and Truth', p. 88.
58 Kendrick, 'Worship in Spirit and Truth', pp. 97–8.
59 Kendrick, 'Worship in Spirit and Truth', pp. 99–100.
60 <http://www.grahamkendrick.co.uk/discography.php>.
61 Graham Kendrick, with Clive Price, *Behind the Songs* (Kevin Mayhew, Stowmarket, 2001).
62 Kendrick, with Price, *Behind the Songs*, p. 58.

49.[63] His most celebrated composition, 'Shine, Jesus, Shine', was composed at a time when Ichthus Christian Fellowship was focusing on the theme of the presence and holiness of God, who dwells in unapproachable light.[64] Although there is a personal story behind the songs, Kendrick reflects on some of the letters he receives, and concludes that now and again,

> there comes a reminder of the way that God can take something as simple as words fitted to a melody, crafted in the most mundane of circumstances and in the shadow of the writer's weakness and inadequacy, yet make it live and breathe and become part of some other worshipper's story.[65]

LEX ORANDI, LEX CREDENDI?

P&W songs play a major role in neo-charismatic worship, and it is through the songs that its theology/theologies is/are expressed. With literally thousands of songs, it is impossible to give any comprehensive theological critique of this genre. Martyn Percy has critiqued some of the Vineyard songs, and Pete Ward has undertaken an analysis of some of the prominent themes of a selection of P&W songs from *Songs of Fellowship*, Book 1, *Graham Kendrick Songbook*, Volume 2, *Songs of the Vineyard*, Volume 1, and *The Survivor Songbook*.[66] A recent collection of essays has scrutinized the top 77 contemporary worship music P&W songs, which were the songs that made up the Christian Copyright Licensing International's Top 25 lists between 1989 and 2005.[67] What, then, were the observations of these studies?

Percy's study of charismatic movements, and particularly John Wimber's writings, focused on the importance of power within the movement, and the leader as an agent of power. He divided the selection of Vineyard songs into four groups:

---

63 Kendrick, with Price, *Behind the Songs*, pp. 163–4.
64 Kendrick, with Price, *Behind the Songs*, p. 152.
65 Kendrick, with Price, *Behind the Songs*, p. 218.
66 Martyn Percy, *Words, Wonders and Power: Understanding Contemporary Christian Fundamentalism and Revivalism* (SPCK, London, 1996); Ward, *Selling Worship*.
67 Robert Woods and Brian Walrath (eds), *The Message in the Music: Studying Contemporary Praise and Worship* (Abingdon Press, Nashville TN, 2007).

1   Love and closeness
2   The power and dominion of God
3   Holiness
4   Of and about praise and worship.

In his judgement, the songs erode the distance between God and humanity, and in 'metaphor, theme and form, a clear stress on submission to power emerges, in the wider pursuit of fulfilment (*sic*) and power for the individual Christian, the Church, and ultimately, the human race'.[68] He suggests that the songs say little about the cross, and fail to articulate anything negative. Christ the King, enthroned in glory reigning with the Father, is emphasized at the expense of Christ in his risen humanity who has known weakness.[69] Trinitarian belief is less than orthodox, and the Spirit seems to be an unstoppable force rather than the third person of the Trinity. The Church is the Church Militant which establishes a mighty Kingdom prior to the return of Christ. Whereas 'Lord' is a kind of metaphor for the power of God, 'You' functions as a metaphor for the love of God. Percy suggests that 'The ideology, helped by the music, establishes and fixes a relationship between God and the believers that is intimate, at times passive, passionate and sensual, and occasionally, almost sexual.'[70]

Pete Ward echoes many of Percy's observations in his analysis. In *Songs of Fellowship*, Volume 1, he notes an absence of reference to the incarnation and ministry of Jesus, his teaching, or even his passion. What is dominant is a vision of the risen and ascended Lord.[71] 'There is also', says Ward, 'an almost sickly sweet sentimentality in the way that many of the songs speak of Jesus. He is "lovely", "pure" and "kind".'[72] Jesus as friend and King, and God as Father and Lord, are prominent. The Christian story is arranged around the central vision of the people of God gathered in the Temple where Jesus is enthroned on high.[73] In Ward's view, the *Graham Kendrick Songbook*, Volume 2, shares a number of themes in common with *Songs of Fellowship*, but there is, in this collection, a greater emphasis on the Church. The waking Church is putting off old things, is prone to failure, and all around is sin and

---

68   Percy, *Words, Wonders and Power*, p. 66.
69   Percy, *Words, Wonders and Power*, p. 79.
70   Percy, *Words, Wonders and Power*, p. 70.
71   Ward, *Selling Worship*, p. 136.
72   Ward, *Selling Worship*, p. 137.
73   Ward, *Selling Worship*, p. 139.

wickedness. However, believers are invited to renew themselves in the Lord. There are also echoes of Kendrick's interest in marching for Jesus. Like *Songs of Fellowship*, there is little reference in this collection to the cross, but there is a clear concern for the vision of Jesus as King, high and lifted on his throne.[74] Ward agrees with much of Percy's assessment of the Vineyard songs, which are not *about* Jesus, but songs *to* Jesus. In Ward's judgement,

> The sentiments expressed are close to those used in popular music for the romantic relationship between a man and a woman. Jesus is spoken of as someone to love. Echoing popular song the believer speaks of loving Jesus, 'most of all because you are you'.[75]

'Lord' is a key metaphor that connotes power and omnipotence.[76] *The Survivor Songbook* of 2002 (part of a series of songbooks published in relation to the Soul Survivor Festival) has distinctive contributions from Matt Redman and Tim Hughes, among others. A key metaphor here is the heart – there is 'heart' to worship. Our hearts are fixed on the heart of Jesus; praise is a sacrificial love, and the cross of Jesus and his blood feature prominently in this collection. There is intimacy, too, and the believer loves the Lord.

The collection edited by Woods and Walrath on the 77 top songs, *The Message in the Music*, confirms some of Percy's and Ward's observations. Lester Ruth noted the dearth of explicit, and in many cases implicit, trinitarian teaching and belief – echoed also by Robin Parry.[77] In keeping with Percy and Ward, Jennell Williams Paris suggests that the American romantic ideal is reflected in some of the songs – like the leading man in the movies, God saves, wins over, and enjoys his one true love. The songs imagine a divine partner who is the ultimate boyfriend, though as Keith Drury discovered, this did not put off too

---

74 Ward, *Selling Worship*, pp. 141–5.
75 Ward, *Selling Worship*, p. 145.
76 Ward, *Selling Worship*, p. 147.
77 Lester Ruth, 'How Great Is Our God: The Trinity in contemporary Christian worship music' in Woods and Walrath (eds), *The Message in the Music*, pp. 29–42. Cf. Lester Ruth, '*Lex Amandi, Lex Orandi*: The Trinity in the most-used contemporary Christian worship songs' in Bryan D. Spinks (ed.), *The Place of Christ in Liturgical Prayer: Trinity, Christology, and Liturgical Theology* (Liturgical Press, Collegeville MN, 2008), pp. 342–59. Robin Parry, *Worshipping Trinity: Coming Back to the Heart of Worship* (Paternoster Press, Bletchley, 2005).

many young males.[78] The songs are frequently lacking in any concern for righteousness and social justice, and only a few of the 77 lyrically and musically contribute at some level to the meaningful expression of pain and suffering.

How far are these observations reflected in two recent CD collections – *Wonder Working God* by Andy Park of Vineyard, and Hillsong's *Songs for Communion*?[79] Park's 11 songs on this CD address the Father, and Jesus, but not the Spirit – though this is not true of his many other CDs, where the Spirit certainly finds generous mention. The most common metaphors for God are Lord and King, but God is also 'creator of all life' and 'helper of the weak'. Jesus is addressed as Messiah, Deliverer, Redeemer, Lamb of God, Emmanuel, Comforter and the Prince of Peace. None of the songs unfold the life and teaching of Jesus, but there is reference to the atonement – 'You shed your blood/And you died for me/You gave me life' ('How Priceless'). Included are two songs that address issues of justice and pain. 'Help Somebody' draws attention to those needing help, and asks worshippers to open their hearts and hands; to take their faith for a ride, and use their prayers to ease somebody's pain. 'Give big bucks, give small change/Give whatcha got and you'll never be the same' . . . 'Show your faith by your deeds'. In 'Friend of the Poor' God is spoken of as friend of the poor, knowing everyone by name; it implicitly asks God's help for all. God's sufficient grace is another theme, with the worshipper surrendering his or her life to God, for God's love is sufficient. God's love covers the worshipper like a blanket, a fleece and as snow, and the whiteness of all these covers the crimson stain of sin. God is a wonder-working God who will bring his reign on earth. Inspired by the Song of Songs, 'Like a Lily' is an intimate song expressing love of God and being in his presence, while 'One Thing I Ask' requests to be in God's presence and sit at his feet.

The Hillsong album contains songs written over a number of years for the church during times of communion, which at Baulkham Hills is once a month. Amanda Bull of Hillsong explains:

---

78 Jenell Williams Paris, 'I Could Sing of Your Love Forever: American romance in contemporary worship music' in Woods and Walrath (eds), *The Message in the Music*, pp. 43–53; and Keith Drury, 'I'm Desperate for You: Male perception of romantic lyrics in contemporary worship music', in Woods and Walrath (eds), *The Message in the Music*, pp. 54–64.

79 Andy Park, *Wonder Working God* (Ion Records, 2009); Hillsong, *Songs for Communion* (Hillsong Church, Hillsong Music Australia), 2006.

In the midst of praise and worship, the service pauses with the Pastor addressing the congregation, sharing a Bible verse and speaking about the meaning and significance of communion and saying a prayer. The congregation receives the emblems. We would then have a time of reflection and personal prayer with an item of worship or DVD presentation focused on Jesus Christ and the Cross. The Pastor would then lead the congregation in partaking of the emblems, followed by a time of worship.[80]

According to Darlene Zschech, the communion songs on this album 'have stirred us time and again to remember, to celebrate, to honour and to worship the One who laid down His life to purchase ours'. The 14 songs are described as 'intimate worship' – all of them are about Jesus, and most are addressed to Jesus. These are Christocentric songs, and although the Father is mentioned, the Holy Spirit is not. Even though they are to be sung at communion, there is no reference to the supper and institution, no reference to the body of Christ, nor is there any reference to the bread and wine. The principal focus is the atoning blood of Christ and his sacrifice. The incarnation and the resulting love of God is the focus of one of the songs. Jesus is the Lamb, exalted King, Saviour, Emmanuel. His wounds have made the worshipper whole and his sacrifice has saved the soul. Jesus is addressed in intimate terms in the song 'Life', where the worshipper describes him as his/her endless love, as being beautiful, and as being the one the worshipper will love all his/her life. The main focus of these songs is the sacrificial blood of Christ which has whitened our sins and evokes our intimate love.

This review of the two albums confirms some of the observations of Percy, Ward and the authors in the Woods/Walrath collection, though Park has certainly addressed the issue of justice and Christian action. By way of defence for the apparent disapproval (Percy) of the romantic/erotic element in many of the songs, they do indeed reflect many of the songs of the secular pop scene, but capture it for God in terms of the Song of Songs and the mystics. It is hardly new to Christian prayer and devotion.

---

80 Amanda Bull, Hillsong Church, email 9 October 2009. Cf. communion at Lakewood Church (see p. 73).

FROM ROARING TO SOAKING:
TORONTO AIRPORT CHRISTIAN FELLOWSHIP

One further landmark in the neo-charismatic renewal is the Toronto Blessing.[81] Also known today as the Toronto Airport Christian Fellowship (TACF), it is a non-denominational, neo-charismatic group in Toronto, Canada, affiliated with the Partners in Harvest churches and Catch the Fire Ministries. Steve and Sandra Long serve as the senior pastors. It was founded in 1988 by John and Carol Arnott (who now pioneer Catch the Fire Ministries), and was for a time affiliated with the Vineyard movement. In January 1994 a Vineyard minister, Randy Clark, visited what was then Toronto Airport Vineyard Church, and a revival with manifestations began. It attracted widespread interest, and became something of a place of pilgrimage. Its influence spread, and it particularly influenced Sandy Millar and Holy Trinity, Brompton, as well as some of the Restorationist leaders in the UK. In addition to conversions and healings, the manifestations included laughter, falling, prostration, and loss of body control. Another manifestation was making animal noises, such as roaring, growling and barking. Collectively these manifestations were called 'slain in the Spirit' or 'drunkenness in the Spirit'. Although Wimber initially supported the stress on these manifestations, the Toronto congregation and the Vineyard eventually parted company in 1995 – Wimber withdrawing the Vineyard endorsement, and the Toronto leadership resigning from the Vineyard. Such manifestations were indeed not new – they have parallels in the eighteenth-century camp meetings, and in the 1801 Cane Ridge revival. However, these manifestations added yet another element to the neo-charismatic worship service. Martyn Percy visited TACF in 1996, and describes the physicality that accompanied the intimate language of the songs:

> At one Toronto intercession meeting I attended, the two women in front of me 'lapsed' into a state of ecstasy. They sat astride their chairs, and then 'rode' them rhythmically with deep and quick pelvic thrusts, their backs arched and their heads in the air, for about 20 minutes. All the while they were breathing deeply, at

---

81 David Hilborn (ed.), *'Toronto' in Perspective: Papers on the New Charismatic Wave of the Mid 1990s* (ACUTE, Paternoster Press, Carlisle, 2001).

times hyper-ventilating, sighing, and crying (with pleasure). Nobody in the prayer meeting found this strange: one of these women later delivered a 'prophetic message' about Jesus coming to his bride soon, and the need to be ready.[82]

More recently, the Arnotts have developed the Catch the Fire Ministries, with a stress on 'soaking'. This is also called 'carpet time', or 'resting on the floor', and recipients are invited to 'marinate in the Spirit' and 'soak in prayer'. The TACF website in 2007 explained that soaking is intimate time spent with Jesus. 'It's you and I enjoying just being with Him. It's about returning to our first love.' It further explained:

> Although 'soaking' includes waiting on the Lord, in this present move of the Spirit it means much more than that. To 'soak' in God's presence is to rest in His love rather than to 'strive' in prayer. As the person receiving a touch from God begins to connect with the reality of the Holy Spirit's presence, he often responds by falling or simply lying on the floor. As he rests expectantly in God's presence, often the Holy Spirit hovers over the person to reveal more of God's love and to renew and repair areas of a person's life. As the believer soaks in God's presence, the Lord takes control and begins to draw his attention to God's word either in the scriptures or through internal audible impressions or pictures he sees in his mind's eye.[83]

According to this site, Carol Arnott compares soaking in prayer to making pickles – we soak in the River of God, and take on the flavour of the Holy Spirit. Catch the Fire Ministries resources include a soaking kit, with DVD and instructions – a special soaking pillow and blanket are also available for purchase.[84]

Soaking CDs are also available and a number are recommended by Catch the Fire Ministries. Laura Rhinehart's *The Soaking Room*,

---

82 Martyn Percy, 'Sweet Rapture: Subliminal eroticism in contemporary charismatic worship', *Theology and Sexuality* 6 (1997), pp. 71–106, p. 84, n. 33.

83 <http://www.tacf.org/tacforghome/CatchTheFireMinistries/SoakingPrayerCenters/Common> (accessed 4/12/2007). The site has now been changed. See <http://www.thehealingcentre.us/pages.asp?pageid=54181>.

84 <http://www.catchthefire.com/community/resources>.

Volume 1 is considered here.[85] The cover of the CD advertises it as 'a compilation of spontaneous songs that were captured (recorded) as they were experienced at various gatherings'.[86] The website explains that soaking

> is all about relationship with our Daddy God, our Husband, Jesus, and our Friend, Holy Spirit. When we know Who He is in us and who we are in Him, we are freed to commune with Him and Heaven is able to touch earth through us and create a living highway for His manifest presence to be released. Our hearts are to simply go where He goes, do what He is doing, and say what He is saying.[87]

It appears that soaking can be part of the worship service, or a pre-worship exercise.

Rhinehart's album, *The Soaking Room*, Volume 1, has seven songs, the shortest lasting 4.55 and the longest 11.36 minutes. The tempo is mainly slow and meditative, and reminiscent of 'cool down' music played in Body Pump workouts at gyms. Percy's observations about intimacy and eroticism find ample illustration in these songs. 'Drink of You' has lyrics (or spontaneous statements) such as 'I want a taste of you', 'I'm pulling you deeper, pulling you closer', 'I am pursuing you', 'Do you want me like I want you?' The song 'Come to the Well' exclaims 'Lord Jesus, I love you/Lord Jesus, so sweet, so kind/How I love to look into your eyes/How I love to gaze on your beautiful face/You are everything I desire/You are everything that I long for'. Lyrics that appear later in the song include, 'I can feel your love swelling, swelling and growing inside me/swelling and growing deeper and wider inside me/Do you feel, feel the swelling inside you/It's expanding/I see walls bursting out, bursting down from the expansion of his love today'. In 'The Father's House', God is speaking and assures the worshipper that 'My house is your house/My table is your table/My bed is your bed . . . Some of you need to eat/some of you need to drink/but some of you need to sleep.' In 'Isa's Song', God will

---

85 Laura Rhinehart, *The Soaking Room*, vol. 1 (Laura Rhinehart Music, 2007), <www.thesoakingroom.com>.
86 Rhinehart, *The Soaking Room*.
87 <http://www.thesoakingroom.com/wb/pages/about-us.php>.

anoint the worshipper and the nations, and in doing so God's love increases in the worshipper. In 'Step into Grace', the worshipper affirms that he or she is a daughter or son of God, and that God's beauty dwells in the worshipper. God speaks affirming that there is no distance and no shame that separates them, and it was a lie if they ever thought that (it is not clear whether God told the lie, or whether it was lack of faith that created the lie of separation from God). This song affirms God's love and release from 'your prison' (sin/guilt/lack of faith?). The lengthy final song of the album repeats that 'we stand firm', 'we chose to believe', 'we chose to stand', and concludes with the hymn 'The Solid Rock'.[88]

Other manifestations of the Toronto Blessing and its aftermath include spontaneous songs in worship, painting worship – where worshippers paint 'in the Spirit', and the 'drunkenness in the Spirit' of John Scotland.[89] On the whole, these are not common in most Third Wave worship services.

CONCLUDING REMARKS

The Third Wave can certainly claim to be postmodern in that it dates from the 1980s, though its pioneers were Boomers raised in modernity, and the neo-charismatic movement might, after all, be simply another PMT – that is, another Pre-Millennial Tension, which is 'the well-documented history of religious paranoia and hysteria that accompanies the end of each millennium'.[90] Andrew Wright notes:

> On the one hand Pentecostals, unlike Methodists and Anglicans, have not adopted a modern scriptural hermeneutic nor acceded to Enlightenment doctrines of progress and critical rationality. On the other hand, Pentecostals have been open to modern technologies, advertising and management techniques. Their commitment to demotic hymnody – no doubt in order to subvert popular culture – has meant in effect that they have been far more at home

---

88 Rhinehart, *The Soaking Room*.
89 <http://www.youtube.com/watch?v=Pkan64ojtHY>; <http://www.youtube.com/watch?v=FqL_Z58ONQE>; <http://www.youtube.com/watch?v=ZHHeeZQx2U8&feature=related>; <http://www.youtube.com/watch?v=pU9ZOINBdi0>.
90 Percy, *Words, Wonders and Power*, p. 153.

with mass media and consumer culture than many of their mainline counterparts.[91]

P&W has been one of the main contributions of the charismatic revivals to contemporary worship, and its influence and popularity cannot be underestimated or ignored. However, this genre, too, can be traced back to movements that belong to the era of modernity. Like pop music, its music is modern, but is able to morph as we move into post-modernity. This raises the possibility that the postmodern songs of P&W are, in fact, not postmodern at all, but a form of modernity surviving and thriving in postmodernity. The music is often criticized for its shallow and simple style, and music styles have long featured in the worship wars.[92] It should be recalled that in Anglicanism there was a great difference in music styles between the partbooks composed for cathedral and collegiate churches which had established choirs, and the music of parish churches with Sternhold and Hopkins, some of whose tunes echoed secular usage. The west gallery music that held sway in most parish churches in the late eighteenth century, with its parish band and singers, was also based on popular ballads and secular music styles. In this sense P&W is not a great innovation. The real question will be whether Gen Y and postmodernity will want to promote a more serious sacred style of music, much as the nineteenth-century Romantic movement did. A new style of music might displace P&W, just as classic hymns and choral music did in nineteenth-century Anglicanism. The vast number of P&W songs that are produced have a counterpart in the vast number of hymns composed from the late seventeenth century through to the end of the nineteenth century. Most fell by the wayside, and only the best and most popular have survived. This will probably also be true of P&W songs. As Bert Polman has said:

> The repertoire of Christian hymnody has always operated on an anthology concept, keeping the best of the old hymns and always open to the best of the new songs. And by all accounts, at least

---

91 Andrew Walker, 'Thoroughly Modern: Sociological reflections on the charismatic movement from the end of the twentieth century' in Hunt, Hamilton and Walter (eds), *Charismatic Christianity*, pp. 17–42, p. 27.

92 Terry W. York, *America's Worship Wars* (Hendrickson Publishers, Peabody MA, 2003). See also Barry Liesch, *The New Worship: Straight Talk on Music and the Church* (Baker Books, Grand Rapids MI, 2001).

some P-W songs appear to be taking their place in that anthology. Stuart Townend and Keith Getty's *In Christ Alone* is probably the best example of a P-W song that will be known by later genera-tions, I suspect, as a 'classic' hymn.[93]

On the other hand, the vast majority of these songs will probably be only a footnote in the history of worship.

93 Bert Polman, 'Praise the Name of Jesus: Are all Praise and Worship songs for the con-gregation?' in Woods and Walrath (eds), *The Message in the Music*, pp. 127–37, p. 136.

Chapter 5

On the margins of the corporate global postmodern culture

Nearly all the worship trends discussed thus far have tended to be North Atlantic/Euro/White initiatives and developments. That is in part because conscious concern with and unconscious developments of postmodern global culture are hard to divorce from their North Atlantic commercial and technological origins. This culture pervades the globe with its international corporate identity, and affects all other regional and local cultures to some degree. Cell phones, iPods and laptops are not the preserve of the so-called developed nations. All national, regional and local cultures are thus in transition as they accommodate or react to the prevailing international culture. Extreme Islamic groups protest against Western, and particularly American, influence on their traditional way of life and standards, and in their efforts to resist this intrusion, the use of the latest developments in weaponry and communication technology have come into play. Many years ago Fatma Mansur suggested that when countries gain independence, reactions to foreign cultures seem to have the Hegelian schema of thesis, antithesis and synthesis.[1] The intruding culture tends to dominate; then a reaction intended to recover the traditional or older cultural norms sets in; but what in fact emerges is a new synthesis. This is probably true also of many new developments in culture and society.

Sensitivity to the fact that liturgical forms and reforms have tended to be European and Western has, in recent decades, led to moves toward indigenization/inculturation/contextualization. In the Roman Catholic Church examples of post-Vatican II (inculturated) liturgies include the Zaire Mass and a Mass for India, though much of the ambitious

---

1 Fatma Mansur, *Process of Independence* (London, Routledge & Paul; New York, Humanities Press, 1962).

proposals for the latter were rejected by the Congregation for Divine Worship.[2] The recent collection of essays *Christian Worship in Australia* draws attention to the quest in that country to incorporate the culture of the First Nation people; and the collection entitled *Worship, Window of the Urban Church* is an example of the localization of worship in urban Great Britain.[3] Such initiatives are also generated by those whose cultural homes or origins are Euro-Atlantic. It is not these types of contextualization that form the subject of this chapter, but rather the worship of communities that stand out as a reminder that within postmodern global culture some worship is almost counter-cultural. The four groups discussed here are extremely different from one another: African Independent Churches; Korean *Minjung* and *Kuk-ak* worship; the Amish; and the North American Appalachian snake-handling sects.

AFRICAN INDEPENDENT CHURCHES

AICs seem to have been an early twentieth-century phenomenon, and since they differ considerably from one another, as do the cultures of Africa, reference here is limited to three well-documented examples of these broad and varied churches. In a South African context, Dawid Venter, in conversation with Stephen Hayes, suggested four classifications of AICs:

- African *Independent* Churches that 'originated in Africa, and are not dependent on any religious groups outside Africa for funding, leadership or control'.
- African *Initiated* Churches that 'were started as a result of African initiative in African countries, but may be affiliated to wider bodies that include non-African members'.
- African *Indigenous* Churches that 'have and retain an African ethos, and whose theology has developed a distinctive local flavour'.
- African *Instituted* Churches, 'whose establishment and growth have taken place on African soil'.[4]

---

2 P. Puthangara, 'Liturgical Renewal in India', *Ephemerides Liturgicae* 91 (1977), pp. 350–66; Bryan D. Spinks, 'The Anaphora for India: Some theological objections to an attempt at inculturation', *Ephemerides Liturgicae* 95 (1981), pp. 529–49.
3 Stephen Burns and Anita Monro (eds), *Christian Worship in Australia: Inculturating the Liturgical Tradition* (St Pauls Publications, Strathfield NSW, 2009); Tim Stratford (ed.), *Worship: Window of the Urban Church* (SPCK, London, 2006).
4 Dawid Venter, 'Concepts and Theories in the Study of African Independent Churches'

AICs usually have a founder who is regarded as more than a prophet, and almost on a par with Christ. The gifts of prophecy, speaking in tongues and healing powers are regarded as important, and in this respect they have certain things in common with neo-charismatics, such as Toronto Airport Church. Their appearance during the last decades of colonial rule has been interpreted as a response to the strains and stresses of modernity, as well as reactions to the intruding colonial culture and religion. Jim Kiernan notes that their reactions to modernity 'vary from closing the hatches to vigorous opposition or partial acceptance – primarily because AICs differ in origin and character'.[5]

Accounts of the Independent Holy Spirit Churches in East Africa have been given by Ane Marie Bak Rasmussen and Cynthia Hoehler-Fatton.[6] Although both studies are concerned with Kenya, the authors cover different groups. Rasmussen focused her studies on the Holy Spirit churches that stem from the Society of Friends missionary Arthur Chilson. One of the students who received the Spirit at Kaimosi in 1927 was Daniel Mundia, and through his preaching, Jacob Buluku received it as well. The split from the Friends African Mission came in 1929. This movement would itself split into four groups: the Holy Spirit Church of East Africa, the Gospel Holy Spirit Church of East Africa, the African Church of the Holy Spirit, and the Lyahuka Church of East Africa, one of which opted to worship on Saturday. Their central beliefs and convictions include the importance of entering a trance, experiencing dreams and visions, and speaking in tongues, all of which may be accompanied with crying, shouting and rolling on the floor. Purification from sin is also an important element, and with that, the driving out of demons. The sacrificial death of Jesus is stressed at the expense of the resurrection.[7] Rasmussen notes that although the first

---

in Dawid Venter (ed.), *Engaging Modernity: Methods and Cases for Studying African Independent Churches in South Africa* (Praeger, Westport CT, 2004), pp. 13–43, p. 16. Stephen Hayes is the author of *Black Charismatic Anglicans: The Iviyo loFakazi bataKristu and Its Relations with Other Renewal Movements* (Studia Specialia, University of South Africa Press, Pretoria, 1990).

5 Jim Kiernan, 'African Independent Churches and Modernity' in Venter (ed.), *Engaging Modernity*, pp. 45–58, p. 45.

6 Ane Marie Bak Rasmussen (published posthumously), *Modern African Spirituality: The Independent Holy Spirit Churches in East Africa 1902–1976* (British Academic Press, London and New York, 1996); Cynthia Hoehler-Fatton, *Women of Fire and Spirit: History, Faith, and Gender in Roho Religion in Western Kenya* (Oxford University Press, New York, 1996).

7 Rasmussen, *Modern African Spirituality*, ch. 5.

impression of the worship of the Holy Spirit Church is that of spontaneity, there is, in fact, a pattern, and a fixed one at that.[8] When people enter the church they kneel and pray aloud to prepare themselves for the service. Then there are a number of hymns, followed by chasing out the devil by clapping and shouting. Members then confess their sins and ask forgiveness. Rasmussen explained thus:

> Because purity of heart is a necessary condition for any real communion with God, purification rites have to take place at the beginning of every meeting and these serve to relieve the members' stress. Any evil affecting them and causing bad feelings towards other people is driven away, and they become free to express their thankfulness and happiness by singing hymns, clapping and dancing. When the worship culminates in the outpouring of the Holy Spirit, further tensions are released as the worshippers give full vent to emotions normally kept under control by the demands of their everyday lives. The extreme emotionalism of the whole service, but particularly of receiving the Holy Spirit, allows Holy Spirit people to forget their problems, to be happy and to express themselves in emotionally satisfying ways.[9]

Prayers are then led by the elders and everyone says the Lord's Prayer, often several times. More hymns follow, and then people who have had dreams and visions can tell the congregation about them. More hymns follow, and then the collection. After more singing, everyone kneels and recites Psalms 1 and 25, and usually the Ten Commandments and Apostles' Creed as well. Preaching follows – often by more than one preacher, and punctuated with hymns. The Holy Spirit is believed to be the real leader of worship. Rasmussen's field studies led her to conclude that not every element appeared in every service, but most of them did. A conspicuous difference between the Holy Spirit Church of East Africa and the African Church of the Holy Spirit is that the former spends more time in intercessory prayer, while the latter has developed purification elements further than others.[10] The hymns are of great

8 Rasmussen, *Modern African Spirituality*, p. 65.
9 Rasmussen, *Modern African Spirituality*, p. 91.
10 Rasmussen, *Modern African Spirituality*, p. 66.

importance, with a very large number of them coming from the Friends' Luragoli hymn book, and the Holy Spirit churches themselves. The manner of singing is rather different from the Friends' slow, quiet manner – for example, the Holy Spirit Church's rendition includes clapping, dancing and jumping. Rasmussen says that their own compositions tend to take up one theme, which is repeated, with a chorus being sung over and over again. She cites the following example (in English translation):

> They are blessed those who pray. (3×)
> Jesus himself has told them.
> *Chorus:*
> *Hallelujah Hallelujah (3×)*
> *When Jesus himself has told them.*[11]

Hymns can be introduced at any point in a service since hymns occur whenever the meeting has movement from one stage of the service to another. No hymn books are used since the hymns are known by heart. Rasmussen noted that during the prayers the doors and windows of the church are closed – an interpretation of Matthew 6.6, though she opined that it was also intended to prevent evil spirits from entering. Psalms 1 and 25, along with the Ten Commandments and Apostles' Creed, were among the important teachings of the missionaries, and we may assume that that is why they have found a place in these services. In addition to purification and the confession of sins, certain other things are done to create an atmosphere conducive to an outpouring of the Spirit, such as rhythmic singing, clapping and drumming, repetitive singing and emotional praying.

> The dancing accompanying the singing becomes more and more lively until people suddenly begin to roll on the floor or stagger around speaking in tongues. Sometimes everyone in the congregation, apart from the majority of elders, is seized by the Spirit. The elders, who feel they ought to listen and observe what is going on, normally remain calm throughout the meeting.[12]

---

11 Rasmussen, *Modern African Spirituality*, p. 68.
12 Rasmussen, *Modern African Spirituality*, p. 83, citing an interview on 3 June 1976.

Finally, a common element among the AICs is the wearing of special clothing for worship. In the churches studied by Rasmussen, the attire was a white robe and turban, with a red cross. Rasmussen and others have noted that some elements here seem to be taken over or retained from traditional East African religions and culture, such as the concern with purification and chasing out demons, as well as the importance of dreams and visions

Cynthia Hoehler-Fatton studied the Ruwe Holy Ghost Church of East Africa, which, together with the Musanda Holy Ghost Church and the Cross Church of East Africa, emerged from the Roho (Spirit) movement associated with Alfayo Odongo Mango in 1934. Mango was appointed to serve as deacon in the Anglican communities – a task made difficult by territorial and land disputes between the Kager and Wanga peoples. After an experience of the Holy Spirit, Mango gradually became estranged from his archdeacon, who eventually expelled him from the Anglican Church. He met a martyr's death when he was burnt to death in his hut after an attack on his community.

Hoehler-Fatton describes a service she attended in Ruwe in 1991.[13] Hymns were being sung even before the worship began. Shoes were removed, and everyone wore a red cross sewn on their white cap. The officiating pastors emerged from the front office, where they had robed for service. Each pastor spread a cloth on the floor in front of himself in preparation for prayer. The hymn 'Cho bithe Sovend Cho Biri Pempi Shesimpu' ('Shortly Before Heaven will be Sealed'), was sung *a cappella* in a special liturgical language – Dhoroho – an encoding of Dholuo.[14] It is, in fact, a translation of the Luo Christian hymn. A second hymn followed. A confession – based on the Church of England 1662 Morning Prayer Confession – was recited. One of the pastors then prayed while people shrieked and moaned as the Spirit came into them. The Lord's Prayer was recited, and then further prayers were said, which made mention of Odongo Mango. Then a hymn followed – 'Brave Warriors who have Won, You Christians, Fight Hard' – which is a reference to the warriors who fought in 1934 when Mango was killed. A reading from Luke 7.1–10 then followed, during which a woman made high-pitched barking noises. A Luo Anglican hymn was sung, followed by a reading from Revelation 4. The next hymn was then followed by a third reading, this time from Hebrews 7. This in turn was followed

---

13 Hoehler-Fatton, *Women*, pp. 139–70.
14 Hoehler-Fatton, *Women*, pp. xx–xxii.

by the hymn 'Behold the Salvific Fire', which again refers to the martyrdom of Mango. Then came the Apostles' Creed, though few members seemed to know it by heart; it was followed by the Lord's Prayer, which everyone knew and could join in saying. The pastor then led more prayers before another hymn was sung. Again, more prayers followed, after which came extempore preaching and instruction – this was continually interrupted by people singing hymns. Several of the pastors preached. A hymn concluded these sermons, after which a woman came with a small wooden cross and addressed the congregation in what seemed to be a prophetic message. Throughout the service, members – particularly women – broke into song. After a number of people had addressed the congregation the senior pastor brought the service to an end. Hoehler-Fatton commented:

> I believe my description here conveys the basic dynamics of Roho congregational worship. The commencement of Roho services is generally characterized by a flexible but nonetheless orderly pro-gression through formal Anglican liturgy components: opening solemn hymns, confession, the Lord's Prayer, Scripture readings, and the creed. These components are interspersed among songs and glossolalia that become increasingly vigorous as worship proceeds. Laity come forward to preach the gospel only after the pastors have done so, and the words of elders are privileged over those of younger members. One notes an ebb and flow between the women's domain of spontaneous song and the ordering authority of male leaders, who attempt to structure and limit that spontaneity. However, the pastors are clearly able to rein in women's expressive worship only up to a point. Communal spiritual power, as cultivated within the Roho collective worship, derives from a dynamic give-and-take between gendered forms of charismatic authority.[15]

A brief account of a service at Ruwe Holy Ghost Church, Singruok Tek St, Bar Sauri, on 8 February 2006 is given by Lenny Kiproneh Mutai. He records as follows:

> Normally in the start of the service, the leader requests the people to stand up and rebuke the evil spirits, this by clapping of hands

---

15 Hoehler-Fatton, *Women*, p. 166.

and stamping their feet. Then the leader leads in a song and accompanied by drums and the songs are sung slowly to bring people closer to God. After the song and the drums slowed down, everybody will kneel down and the leader leads people for the Lord's Prayer three times and people can pray in their own voices. This enables each one to talk to God according to his own needs.

When the leader sees that almost everybody has finished, he/she leads in a loud prayer, and after that people stand and join in a song and drum beating. This time as they sing, they await the fall of the Holy Spirit and those gifted in prophecy will talk in their language. When the Holy Spirit works through people, miracles are witnessed in the church. Those who prophesied leave people with fear, as they prophesy of their sins they have done at home or the church, the drunkards and those who practise sorcery are recognized.[16]

He notes that the Roho Church is one of the fastest-growing churches in Kenya.

Perhaps one of the largest AICs of Nigerian origin is the Cherubim and Seraphim movement. The various branches and churches of this movement trace their origins to the itinerant preacher Moses Orimolade Tunolase, or Baba Aladura, and the young woman visionary Christianah Abiodun Akinsowon of Saba Court, Lagos, whose vision of June 1925 resulted in the two figures founding the movement.[17] Orimolade was the 'supreme founder', and Abiodun was the spiritual daughter. Abiodun's visions were reminiscent of the apocalyptic visions of 1 Enoch, focusing on angelic beings and heaven. Originally it was a movement, with members belonging to various churches and coming together for special events. Michael the archangel was announced as the Captain of the society, and later, after a number of splits, Orimolade named Gabriel as the Deputy Captain. Orimolade elected 70 disciples, 25 of whom were women. A Praying Band was appointed to assist Orimolade with praying, and then 12 elders or Patriarchs, as well as

---

16 See Jim Harries, lecturer, *Visits to AICs, submitted to the African Literature Profile of Kima International School of Theology*, January to March 2006, <http://www.jim-mission.org.uk/articles/visits-to-aics.pdf> (accessed 5/11/09), pp. 16–18. This document is useful for brief accounts of worship in a number of AICs in Kenya.
17 Here I am dependent upon J. Akinyele Omoyajowo, *Cherubim and Seraphim: The History of an African Independent Church* (NOK Publishers, New York and Lagos, 1982).

some younger men, were appointed as 'the Army of Salvation'. A tradition holds that Jesus pleaded with God for 40 years to establish the Society on earth, which is expressed in the lyrics of one of their popular hymns:

Forty years was Baba Aladura entreated,
that this glorious order be instituted,
and for forty years, the Son pleaded for
the Seraphim Society to be founded.[18]

The Society soon split into differing factions, beginning with a rift between Orimolade and Abiodun, and eventually resulting in the Cherubim and Seraphim Society, the Eternal Sacred Order of the Cherubim and Seraphim, the Praying Band, the Western Conference, the Holy Flock of Christ and the Eternal Sacred Order of the Cherubim and Seraphim, Koro Agbede. Subsequent splits have also occurred.

Among the beliefs of the Cherubim and Seraphim, Omoyajowo stresses that it sees itself as the fulfilment of the prophecy of Joel 2.28 – a number of hymns express the eschatological self-image of the Cherubim and Seraphim. Reginald Heber's hymn 'Holy, Holy, Holy' is a favourite in the Society. Omoyajowo observes that the liturgical practices seem borrowed from a number of traditions and churches, reflecting the fact that originally the Society had members who continued to belong to other churches. Old Testament purification rules are important, particularly regarding menstruation, which excludes women from worship. On Holy Michael's Anniversary, a sword plays a prominent part in the service, and staffs are also used – for prayers by the leaders and anointed members. White praying robes are worn for worship. The ordinary members also wear yellow bands, while other members wear red or blue according to rank. Candles, incense and holy water are used in the services. A Sunday Thanksgiving Service is provided on the website of the Cherubim and Seraphim Movement in the USA – a movement derived from the Western Nigerian Province, which traces its ancestry back through J. O. Coker, one of the 70 appointed by Orimolade.[19] A separate service for protection is provided

---

18 Cited in Omoyajowo, *Cherubim and Seraphim*, p. 47.
19 See <http://www.csmovementchurchusa.org/>, select 'programs'. For another Cherubim and Seraphim group, Glorious Morning Star, on YouTube, see <http://www.youtube.com/watch?v=DxxS81U68iw&feature=related>.

there as well, and is a reminder of the importance of this theme in many African cultures. The Sunday Thanksgiving Service is structured thus:

A   Preparation. With a vestry prayer, processional hymn, introit, call to worship and opening hymn.

B   Prayer of Confession and Declaration of Forgiveness. This has a reading of Psalms 51, 99 and 24, with an opening prayer for forgiveness of sin and a spirit of repentance, purification and sanctification, and the manifestation of the Holy Spirit in the lives of the worshippers. The Lord's Prayer follows and the 'Seal'.

C   Appreciation and Thanksgiving. This has thanksgiving hymns and prayers.

D   The Ministry of the Word. Two lessons are read, and the choir sings Gloria after each reading (presumably referring to the Gloria patri rather than the Gloria in excelsis).

E   The Apostles' Creed, led by a church elder.

F   Prayer of Intercessions, including anointing of the Spirit.

G   Church General Announcements.

H   Appreciation and Response, with congregational prayers of thanksgiving and prayer for visitors.

I   General and Offertory collections.

J   The Word/Sermon with a hymn before the sermon.

K   Dispersal, with closing and offertory hymn, closing prayer, vesper by the choir, benediction and grace by a church elder, and recessional hymn.[20]

Notes mention that the procession is led by the incense-bearer and that incense must be placed on the altar throughout the worship. A service of communion, which is celebrated four times a year – Christmas, Maundy Thursday, Pentecost and Trinity Sunday – is also provided. This service includes an opening hymn, Psalm 51, and opening prayers as in the Sunday Thanksgiving Service. There is one reading, which comes from Matthew 26.17–29, and then the Apostles' Creed is said. Three prayers follow: one for spiritual power (male member); grace for true communion (female member); and protection of all members (male member). A hymn precedes the sermon, which is followed by the

---

20 <http://www.csmovementchurchusa.org/pdf/csprograms.pdf>.

sanctification of the elements (by seven elders) and the administration (all the elders in the chancel). The service ends with a closing hymn and prayer. What neither of the orders is able to convey is the joy and vibrancy in the celebration – a mixing of formality with informality. The YouTube citations noted are helpful, therefore, in showing how the services are conducted in this particular type of Cherubim and Seraphim community.

The descriptions above represent only the tip of the iceberg of the many and varied AICs. The origin of some of them, following the Great War (1914–18), along with the beginning of the questioning of colonialism, are interesting factors in the development of these churches. They represent an adaptation of the gospel to the local culture and passive frustrations with European influence and dominance. It is interesting that in the Cherubim and Seraphim in Nigeria, polygamy is still practised. The AICs represent a protest against Western European modernity and Western European Christianity. They are alive, well and growing in the midst of global postmodern culture, and their beliefs and culture of an enchanted world seem less out of place in postmodernity than in the culture of modernity.

KOREAN *MINJUNG* EUCHARISTS AND *KUK-AK* WORSHIP

The word *minjung* consists of two Chinese characters, *min* and *jung*, and means people of the masses, which was a common term used in Korea to describe the majority of ordinary agricultural communities – a version of the Israelite 'People of the Land'. The agricultural communities were dependent on rice, and in ancient Korean shamanism a common meal of rice became vested with religious meaning. This attracted further religious meanings with the influence of Buddhism and Confucianism. However, the word *minjung* took on a new connotation in the 1970s, when it developed as a conscious protest by the marginalized and poor against the oppression they suffered under the regime of Park Jung Hee, and later under General Jeon Du Whan. The plight of the socially and economically weak also worsened under the economic reforms demanded by the IMF in the 1990s. *Minjung* emerged as a Korean liberation theology, concerned with political and economic reform. According to Yeong Mee Lee, the term was first used in an academic theological sense in 1975 by Ahn Byung Mu and Suh Man Dong.[21]

Minjung theology likens the plight of the poor to the Exodus people of Israel, and those who were oppressed by the rich, whose actions were condemned by the Old Testament prophets. Jesus is regarded as a Galilean *minjung* person. The traditional Christian churches were criticized for not speaking out on behalf of the poor. As a result some *minjung* churches came into being as working-class communities shepherded by working-class pastors. Central to the worship life of those churches has been the recovery of a common meal, usually featuring rice, and partaken of in association with the celebration of the Lord's Supper. The use of Korean folk tunes to accompany hymns also became central to this type of worship. Although it is possible to see this movement primarily in socio-economic terms, it is also, in part, an attempt to preserve a culture that has been eroded by modern industrial culture.

As with Africa, worship patterns in Korea were introduced by the Western missionaries of the late nineteenth century. Presbyterianism, for example, was introduced from the USA, and the nineteenth-century patterns of worship were already an American Frontier adaptation of the earlier classical Reformed rites. Korean Presbyterianism never received Calvin or John Knox, but did receive nineteenth-century American forms of worship. These were in stark contrast to many of the cultural religious assumptions of Korean people. The *minjung* movement has also challenged Koreans to think about what contextualized Korean Christian worship might be.

Although the order of worship of *minjung* congregations varies from congregation to congregation, Seong-Won Park provides the following as a typical order:

Prelude

Call to Worship

Invocation

Hymn: 'Come Here, O Lord!'

---

21 Yeong Mee Lee, 'A Political Reception of the Bible: Korean minjung theological interpretation of the Bible', *SBL Forum* (cited October 2005), <http://sbl-site.org/Article.aspx?ArticleID=457> (accessed 11/9/09).

Confession of Faith

We believe in God who made this world beautiful.

We believe in Jesus Christ who, according to the will of God, lived with *Minjung*, suffered, was crucified, but won the victory by resurrection.

We believe in Holy Spirit who, as Spirit of Love, Justice and Peace, is at work with *Minjung* on earth.

We believe that the Kingdom of God will be built in this world and we will enjoy the eternal life in the Kingdom of God to come.

Hymn: 'Joy and Hope of Labour is . . .'

Prayer

Bible Reading   Hebrew (*sic*) 13.12–13

Anthem

Celebration of Resurrection

The Workers who are forced to be slaves by the power of death!

Bible Reading	Job 24.9–12
Poem Reciting	'Dream in childhood'
Song	'A Story of Life'

The Workers who struggle in solidarity to prevail over power of death.

Bible Reading	Isaiah 10.1–2
Poem Reciting	'To be working with strong arm'
Song	'Iron Worker'

Ours is the day of Resurrection and Victory.

Bible Reading 1	Amos 5.7, 10, 11
Bible Reading 2	Luke 1.51–53
Bible Reading 3	Luke 4.18–19
Poem Reciting	'You must be our love'
Song	'Song for Labour's Liberation'

Intercession for the resurrection and the liberated World

For ourselves and the Church outside the Camp
Response: 'Song of the Worker'

For the liberation of workers
Response: 'Song of Labours Union'

For democratization and unification of the country
Response: 'A patriotic way'

Hymn   'We Must Go!'

Message   'Let's meet outside the Camp'

Hymn   'Comrades! Here I am.'

Communion

Institution

Peace

Eucharistic Prayer

Communion

Thanksgiving Prayer

Hymn   'Let's Go Together This Way!'

Offering and Prayer

Announcement

Hymn   'True Love'

Poem Reciting 'Friends who have disappeared'

Preparation for the following week in silence

Benediction.[22]

Park draws attention to the concern to link worship with the struggles of daily life, and the concern for worship to engage with daily life.[23]

This 'generic' order may be supplemented by two specific accounts given by Dong-sun Kim.[24] Kim stresses the place of the common meal, and how it complements the Eucharist. For many pastors, he says, the community of Jesus has been called a 'rice-table community'.[25] He writes:

---

22 Seong-Won Park, *Worship in the Presbyterian Church in Korea: Its History and Implications* (Peter Lang, Frankfurt am Main, 2001), pp. 128–9.
23 Park, *Worship*, pp. 129–30.
24 Dong-sun Kim, *The Bread for Today and the Bread for Tomorrow: The Ethical Significance of the Lord's Supper in the Korean Context* (Peter Lang, Frankfurt am Main, 2001).
25 Kim, *Bread for Today*, p. 157.

The common meal is shared in general without any particular formality. The main reasons for it are: (i) to help the congregation to experience the inner meaning of a common meal through the body rather than through the words; (ii) to make them envision a new community themselves; and above all (iii) to give them the opportunity of training to find out for themselves how to participate in the kingdom of God movement.[26]

Kim believes that the common meal makes the congregation reinterpret their own table tradition in the light of the table community of the historical Jesus. However, the meal is not a substitute for the Eucharist; perhaps with echoes of 1 Corinthians 11 it is a meal celebrated alongside the Eucharist. Kim's first example of a *minjung* eucharistic service is that of Eewood Church, which borrowed considerably from the World Council of Churches' Lima Liturgy. Kim notes that the worship service mainly progresses not with the pastor alone, but with the common participation of the pastor and congregation. Worship is usually called *madang*, which in Korean refers to an open round stage for the Korean mask dance – a Korean type of opera.[27] The service is divided into five *madang*:[28]

1 *Madang of Entrance*: entrance psalm, greeting, confession and absolution, Gloria.
2 *Madang of the Word*: prayer, Scripture lesson, Alleluia, homily, silent prayer and confession of faith. The latter has the following text:

> We believe in God, the source of truth and life, who is labouring through the minjung. We believe in Jesus Christ, the Liberator of the minjung, who was conceived by the Spirit of Liberation, was born as the son of a minjung, practiced the movement of minjung liberation against oppressors of the minjung, and was crucified to death. He rose again with the minjung from the unjust power and cut the chain of death. He is continuing the kingdom of God movement through the

---

26 Kim, *Bread for Today*, p. 158.
27 Kim, *Bread for Today*, p. 164. For the influence of the mask dance, see Commission on Theological Concerns of the Christian Conference of Asia (ed.), *Minjung Theology: People as the Subject of History* (Orbis Books, Maryknoll NY, 1983).
28 Kim, *Bread for Today*, pp. 166–7.

minjung; He shall come again to consummate history as the Messiah of the minjung. And we believe in the Holy Spirit, the Spirit of liberation, who gives power and courage to conquer the world.

We believe that a church is a sharing, serving, and confessing community. God makes us serve one another through the forgiveness of our sins.

We are called to expand this community into the world until the minjung become the subjects of it.[29]

3 *Madang of the Eucharist*: invitation and response, dialogue, preface, first epiclesis, institution narrative, anamnesis and commitment, second epiclesis; Lord's Prayer, Peace, breaking of the bread, communion, thanksgiving prayer.

4 *Madang of Offering and Sharing*: offering and hymn; sharing of life (testimonies).

5 *Madang of Mission*: hymn of mission, and blessing.

The eucharistic prayer is *based* on Lima, but has very different wording in places. Kim cites one of the hymns for communion:

1 Sharing of this bread is sharing of our love,
   Now you and I are comrades in the same laugh.
2 Sharing of this wine is sharing of our love,
   Now you and I are comrades in the same cry.
   (refrain)
   As you and I are from the same heaven,
   We are of the same blood.
   As you and I live under the same heaven,
   We are going to the same place.[30]

Kim summarizes the theological meaning as follows:

When the congregation celebrates the eucharist as a sign of confession that Jesus is present in their sufferings, they can taste the life of the resurrection. Because the sufferings of the minjung are very real, their partaking of the body and blood of Christ is

---

29 Cited by Kim, *Bread for Today*, pp. 167–8.
30 Kim, *Bread for Today*, p. 172.

directly related to their real lives: this attitude prevents their hope from being reduced to an abstract one; rather it makes the hope eschatological. The life of the resurrection is tangibly experienced in the common meal which is shared right after the worship; and this experience again gives a more profound meaning to the eucharist and makes it not merely spiritualised or ritualized.[31]

A second example given by Kim is of Gogee Church, which is a small rural church in Yongin District. Here a celebration was planned over three Sundays. On the first Sunday there was a common meal for the congregation; on the second Sunday, a thanksgiving with a communal meal, including rice cakes and rice wine, was arranged for everyone in the village. There was a Eucharist on the third Sunday, and fruits that were brought to the service were arranged in the form of a cross, with the congregation sitting on the floor facing one another, rather than facing the pulpit. Sins were confessed, and people then had a time of silence to contemplate the cross. As the Eucharist was celebrated in silence, the congregation took the fruits from the cross which symbolized the cross in their lives. The following song concluded the service:

> We love one another with the love of the Lord.
> We love one another with the love of the Lord.
> As brothers and sisters,
> Seeing the glorification of the Lord;
> We love one another with the love of the Lord.[32]

Reference has been made earlier that *minjung* worship frequently uses traditional Korean music and tunes, and fits biblical words to them. One of the leaders of *minjung* theology, Ahn Byoung Mu, founded the Hyang-lin Presbyterian Church in Seoul. In recent years this church has pioneered contextualized worship, and in particular *Kuk-ak* worship – *Kuk-ak* is the term for Korean traditional music.[33] Whereas *minjung* worship focuses on the urban labourers and the poor, *Kuk-ak* worship attempts to bring a new way of worship to all Korean Christians. The

---

31 Kim, *Bread for Today*, p. 175.
32 Kim, *Bread for Today*, pp. 179–82.
33 I am indebted to my STM student Jooil Park for this information, and his essay 'Kuk-ak Worship in Korea', May 2009.

service in Hyang-lin Church on 3 May 2009 was summarized by Jooil Park as follows:

> Striking a *Jing*/ Waiting for the Presence of Holy Spirit.
>
> Invocation
>
> Opening Hymn/ *Kuk-ak* Hymn No. 167, 'O Merry This Day'
>
> Versicle/ from Psalm 121, sung to a 4.4 rhythm . . .
>
> Gloria/ *Kuk-ak* Hymn No. 4, 'Enjoy Glory'
>
> Pastoral Prayer
>
> Silent Prayer
>
> Prayer Response
>
> Hymn of Confession/ *Kuk-ak* Hymn No. 217, 'Fragrant Neighbors in This Land'
>
> Anthem/Choir
>
> *Ha-nl* (Heaven)'s (*sic*) Word Reading/ Genesis 1:26–2:4; Ephesians 6:1–14 (a reader from the congregation)
>
> Waiting for the *Ha-nl* (Heaven)'s (*sic*) Will/*Kuk-ak* Hymn No. 10, 'Illuminate Us'
>
> Unfolding the *Ha-nl* (Heaven)'s (*sic*) Will/Rev. Hun-jung Jo
>
> Response Song/ Hymn No. 559, 'All Seasons are Springlike'
>
> Offering Song/ *Kuk-ak* Hymn No. 18, 'With the First Fruit'
>
> Offering Prayer
>
> Resolution Hymn/ *Kuk-ak* Hymn No. 151, 'Faithful are the Lord's Family'
>
> Sending to the World/ Rev. Hun-jung Jo
>
> Benediction/ 1 Cor. 13:13, all together
>
> Response Song/ Choir
>
> Striking a *Jing*
>
> Communal Lunch.[34]

---

34 Park, 'Kuk-ak Worship'.

Jooil Park has explained parts of this service as follows. The *Jing*, a type of gong, is a traditional Korean percussion instrument. The beat and rhythm of Korean music is based on a breath rather than on heartbeats – consequently the *Jing* speaks to the soul. The sound of the *Jing* also opens the communal meal. *Ha-nl* is the term used as a substitute for God. The Korean word for God is *Ha-ne-nim*, and is a traditional Korean term for the One who is in heaven, but it has become associated exclusively with Christian use. Hyang-lin *Kuk-ak* worship has adopted *Ha-nl* in the belief that it signifies the God of all. At the benediction the pastor joins the congregation, all hold hands and say the benediction together. This, of course, signifies the priesthood of all believers, but also echoes the communal spirit of traditional Korean agricultural society. The service represents a modest attempt to reintegrate Korean tradition and Christian gospel, owing its development to both *minjung* theology and the concern for an expression of something genuinely Korean in worship.

THE AMISH AND WENGER MENNONITES

Living within American postmodern culture, but keeping a cultural distance from it, are the Amish and Wenger (Old Order) Mennonites. There are distinctions between these groups, with the Amish being a subgroup of the larger Mennonite or Anabaptist movement. The separation of Amish from the wider movement took place in 1694 in Switzerland and South Germany when followers of Jacob Ammann excommunicated those who, in Ammann's opinion, were disregarding the Meidung (shunning of those who had lapsed), and had suspect ideas of salvation.[35] Large groups of Amish and Mennonites emigrated to the USA in the eighteenth century due to religious wars, poverty and persecution in their homelands. Although Mennonites are still found in their native Europe, the Amish there became extinct, and exist now only in the USA and Canada. To outsiders, the Amish are probably the better known, but both groups are distinguished by their distinctive dress, their agricultural and cottage industries (they are well known for the manufacture of furniture and fine quilts), the shunning of most modern technology, and the preservation of a German dialect within their community and in their worship. Both Amish and the Wengers are

---

35 See Milton Gascho, 'The Amish Division of 1693–1697 in Switzerland and Alsace', *The Mennonite Quarterly Review* 11 (1937), pp. 235–66.

known for their repudiation of automobiles, having retained the horse and buggy for travel within their communities. Donald Kraybill and James Hurd comment:

> The automobile, supreme badge of modernity, symbolically and literally articulates the core values of contemporary culture – independence, individualism, mobility, power, status, and speed. The Wenger rejection of this prince of progress keeps them in a different world, a local world anchored in face-to-face conversations, a slower world paced by the speed of a plodding horse, a communal world where neighbors see each other daily, an Old Order that boldly spurns the relentless press of progress.[36]

The original sixteenth-century Anabaptists taught a life of simplicity and humility, as well as detachment, and their communities negotiate these principles with contemporary North American culture. It is a way of life that is under threat because of the shortage of new land for farming in their traditional enclaves, such as in Lancaster County, Pennsylvania, in Indiana and Ohio, and the smaller communities in Iowa, Missouri and Minnesota. Their communities constantly wrestle with what may or may not be adopted from the stream of new technologies available in American life. Debate about the use of tractors, and what type of tyres, led to splits among the Wenger Mennonites. The iPhone and internet, along with television, are not part of their conservative home culture, but Wengers will allow computer printouts for business. Kraybill and Hurd observe that although they employ some modern tools for productive purposes, they do not use them to open portals of cultural influences from the outside world:

> Today, many evangelical churches see change as indispensable, even desirable, as they seek to adapt religious patterns to changes in contemporary culture. By contrast, the Wenger Church honors tradition and resists change. Church organization, leadership roles, and even churchhouse architecture keep continuity with the past.[37]

---

36 Donald B. Kraybill and James P. Hurd, *Horse-and-Buggy Mennonites: Hoofbeats of Humility in a Postmodern World* (Pennsylvania State University Press, University Park PA, 2006), pp. 73–4.
37 Kraybill and Hurd, *Horse-and-Buggy Mennonites*, p. 97.

The foundation of Amish and Wenger Mennonite life is worship. One major difference is that the Amish do not build church buildings, but rotate among the homes of the congregation. The Amish also do not meet every week for communal worship.

Two books that are fundamental to the worship of the Amish are the *Ausbund* and *Die ernsthafte Christenpflicht*. The former is a collection of hymns – its eighteenth-century editions combine what are actually three separate collections. The oldest known edition of the *Ausbund*, printed in 1564, contains 53 hymns.[38] Many of them seem to have been composed by Anabaptists who were imprisoned in Passau between 1535 and 1540. The next surviving edition, printed in 1583, has 131 songs, but only the latter 51 correspond to the songs of the 1564 book. Later still, a section was added after the Passau section.[39] Some Amish communities use other collections (*Ein Unpartheiische Liedersammlung*, 1860; *Unpartheiische Liedersammlung*, 1892). There is considerable overlap in the songs contained within these books, but since the tunes are transmitted orally, there is no music contained in them.[40] The songbooks are owned by the community and kept by the Vorsänger, who always announces the first hymn during worship.

> At the end of a service he gathers up the books, packs them in a suitcase or box prepared for the purpose, and takes them home with him. When he brings them to meeting two weeks later, each book contains a piece of yarn marking the first hymn to be sung in the service.[41]

Die ernsthafte Christenpflicht is a collection of prayers, the first known printing being 1739, but containing some prayers known to have been composed by Kaspar Schwenckfeld (*c.* 1490–1561) and the Lutheran

---

38 Harold S. Bender, 'The First Edition of the Ausbund', *The Mennonite Quarterly Review* 3 (1929), pp. 147–50. For a popular account of the history see Benuel S. Blank, *The Amazing Story of the Ausbund* (Carlisle Printing, Sugarcreek OH, 2001).

39 For individual compositions, see A. J. Ramaker, 'Hymns and Hymn Writers among the Anabaptists of the Sixteenth Century', *The Mennonite Quarterly Review* 3 (1929), pp. 93–131.

40 For an analysis of the intonation of Amish worship, see Werner Enninger and Joachim Raith, *An Ethnography-of-Communication Approach to Ceremonial Situations: A Study on Communication in Institutionalized Social Contexts: The Old Order Amish Church Service* (Franz Steiner Verlag GMBH, Wiesbaden, 1982).

41 John Umble, 'Amish Service Manuals', *The Mennonite Quarterly Review* 15 (1941), pp. 26–32, p. 27.

Johann Arndt (1555–1621).[42] The Amish bishop/presiding minister uses prayers from this book in the Sunday worship. Both books are still printed in the old Gothic fonts and in High German language. Werner Enninger and Joachim Raith comment that the script creates an awareness of being close to linguistic originals, and 'constitutes an act of asserting the cultural identity of a minority exposed to the pressures of a cultural contact situation'.[43]

The community has wooden benches which are brought to the home where the worship service is to take place. There is a particular seating order, with men and women sitting separately, and in order of age. The ministers begin the worship seating ritual by walking in followed by the older men. The seating ritual progresses until the young children, regardless of their sex, are seated with either their father or their mother. When everyone is seated, the deacon distributes the hymnals owned by the church district. The Vorsänger announces the first hymn, and then sings the first syllable as a solo, after which the assembly joins in unison and *a cappella*. This is repeated line by line. Over a period of time most *a cappella* congregational singing (e.g. psalms in Gaelic in the Free Church of Scotland) becomes slower and slower, and the singing of the song (usually only a few stanzas of the song) takes the Amish community some 20–30 minutes. The second hymn is always a particular hymn, the *Loblied/Lobgesang*, 'O Gott Vater Wir Loben Dich'.

During the first hymn the ministers withdraw to a separate place for the Abrath, or meeting. They discuss which parts of the service each will take, and any church business that needs to be taken care of. The congregation continues singing until the ministers return. When they return, they sit in order determined by the part of the service each one of them will take. If the ministers return during the *Loblied*, it is sung to the end, but if the congregation has started a third hymn, it will conclude with the stanza then being sung.

One minister then gives the Anfang, or introductory sermon.[44] This

---

42 Robert Friedmann, 'Mennonite Prayer Books', *The Mennonite Quarterly Review* 17 (1943), pp. 179–206.

43 Enninger and Raith, *Ceremonial Situations*, p. 35.

44 For a summary of such a sermon, see John A. Hostetler, *Amish Society*, third edn (Johns Hopkins University Press, Baltimore and London, 1980), pp. 211–13. See also Stephen Scott, *The Amish Wedding and Other Special Occasions of the Old Order Communities* (Good Books, Intercourse PA, 1988), which has a description of a typical Amish Sunday; see also Calvin George Bachman, *The Old Order Amish of Lancaster County* (Pennsylvania German Society, Lancaster PA, 1961), pp. 121–9.

concludes with the words 'Und wann dir einig sind lasset uns bede' (If you are all agreed, let us pray). All kneel to pray – *Ein Gebät for der Predigt* (A Prayer before the Sermon) is usually selected from *Die ernsthafte Christenpflicht*.[45] They rise, and the deacon reads the Scripture – an entire chapter – which is read in a singsong, chant-like manner. There is a seasonal lectionary that is followed, though some variations exist between the communities.[46] The main sermon is now given, introduced with, 'Grace be with you and peace from God our Father'. The delivery has a particular style, rising to a high pitch, and then suddenly dropping at the end of each phrase. At the end of the lengthy sermon (perhaps two hours), a second chapter of Scripture is read by the preacher. This is followed by Zeugnis (testimony) when other ministers comment on, or correct, what the preacher has said. The main preacher gives closing remarks, and then all kneel for the concluding prayer which is taken from *Die ernsthafte Christenpflicht*.[47] The assembly stands for the benediction, and announcements follow, including the place of the next service. The Vorsänger then starts the closing hymn. As the assembly departs, the youngest members leave first, and the men and women leave separately.

One of the reasons for the Amish split in 1694 was over the frequency of the Lord's Supper, and foot-washing. The Mennonites thought once a year was sufficient for the Lord's Supper, and did not think foot-washing had to be part of the celebration. Ammann insisted on two celebrations a year, which would include foot-washing. There is a preparatory service and personal examination. At the end of the main sermon, ministers leave and return with bread and wine. After prayer, the bishop and ministers give communion, with the communicants bowing their knees in reverence. After the bread and wine are distributed, the bishop proceeds by asking for Zeugnis in the usual manner. Some of the formulae/prayers said at communion have been handed down in ministers' manuals. The nineteenth-century Unzicker manuscript, which records an older tradition, has the following:

---

45 Enninger and Raith, *Ceremonial Situations*, p. 55. Writing in 1984, they claimed that there was no English translation, but that is no longer the case. Leonard Gross (ed. and trans.), *Prayer Book for Earnest Christians* (Herald Press, Scottsdale PA, 1997), p. 92.
46 See Umble, 'Amish Service Manuals'.
47 According to Enninger and Raith, *Ein anderes Gebät* or *Ein ander andächtig allgemein Gebät*, ET in Gross (ed. and trans.), *Prayer Book for Earnest Christians*, pp. 51 and 94.

After one has narrated the account of the death of our Lord until the Ascension, then he reads from the Gospel the usual part of the sixth chapter of John. Then also afterwards an explanation is made of what the communion signifies, how a person is to prepare himself for it and so on and that one [the presiding bishop] intends to make the beginning with the breaking of the bread.

Then one says, 'Our Lord Jesus in the night when he was betrayed took the bread and thanked his Heavenly Father. We wish to do likewise with an earnest prayer.'

After the prayer of thanksgiving then one says

After he had given thanks he broke the bread and gave it to his disciples and said, 'Take and eat, this is my body which is given for you. This do in remembrance of me.' Accordingly I also intend to make a beginning with this bread and this in the hope and in the belief that he through his bitter suffering and death has purchased and redeemed us from the curse and fall of Adam. Also in the hope and in the confidence that he will be thanked for this by us and our posterity forever. And also in the hope and faith that he will raise us up at the last day and lead us with him into his everlasting kingdom. And whoever stands with me in such a hope let him also come after me and eat of this bread and this in memory of the bitter suffering and death of our Lord and Saviour Jesus Christ as has been set forth in your hearing.

With the cup one says

After he had broken bread he took the cup and thanked his Heavenly Father. Let us also thank him with an earnest prayer!

After the thanksgiving one says

After he had given thanks, he gave the cup to his disciples and said, 'Take it and drink all ye of it. This is the cup of the New testament in my blood which was shed for you for the forgiveness of sins.' Accordingly, I also intend to make a beginning with this drink and this in the hope and in the faith that he by his bitter suffering and death and by the shedding of his innocent blood has purchased and redeemed us from the curse and fall of Adam. Also in the hope and in the confidence that he will be thanked for this by us and our posterity forever. Also in the hope and in the faith that he will raise us up at the last day and lead us with him into his everlasting kingdom. And whoever stands with me in such a hope let him come after me and drink of this drink and this in memory of the bitter suffering and death and innocent shedding of the blood of our Lord and Saviour Jesus Christ as has been set forth in your hearing.[48]

The reference to 'earnest prayers' seems to be to those provided in *Die ernsthafte Christenpflicht.*[49]

After the final prayer, a hymn is announced, and the each member of the assembly is invited to wash the feet of the person nearest to her/him, and exchange a kiss of peace.

The hymn sung during this is 'Von Herzen woll'n wir singen' from the *Ausbund.*[50]

Wenger worship follows a similar order, though there are differences. First, unlike the Amish, the Wengers and other Mennonites have purpose-built churches. There is a ministers' bench, a singing table, and a preacher's table, and men and women sit separately with women on the left and men on the right. Their hymn book is the *Umpartheyisches Gesangbuch*, with hymns led much like the Amish. The service as outlined by Kraybill and Hurd, and Scott, is identical to the Amish ritual.[51] The Wenger congregations surveyed by Kraybill and Hurd celebrated the Eucharist twice a year and have foot-washing, as the Amish.[52]

Here is worship that tries to be oblivious to time, and that has little interest in modern culture, other than the printing press. Dress, sexual etiquette, language and Gothic script are a ritual expression of a way of life that lives on the edge of postmodernism, and has little interest in it. Amish and Wenger worship thus becomes deeply counter-cultural.

APPALACHIAN MOUNTAIN RELIGION AND TAKING UP SERPENTS

In recent decades considerable interest has been shown in the rural Holiness and Baptist communities in the Appalachian Mountains, which stretch across several south-eastern states of the USA. On the whole they have not been the object of interest of liturgical scholars but of ethnologists and sociologists. In an important study of these mountain churches, Deborah McCauley writes:

---

48 John Umble (ed.), 'An Amish Minister's Manual', *The Mennonite Quarterly Review* 15 (1941), pp. 95–117, p. 107.

49 See Gross (ed. and trans.), *Prayer Book for Earnest Christians*, pp. 101–3.

50 Charles Burkhart, 'The Church Music of the Old Order Amish and Old Colony Mennonites', *The Mennonite Quarterly Review* 27 (1953), pp. 34–54, p. 36.

51 Kraybill and Hurd, *Horse-and-Buggy Mennonites*, pp. 127–8; Scott, *The Amish Wedding*, p. 91.

52 Kraybill and Hurd, *Horse-and-Buggy Mennonites*, pp. 137–8.

Appalachian mountain religion is one of the very few uniquely American regional religious traditions to which Protestantism in the United States can lay claim. It is made up of church traditions found almost entirely in the region's mountains and small valleys. Generally, they do not exist beyond Appalachia, except through out-migration. These church traditions, nearly invisible to the outside world and to much of the Protestant mainstream even within Appalachia, make up what is exclusive to religious life in Appalachia.[53]

McCauley says that this '[m]ountain religion is essentially an oral religious tradition because it is known primarily through its oral literature and material culture', and these contribute to its apparent invisibility.[54] It has been depicted as a religion of the poor and the oppressed, which McCauley questions. The religion is marked by conservative tradition, along with charity and feelings that take priority over 'knowledge'. The churches teach that the image of God in each person lives in the heart, and that the Holy Spirit dwells in the heart. One listens to the heart, not the head. McCauley writes:

> Throughout mountain religious life, there is a dominant emphasis on the purity of God-generated or God-instituted emotion or religious experience, unmediated by direct human manipulation. Expressive and ecstatic worship traditions have a very long heritage in mountain religious life, reaching back to the earliest years of the first settlements on the Appalachian frontier near the beginning of the eighteenth century. These traditions involve intensely physical and emotional behavior in the worship environment where spontaneity is highly valued because it marks the immediate presence of the Holy Spirit. Such emotional expressions, to a greater or lesser degree, cut across almost all mountain church traditions, from the most doctrinally conservative to the more free-flowing.[55]

---

53 Deborah Vansau McCauley, *Appalachian Mountain Religion: A History* (University of Illinois Press, Urbana and Chicago, 1995), p. 2.
54 McCauley, *Appalachian Mountain Religion*, p. 6.
55 McCauley, *Appalachian Mountain Religion*, p. 15.

There are, in fact, a great many denominations or sub-denominations in this vast rural area, including Missionary Baptists, Free-Will Baptists, Union Baptists, Primitive Baptists, Regular Baptists, Old Regular Baptists, as well as a host of independent and non-denominational independent Holiness Churches. Precise details of worship differ, but generally these (usually small) congregations tend to follow a particular style of worship. The worship usually begins with hymns, the first chosen by the pastor/elder, and others chosen in turn by members of the congregation. The pastor/elder might comment on the stanzas of a hymn before another hymn is sung. There is usually a prayer time, perhaps with a call for those near the 'altar' to kneel, and people praying as the Spirit directs. There may be a special hymn-singing slot, a time for healing, an offering, a Scripture reading and message, an impromptu prayer, an altar call and a final hymn. The message is delivered in a particular chant style. When communion is celebrated, it usually includes foot-washing.[56]

Within these many churches, the snake-handling Holiness Churches have received the most attention, and for obvious reasons. In these particular communities – divided between the Oneness or Jesus Only group (primarily located in West Virginia, Virginia and Kentucky, and who baptize in the name of Jesus), and the Trinitarian groups, mainly in Georgia and south-east Tennessee – members receive 'anointing' in worship, handle poisonous snakes, drink poison and touch fire. To most people outside of this tradition, these are not enticing practices, and given that fatalities occur, they are not particularly conducive to church growth. These communities focus on Mark 16.17–18, and usually append the phrase 'with Signs Following' to the name of their church, such as 'The Dolly Pond Church of God with Signs Following'.

The precise origin of Appalachian snake-handling is disputed, but most writers suggest that it was with George Hensley in Tennessee, either in 1908 or 1913.[57] Hensley was co-founder of the Dolly Pond Church, which was a Trinitarian church. Jimmy Morrow, a pastor in the

---

56 See the accounts in McCauley, *Appalachian Mountain Religion*; Howard Dorgan, *Giving Glory to God in Appalachia: Worship Practices of Six Baptist Subdenominations* (University of Tennessee Press, Knoxville, 1987); Jeff Todd Titon, *Powerhouse for God: Speech, Chant, and Song in an Appalachian Baptist Church* (University of Texas Press, Austin, 1988). There are some churches that practise foot-washing separately from communion.

57 Thomas Burton, *Serpent-Handling Believers* (University of Tennessee Press, Knoxville, 1993), pp. 33–8.

Jesus Only group, claims that it originated in the 1890s with the prophetess Nancy Younger Kleinieck in West Virginia, and that Hensley had witnessed the handling of serpents when he was a boy.[58] Whatever the precise origin, it was certainly George Hensley who gained publicity and notoriety to this gift of the Spirit, and once the ritual started, it spread quickly. In the view of Burton this was because of a fervent fundamentalist religious community with a traditional approach to biblical interpretation, and one that espoused traditional values that would evoke and reinforce the practice.[59] Snake-handling has been outlawed in many States, but still persists in spite of the law.

The 1967 documentary by Peter Adair, entitled 'Holy Ghost People', featured a snake-handling service at Scrabble Creek, West Virginia.[60] The service had some preliminary singing prior to the arrival of the presiding pastor/elder, and during the gathering members greeted one another with a holy kiss. After a brief exhortation there were prayers for various people, during which everyone prayed aloud, with some people kneeling in groups, while others were lying on the floor, or jerking their bodies. Testimonies were offered, followed by a duet accompanied with a guitar. A testimony of a vision followed, and then came singing with clapping, during which a woman was dancing and twirling around in circles. Then, as the singing and dancing continued, snakes were handled. One man collapsed in the Spirit and writhed on the floor, and a woman also collapsed on the floor. More singing and testimonies followed, and then an offering was taken. The presiding elder then handled a snake, and was bitten, and the service came to a conclusion with communal prayer.

In more recent times, David Kimbrough describes a service he attended as part of his study, which was published in 2002.[61] As the congregation gathered, they shook hands, hugged and exchanged a holy kiss. The musical instruments which were brought in included acoustic and electric guitars, fiddles, steel guitars, harmonicas, drums, banjos and cymbals. Wooden boxes containing snakes were brought in – the boxes are usually inscribed with Mark 16.17–18. The service began

---

58 Jimmy Morrow with Ralph W. Hood, Jr, *Handling Serpents: Pastor Jimmy Morrow's Narrative History of His Appalachian Jesus' Name Tradition* (Mercer University Press, Macon GA, 2005), pp. 1–15.
59 Burton, *Serpent-Handling Believers*, p. 7.
60 <http://video.google.com/videoplay?docid=1536399379687877393#>.
61 David Kimbrough, *Taking Up Serpents: Snake Handlers of Eastern Kentucky* (Mercer University Press, Macon GA, 2002), pp. 16–22.

with everyone singing a song called 'Feel Like Traveling On', during which some members raised their hands and spoke in tongues, while snakes were handled. After 45 minutes of singing and snake-handling, the excitement subsided, and testimonies were given. A time of prayer ensued for about 15 minutes, with everyone praying the requests that had been voiced, and some people speaking in tongues. The minister then requested a song, and a woman arose and began singing 'Can't nobody hide from God', as the instrumentalists joined in this ten-minute rendition. One man handled a snake during the song, and after the song the minister delivered the message in the traditional breathless, chant style, during which his body shook.[62] A number of testimonies were given, and a woman was anointed with olive oil and prayed for. During the song 'I Wanna Live so God Can Use Me', snakes were once again handled. One man grabbed a fire bottle, lit it and held it to his face for a minute – and received no burns. People then began to depart. A similar service is described by Fred Brown and Jeanne McDonald at Rock House Holiness Church of God, Macedonia, Alabama, on 3 October 1998, during which the guest preacher, John Wayne 'Punkin' Brown, was bitten – he died five minutes later.[63]

A key factor in taking up serpents, drinking poison and handling fire is to be 'anointed' with the Spirit. To attempt these things when the anointing has not happened is regarded as taboo. The 'anointing' is described by Anna Prince, whose father Ulysses was a snake-handling pastor, as was her brother Charles Prince, who died from a fatal snake bite. Anna Prince says:

> It's a spiritual trancelike strand of power linking humans to God; it's a burst of energy that's refreshing, always brand new; it brings on good emotions. One is elated, full of joy. You know you're right with God, totally in tune with God; everything is right with everyone on earth. It's a delicious, wonderful feeling going through your body; it's a roar of happiness; you want to laugh,

---

62 For the auctioneer-style of Pastor Jimmy Morrow, of del Rio TN, see <http://www.youtube.com/watch?v=wEm7u0LanzU>.

63 Fred Brown and Jeanne McDonald, *The Serpent Handlers: Three Families and Their Faith* (John F. Blair, Winston-Salem NC, 2000), pp. 10–15. See also Paul F. Gillespie (ed.), *Foxfire 7* (Anchor Press, Garden City, 1982), pp. 370–428; Dennis Covington, *Salvation on Sand Mountain: Snake Handling and Redemption in Southern Appalachia* (Penguin Books, New York, 1995).

jump. It's a power surge that is near to a light electrical shock and a sexual orgasm simultaneously felt, but it is not sexual or electrical, just a similar sensation. It's close to sexual without being sensual; it's loving, not making love. Love surges through the body in waves; one knows no enemies; one wants to dance in happiness or hug somebody. It's addicting – once you feel it you want to feel it again; it causes people who get hooked on the feeling to band with others who feel it in order to get a bigger and deeper high. One feels akin to God, free of guilt, pain, shame or 'pull-downs' that normally plague a person. The anointed one is nearly unearthly for a few minutes.[64]

Music and dance/movement seem to be important ingredients in setting the scene for the anointing of the Spirit to take place.[65] The style is country-western and bluegrass, and is characterized by improvisation and free melodic and textual variation. According to Scott Schwartz, it is probably borrowed from what the musicians hear on commercial radio and television stations, and is therefore familiar to them, as well as to the church members.[66] Schwartz notes that the performance of a single piece will frequently last 15–20 minutes. The music is not written down – the musicians and singers simply play and sing from memory. The style of preaching 'in the Spirit' has a number of things in common with African American preaching styles – perhaps reaching back to their Camp Meeting origins. Brown and McDonald note:

> Their speech, which might sound ignorant to the uninformed ear, is the result of a long cultural heritage. It includes a dose of Scots-Irish dialect of their ancestors, a smattering of Biblical terms, and a generous helping of colorful idioms handed down through the generations. Their grammatical constructions, syntactic patterns, and idiosyncrasies of language also stem from the geographic isolation of the mountains in which they live. This isolation has tended to preserve and concentrate all these linguistic features into a rhythmic, lilting expression unique unto itself.[67]

---

64 Burton, *Serpent-Handling Believers*, p. 140.
65 The music does not affect the snakes since they do not have auditory organs that can detect airborne sounds.
66 Scott W. Schwartz, 'Music of the Serpent-Handling Service' in Burton, *Serpent-Handling Believers*, pp. 146–8.
67 Brown and McDonald, *The Serpent Handlers*, p. xv.

One major question is 'why did snake-handling arise in this region?' Some sociologists have suggested that it is a ritual response to exploitation and poverty. The subsistence farming of these mountain areas was on land rich in minerals, particularly coal. Coal-mining companies bought the land at what seemed to the farmers a good price, but this eventually left the farmers with insufficient land to remain self-sufficient, and farming gave way to working in the coal mines with poor wages. In a disenfranchised and poor community, taking up serpents was a way of expressing spiritual empowerment. Kimbrough writes:

> The serpent became the intermediary between the conflicting economies not only because it represented evil and death but also because victims of the capitalist system still viewed the mountain economy in personal rather than commodity terms; that is, they saw capitalism as exploitative. The capitalist system that coal mining introduced was a frightful distortion of the mountain social and economic order, and snake handling represented a form of supernatural retaliation.[68]

Although McCauley has challenged the stereotyping of the Appalachian mountain religion as poor and ignorant, a lot of the snake-handling communities do seem to consist of those dwelling in or near mining districts, and many of the men have worked in the mines. The area is not noted for its affluence, and leading worship is considered to be a gift of the Spirit, not a seminary-learned skill. However, Burton points out that although it 'originated in rural areas of the South among people with little education who shared a low socioeconomic status . . . serpent-handling can be found among relatively prosperous, even wealthy, individuals and in . . . middle-class industrial centers'[69] as well. He suggests that the spiritual dimension needs to be taken seriously.

Charles Lippy stresses two important features of religiosity or spirituality of Appalachian religion that are important in this context:

1 A sense that the world of everyday life is a realm of power, an arena where supernatural forces of good and evil are operative. Popular religiosity revolves in part around gaining access to divine supernatural power that assures triumph over the forces of evil.

---

68 Kimbrough, *Taking Up Serpents*, p. 96.
69 Burton, *Serpent-Handling Believers*, p. 132.

2 An understanding that life transpires simultaneously in two dimensions of time, the present and the future, and on two levels of reality, the 'here and now' and the hereafter. For those trapped in Enlightenment modes of thinking, in each case the former element is identified with empirical reality and represents all that can be known. But for those imbued with power, the future beyond this life that will come on a higher plane not only transcends empirical reality, but is far superior to it.[70]

In other words, the religious culture does accept a supernatural, enchanted world. To those trained in biblical criticism, it seems bizarre that verses of the longer (and later add-on) ending of Mark's Gospel would be taken as the core of the Gospel, and troublesome that the King James English rendering of the Greek might perhaps have been more accurately rendered as 'take away' or 'remove' rather than 'take up'. In a postmodern culture the idea that there is one meaning for this pericope seems to be less important, but regardless of that, the strong belief in the spiritual world of evil means that snake-handling becomes a sign (*semeion*) that is, in a sense, sacramental. As Mary Lee Daugherty observes:

Their Bible is the King James Version, and they know, through their own experiences, that their faith in the healing and saving power of Jesus has been tested and proved beyond question and doubt. It still functions sacramentally for them as a 'sign'. It is a ritual about life, death, and resurrection through faith in Jesus.[71]

Although Pastor Jimmy Morrow claims that snake-handling is found in 15 states, and is growing, most research suggests the opposite.[72] It is handed down through families, and so depends on kinship. But with better education and greater economic opportunities for the younger generations, the loyalty to snake-handling seems to be waning.[73] While

---

70 Charles H. Lippy, 'Popular Religiosity in Central Appalachia' in Bill J. Leonard (ed.), *Christianity in Appalachia: Profiles in Regional Pluralism* (University of Tennessee Press, Knoxville, 1999), pp. 40–51, pp. 41–2.
71 Mary Lee Daugherty, 'Serpent Handlers: When the sacrament comes alive' in Leonard (ed.), *Christianity in Appalachia*, pp. 138–52, p. 147.
72 Morrow and Hood, *Handling Serpents*, p. 128.
73 Mary Lee Daugherty, 'Serpent Handlers', p. 151.

a valid expression of faith in a postmodern world, it is not itself attractive to postmodern people. Like the Amish, its continued existence is counter-cultural, but unlike Amish furniture it is unlikely that there will be a great market for it.

CONCLUSION

Some Christian Churches actively try to adopt practices that they think are postmodern, but postmodernity is very much bound up with global commercial culture. The AICs, *Minjung* and *Kuk-ak*, as well as Amish and Wenger, and the snake-handlers, are an important reminder that local culture and counter-culture are also important elements in the worship varieties of the Worship Mall.

Chapter 6

What is Celtic about contemporary Celtic worship?

> One of the characteristics of Celtic Christianity is that it makes no distinction between sacred and secular, spiritual and material. The whole world, having been created by God, is infused with holiness, rendering every moment an opportunity to be touched by God. Join us, enveloped by the beauty of Shrine Mont, as we use all our senses to open ourselves more fully to God in our daily lives.[1]

This quotation from a flyer for a retreat sponsored by the Episcopal Church Women of the Diocese of Virginia usefully encapsulates the common perception of what is described as Celtic Christianity or Celtic spirituality, and its marketability. It is described as if it has characteristics that are in marked contrast to other forms of Christianity, and as such, as something that is a desirable commodity for any spiritual shopper looking for something new and fulfilling. Within this apparent rediscovery of Celtic Christianity there is also a new industry in Celtic worship. Donald Meek writes:

> Liturgies which claim to be 'Celtic' are being produced to meet the needs of those who may wish to incorporate 'Celtic' prayers and other items into their worship . . . In short, 'Celtic Christianity' is a major growth industry, which appears to be thriving at many levels.[2]

---

1 The Episcopal Church Women of the Diocese of Virginia, 'A Prayer and Worship Retreat', <www.rlva.org/documents/2008/AprilHarbinger.doc>.
2 Donald E. Meek, *The Quest for Celtic Christianity* (The Handsel Press Ltd, Edinburgh, 2000), p. 5.

Here I will explore this renewed interest in things Celtic, and look into just how Celtic the contemporary liturgical forms that claim to be Celtic worship really are.

Interest in things Celtic is not a new phenomenon. Ian Bradley, in his *Celtic Christianity: Making Myths and Chasing Dreams*, has described how from the seventh century onwards there have been particular epochs in which outsiders and exiles, rather than native Celts, have attempted to identify and celebrate its distinct ethos and character. Bradley notes that distance – geographical and chronological – lends enchantment to the quest.[3] Furthermore, such quests are not neutral or indifferent; they have usually been inspired by some contemporary need – spiritual, political or cultural – which has coloured the reconstruction of what constituted 'Celtic'. Thus, for example, some sixteenth- and seventeenth-century Anglican writers invoked an imagined 'Celtic' Church, which, like the Church of England, was an Episcopal church independent of Rome and Romanism. Archbishop James Ussher, in his *Discourse on the Religion Anciently Professed by the Irish and the British* (1623), argued that the Protestant Church of Ireland was a descendant of a 'Protestant' Celtic Church which had survived untainted by Romanism. Both the eighteenth and nineteenth centuries also birthed quests for the authentic 'Celtic' spirit.[4] Thus the present industry in things 'Celtic', which has marked the last decades of the twentieth century and continues unabated into the twenty-first, is simply the latest in a whole history of such quests, albeit with its own particular current agendas and concerns.

The term 'Celtic spirituality' in much contemporary usage seems to be a broad umbrella term, and may include elements not only inspired by a perceived Christian tradition, but also by Celtic paganism, Druidry and Celtic-influenced New Age movements. In a very perceptive essay on this term, Marion Bowman noted that the term 'Celtic spirituality' adds a particular 'flavour' to a chosen form of religiosity, which is sometimes highly individualistic, but that there is no authoritative, universally accepted version of the 'truth' about the Celts. Rather, there are shifting ideas and images, scholarly and popular, all of which have contributed to the immensely varied and vibrant phenomenon of contemporary Celtic spirituality.[5] Bowman writes:

---

3 Ian Bradley, *Celtic Christianity: Making Myths and Chasing Dreams* (Edinburgh University Press, Edinburgh, 1999), p. 3.
4 Bradley, *Celtic Christianity*, chs 3 and 4.
5 Marion Bowman, 'Contemporary Celtic Spirituality' in Joanne Pearson (ed.), *Belief*

For some, it seems that Celts and the Celtic past have come to epitomize that which is lost but longed for in contemporary society. The remedy for dissatisfaction with the present is being sought in a particular (some would say distorted) reflection of the past.[6]

She notes the wide-ranging interest in Celtic languages, Celtic music, Celtic artefacts, Celtic art, Celtic ceremonies and Celtic worship, but observes that this has given rise to the idea that there is such a thing as a single, common Celtic culture or spirit. She points out:

From Celtic literature appearing in English for an English-speaking audience has emerged a sort of hybrid 'Celtish', which reflects the style of English to emerge in translations of Celtic literature, involving formulaic – frequently threefold – repetition, metrical forms, short lines and archaic turns of phrase (e.g. 'Power of storm be thine, Power of moon be thine, Power of the sun . . .'). Thus, to the linguistically uninitiated, Celtic literature comes in a homogenized package, with Irish, Welsh, Cornish and Gaelic writings (which we rarely see in their varied original versions) seeming all the same. Similarly, there is a collapsing of chronology, as translations of early medieval, nineteenth- and twentieth-century texts frequently appear together without differentiation, often with the implication that these are all 'ancient' writings. (The antiquity and influence of oral tradition is undoubtedly an important factor, but the fact remains that the texts themselves are often of far more recent date than is implied.) . . . It is no wonder, then, that Celtic writings seem 'timeless', for they are often presented in a completely atemporal manner; and because of the pervading 'Celtish' style, Celtic prayers, blessings and ritual/liturgical speech being written now, whether Christian, Druid, New Age or Pagan, frequently sound similar – and that in turn all feeds back into the impression of the 'sameness' and solidity of Celtic spirituality.[7]

Beyond Boundaries: Wicca, Celtic Spirituality and the New Age (Ashgate/Open University, Aldershot and Milton Keynes, 2002), pp. 55–101, pp. 63–4.

6 Bowman, 'Contemporary Celtic Spirituality', p. 60.

7 Bowman, 'Contemporary Celtic Spirituality', pp. 68–9.

The crucial point here is that there is in fact a difference between Scottish Highland and Island culture, and Irish, Welsh and Manx cultures. Furthermore, writings, whether devotional or not, are not atemporal. This point leads us to the fact that, as Bradley, Meek and Bowman all note, a major source and inspiration for 'Celtophiles' is Alexander Carmichael's collection of orally transmitted folk hymns, private prayers, incantations, spells and charms, published in six volumes from 1900 under the title *Carmina Gadelica*. Carmichael was a Gaelic speaker, and as a civil servant was posted as exciseman to the Hebrides. There he set out to record the oral folklore. None of this material, we should note, is from public worship. As with much oral tradition, it was undatable, and the concerns in many of the spells and charms with the saints (and kept alive by some Protestants as well as Catholics) witness to a powerful folk religion. His view that some of the hymns might have been composed in the cloistered cells of Derry or Iona is probably wishful thinking. However, the collection is specifically Hebridean. Furthermore, Carmichael was far from a disinterested recorder of oral tradition. He certainly edited, improved and at times rewrote his material – particularly when there was more than one version – and in some instances it is thought that he invented extra verses or extra lines.[8] Yet, in contemporary Celtic spirituality the assumption of the collection's authenticity and antiquity is accepted, or at least assumed, and for many, the English translations provide authentic paradigms of Celtic style and phraseology which can be used or imitated in contemporary prayers and spiritual writings. An example from the collection is as follows:

> God with me lying down,
> God with me rising up,
> God within each ray of light,
> Nor I a ray of joy without Him,
> Nor I a ray of joy without Him.

---

8 Alexander Carmichael, *Carmina Gadelica: Hymns and Incantations*, ed. C. J. Moore (Floris Books, Edinburgh, 1992). The defensive Preface by John MacInnes comments: 'There are elements of fabrication undoubtedly: perhaps few texts in *Carmina* are totally free of some editorial repair-work and some, including the "Invocation of the Graces," may have it to a very high degree. But throughout the collection, the core of the material is the treasure-trove of oral literature that Carmichael discovered in Gaelic Scotland.' *Carmina*, p. 17.

Christ with me sleeping,
Christ with me waking,
Christ with me watching,
Every day and night,
Each day and night.

God with me protecting,
The Lord with me directing,
The Spirit with me strengthening,
For ever and for evermore,
Ever and evermore, Amen.
Chief of chiefs, Amen.[9]

My concern here is focused on the Celtic Christian tradition, and with what can be said historically about Celtic liturgy; and with contemporary liturgies that are described as Celtic. Before turning to Celtic worship, however, something needs to be said briefly about perceptions of Celtic spirituality.

PERCEPTIONS OF CELTIC SPIRITUALITY

The quotation from the Episcopal Church Women's flyer already gives some hints at the popular understanding of the characteristics of Celtic Christianity. These views have been made popular by authors such as Nora Chadwick in her 1971 book, *The Celts*; Esther de Waal's *God Under My Roof* (1984), and *The Celtic Vision* (1988); and Robert Van de Weyer's *Celtic Fire* (1990). Donald Allchin joined with Esther de Waal in *Threshold of Light* (1986), and Allchin himself has produced anthologies of Welsh prayers and devotions.[10] These are respected names, and therefore few have questioned whether the views might be flights of fantasy more than core fact. In the case of de Waal, her naive fundamentalist trust in the authority of *Carmina Gadelica* seems to have been

---

9 Carmichael, *Carmina*, p. 36.
10 Nora Chadwick, *The Celts* (Penguin Books, Harmondsworth, 1971); Esther de Waal, *God Under My Roof* (Fairacres Publications, Abingdon, 1984); *The Celtic Vision* (Darton, Longman & Todd, London, 1988); Robert Van de Weyer, *Celtic Fire* (Darton, Longman & Todd, London, 1990); Donald Allchin and Esther de Waal, *Threshold of Light* (Darton, Longman & Todd, London, 1986); Donald Allchin, *God's Presence Makes the World: The Celtic Vision through the Centuries in Wales* (Darton, Longman & Todd, London, 1997).

accepted without question by her many readers. These works together with a host of similar writings, many inspired by these writers and repeating their views, have given rise to the current common perception of what characterizes Celtic Christianity. First and foremost, it is seen as having a strong emphasis on the environment and the holiness of the created order, and extolling the great outdoors; here is the original Green Church, a veritable farmers' market of spirituality. Linked to this close-to-nature lifestyle, the Celtic Church is seen as having a simple structure, with abbots rather than diocesan bishops. In distinction from the Augustinian mission, it is perceived as being independent of Rome, and therefore having an ecumenical dimension, and a gift for tolerance. Donald Meek suggests that in the religious sphere the term 'Celtic' conjures up beautiful stone crosses, splendidly executed manuscripts, remote islands away from noise and special individuals called saints, with the result that 'People not only "see" Celtic things; they "feel" them: peace and tranquility in distant islands and "peripheral" rural areas; purity of environment; an indefinable loveliness in wind and sea and sky; dazzling sunrises and soothing sunsets.'[11]

In his liturgical collection entitled *heart2heart*, John Birch, for example, who relies on Michael Mitton's *Restoring the Woven Cord*, itself inspired more by the themes of *Carmina Gadelica* than any serious study, writes:

> To the Celtic Church their God was a personal loving God totally involved in the whole of the Created world, which he had breathed into existence.
>
> God was with them when they pulled weeds out of their gardens. He was there when they milked their cows; when they gave birth and when they lay down in the darkness of their simple huts in the cold of the evening.
>
> The Celts knew that their God was involved in all of His Creation.[12]

---

11 Meek, *Quest*, p. 9.
12 John Birch, *heart2heart: Contemporary Prayers, Litanies and Liturgies for Christian Worship* (Moorleys, Ilkeston, 2004), p. 5. Michael Mitton, *Restoring the Woven Cord: Strands of Celtic Christianity for the Church Today* (Darton, Longman & Todd, London, 1995).

According to Meek, such views represent a romantic, postmodern concept of the past, which compensates for a pessimistic view of the future.[13] Certainly such 'warm and fuzzy' perceptions seem very far from what we do know historically about the Celtic Churches. There is, for example, little evidence that Celtic priests and religious were any more interested in nature than were their Anglo-Saxon counterparts, and the so-called nature prayers in *Carmina Gadelica*, reflecting Hebridean folk religion, have some counterparts in Anglo-Saxon charms and spells.[14] Patrick Ford argued that one of the longest 'nature' poems is in fact a grammatical exercise to demonstrate the working of forms of the infixed pronoun found in Early Irish.[15] Thomas O'Loughlin notes that in the writings of Patrick, the closeness of God is of a stern and all-seeing master, to be reverenced with awe and trembling.[16] The founding of large monasteries by the Celtic churchmen, far from being an ancient eco-friendly action, was in fact the first step towards urbanization. The organization of monastic houses under abbots was as highly hierarchical as the diocesan parochial system, and in some ways more so. All our evidence points to the fact that in spite of local custom and usage, far from being isolated, the Celts were in constant touch with Rome and the rest of the Western Church, and saw themselves as very much a part of it, both receiving from it and contributing to it. The Irish monk Columbanus defended the Irish Easter calculation, but wrote to Pope Boniface stating that all the Irish were pupils of Sts Peter and Paul, and that 'Our possession of the catholic faith is unshaken: we hold it just as it was first handed to us by you, the successors of the holy apostles.'[17] One of the greatest contributions the Celtic Church made was in the Irish Penitentials, which show great suspicion,

---

13 Meek, *Quest*, p. 30.
14 See Karen Louise Jolly, *Popular Religion in Late Saxon England: Elf Charms in Context* (University of North Carolina Press, Chapel Hill, 1996); Edward Pettit, *Anglo-Saxon Remedies, Charms, and Prayers from British Library Ms. Harley 585* (The Edwin Mellen Press, Lewiston, Queenston and Lampeter, 2001). See also Oliver Davies, *Celtic Christianity in Early Medieval Wales: The Origins of the Welsh Spiritual Tradition* (University of Wales Press, Cardiff, 1996).
15 P. Ford, 'Blackbirds, Cuckoos, and Infixed Pronouns: Another context for Early Irish nature poetry' in R. Black, W. Gillies and R. Ó Maolalaigh (eds), *Celtic Connections* (Tuckwell Press, East Linton, 1999), cited in Meek, *Quest*, p. 85.
16 Thomas O'Loughlin, *Celtic Theology: Humanity, World and God in Early Irish Writings* (Continuum, London and New York, 2000), p. 34.
17 Columbanus, Epistle V, 3 in G. S. M. Walker, *Sancti Columbani Opera* (Dublin Institute for Advanced Studies, Dublin, 1957).

if not out-right hostility, to the body and sexuality. Dáibhí Ó Cróinín commented:

> [T]here was apparently no crime that could not be thought of: heterosexual and homosexual relations (male and female), the regulation of 'proper' methods of intercourse, aphrodisiacs and potions, physical relations, bestiality (Columbanus has two canons on the subject, one for clerics or monks, the other for laymen), wet dreams, stimulation, abortion, contraception, abstinence from sexual relations, and an endless litany of reprobate behaviour that ranged from drinking in the same house with a pregnant woman to keening or wailing for the dead.[18]

The negative concern for the body in the Penitentials is the very opposite of contemporary postmodern interest in the human body.[19] Thomas O'Loughlin concludes: 'certain popular presentations of the theology that came from the Celtic lands which present it as "female-friendly", "feelings-friendly", "affective" and "an Augustine-free zone" are somewhat wide of the mark.'[20]

In terms of resources of Celtic prayers and liturgies, these too continue to grow like Topsy. There are collections on the market which, in turn, inspire more home-grown products. Among the earliest of the current quest were *The Sun Dances* and *New Moon of the Season* from the Christian Community Press (1960), and G. R. D. McLean's *Poems of the West Highlands* (1961).[21] The former were extracts from *Carmina Gadelica*, and the latter contained material from *Carmina Gadelica* turned into verse. As previously noted, Esther de Waal also culled her material from Carmichael's work. Additionally, a significant contribution has been made by David Adam, former Vicar of Lindisfarne, in such works as *The Edge of Glory: Prayers in the Celtic Tradition* and *Tides and Seasons: Modern Prayers in the Celtic*

---

18 Dáibhí Ó Cróinín, *Early Medieval Ireland 400–1200* (Longmans, London, 1995), p. 199.

19 See, for example, David Brown's treatment, *God and Grace of Body: Sacrament in Ordinary* (Oxford University Press, Oxford, 2007).

20 O'Loughlin, *Celtic Theology*, p. 126.

21 *The Sun Dances* (Christian Community Press, London, 1960); *New Moon of the Season* (Christian Community Press, London, 1960); G. R. D. McLean, *Poems of the West Highlands* (SPCK, London, 1961).

Tradition, which contain short rhythmic prayers imitating the style of *Carmina Gadelica*, though including material from such diverse non-Celtic people as Aquinas, Ignatius Loyola and Robert Runcie.[22] The Northumbria Community, which was established in 1992, has produced *Celtic Daily Prayer* and *Celtic Night Prayer*.[23] Ray Simpson, of the Community of Aidan and Hilda, and who left his parish ministry to live on Lindisfarne, published *Celtic Worship through the Year* (1997).[24] Perhaps best known are the worship services that come from the Iona Community. Philip Newell produced *Each Day and Each Night* (1994), which again has *Carmina Gadelica* as a main inspiration, and for which Newell claimed, 'These "Songs and Prayers of the Gaels" had been forged by crofters and fishermen in the often wild and harsh conditions of the Western Isles, and been passed down in the oral tradition for hundreds of years.'[25] The songs from the community, the Wild Goose Worship Group, while having little in common with the Celtic chant of Columba, or Columbanus, draw on contemporary understanding of Celtic song, imagery and rhythm. More recently, Brendan O'Malley has compiled *A Celtic Primer* (2002), which contains Morning and Evening Prayer, Compline, hymns and a Celtic Eucharist.[26] There are smaller compilations such as that of John Birch. The Church of Scotland's *Common Order* (1994/1996) claims to have some of its services based on the Celtic tradition. This list is certainly not exhaustive, and on the internet many groups and churches post their Celtic forms of worship. However, before looking at some of these in more detail, let us first consider what we do know about the worship of the Celtic Church(es) of late antiquity and the early medieval period.

---

22 David Adam, *The Edge of Glory: Prayers in the Celtic Tradition* (Triangle/SPCK, London, 1985); *Tides and Seasons: Modern Prayers in the Celtic Tradition* (Triangle/SPCK, London, 1989).
23 *Celtic Daily Prayer: A Northumbrian Office* (Marshall Pickering, London, 1994); *Celtic Night Prayer* (Marshall Pickering, London, 1996).
24 Ray Simpson (comp.), *Celtic Worship through the Year: Prayers, Readings and Creative Activities for Ordinary Days and Saints' Days* (Hodder & Stoughton, London, 1997).
25 Philip Newell, *Celtic Prayers from Iona*, USA title of *Each Day and Each Night* (Paulist Press, New York, 1997), pp. 5–6.
26 Brendan O'Malley (ed.), *A Celtic Primer: The Complete Celtic Worship Resource and Collection* (Morehouse Publishing, Harrisburg PA, 2002).

CELTIC CHURCHES OF LATE ANTIQUITY AND THE EARLY MEDIEVAL PERIOD

One of our main sources is the Stowe Missal, which provides us with a baptismal rite as well as the ordinary and some propers of the Mass.[27] Probably written at Tallaght, *c.* 792, and associated with the monastic revival, the *Celi Dé*, the work clearly shows Gallican influences. The baptismal rite is mainly Roman material, but with the Gallican ritual shape. It has one anointing, and the *pedilavium*, and as one might imagine has material in common with the Bobbio missal. Since, however, contemporary Celtic worship shows little interest in creating baptismal rites, but is mainly concerned with Eucharists, Daily Offices and litanies, it is these that we will further consider.

The Mass in the Stowe Missal is mainly that of the Gelasian rite, and the canon missae is labelled 'Canon Dominicus Papae Gelasii'. Yet there are some significant departures from the Gelasian sacramentary. The rite commences with a Litany of the Saints, preceded by an antiphon; though some additions were made here by an editor, Moél Caích; there is a prayer ascribed to St Augustine, which later is found as a vesting prayer in French sources. Some prayers were said after the Epistle, including a form of prayers for the people, entitled 'Deprecatio sancti Martini', prior to the Gospel. It has a striking Preface, and certain peculiarities within the canon, and includes names of Irish saints and bishops, including Maelruen, the founder of the *Celi Dé*. Also included is an extremely complex ritual with formulae for the fraction, with the broken bread laid out in a cross on the paten. It has been suggested that items in the Derrynavlan Hoard – a two-handled chalice of about 21 cm, a paten of about 36 cm in diameter, a strainer and a large bronze bowl – were the type of communion vessels designed for distribution of communion as directed by the Stowe rubrics.[28] A long series of anthems, antiphons and alleluias are sung, and these are also found in the Antiphonary of Bangor. Thomas O'Loughlin comments:

---

27 B. MacCarthy (ed.), *On the Stowe Missal: The Transactions of the Royal Irish Academy*, vol. XXVII (1886). ET in *Celtic Missal*, translated and rubricated by Kristopher G. Dowling (Ascension Western Rite Orthodox Church, Akron OH, 1997). See also Jane Stevenson and F. E. Warren (eds), *The Liturgy and Ritual of the Celtic Church* (The Boydell Press, Woodbridge, 1987).

28 Próinséas Ní Chatháin, 'The Liturgical Background of the Derrynavlan Altar Service', *Journal of the Royal Society of Antiquaries of Ireland* 110 (1980), pp. 127–48.

The meal then properly begins when the piece of the broken loaf is given to be eaten, and the blessed chalice is handed to the participant to be drunk from; and it is with that perspective in mind that we should look at this chant (wholly in Moél Caích's hand) for use while the people are eating and drinking at the Lord's table. This process probably took quite a time, moving, eating, drinking, and then tidying up and cleaning of the vessels – so this sequence of antiphons and psalms was probably long enough to cover the length of time even the largest congregation would need, as well as providing a time for reflection after people had received a portion of the loaf and cup – while it could easily be curtailed if the group was smaller.[29]

The evidence for the Daily Office in Ireland has been studied in some depth by Peter Jeffery.[30] He notes first the Office of the Three Fifties, which entailed the recitation daily of the entire Psalter in three groups of fifty, with some canticles and the Lord's Prayer. Other Offices, such as recorded in the Voyage of St Brendan, were derived from Cassian, and consisted of set psalms. The next group are the Offices of the Irish monasteries on the Continent, and here he draws on Columban's rule. These seem to be in the spectrum between contemporary Gallican practices and the prescriptions of Cassian. The largest source, however, is the Bangor Antiphoner. Jeffery notes that this is not an antiphoner in the modern sense, but is an appendix or supplement to a psalter, containing the non-psalmic material needed to celebrate the Office. It contains canticles, hymns, collects and antiphons. He concludes that it represents St Columbanus' Office as it developed after his time at a Continental centre, under the influence of Gallican and north Italian traditions such as we might expect to find at Bobbio.[31] The more recent study by Patricia Rumsey notes the difference in the understanding of the Offices in the Voyage of St Brendan and the rules of the *Céli Dé*, with the latter putting a heavy emphasis on penance and asceticism at

---

29 O'Loughlin, *Celtic Theology*, p. 143.
30 Peter Jeffery, 'Eastern and Western Elements in the Irish Monastic Prayer of the Hours' in Margot E. Fassler and Rebecca A. Baltzer (eds), *The Divine Office in the Latin Middle Ages: Methodology and Source Studies, Regional Developments, Hagiography* (Oxford University Press, Oxford, 2000), pp. 99–143.
31 Jeffery, 'Eastern and Western Elements', p. 127.

all times.[32] However, we should note the obvious: the texts are in Latin, and do not represent a totally different form or style of the Divine Office from other contemporary Latin sources.

An important para-liturgical product of Irish Christianity is the composition of Irish litanies. These were edited by Charles Plummer in 1925 for the Henry Bradshaw Society, and Plummer gives both the Gaelic texts and English translations.[33] The manuscripts in which these are found range from the twelfth to the fifteenth and sixteenth centuries, though Plummer thought their composition was significantly earlier, some perhaps originating in the sixth century. Both the format and style of these litanies are quite varied, and certainly some of them are quite evocative in style and phraseology. They include a Litany of Confession, of the Saviour, of the Virgin and All Saints, of Jesus I and II, of the Virgin, of Irish Saints I and II, of the Trinity, of St Michael, of the virgins, a metrical Litany of the Virgin Mary and a Litany of Creation. Some quotations will illustrate the varying styles. The Litany of Jesus II:

O holy Jesu:
O gentle friend;
O Morning Star;
O mid-day Sun adorned;
O brilliant flame of the righteous, and of righteousness, and of
   everlasting life, and of eternity;[34]

The Litany of the Trinity (British Library manuscript Additional 30, 512):

O God of the earth,
O God of fire,
O God of the excellent waters,
O God of the tempestuous and rushing (?) air,
O God of the many languages round the circuit of the earth,

---

32 Patricia M. Rumsey, *Sacred Time in Early Christian Ireland: The Monks of the Nauigatio and the Céli Dé in Dialogue to Explore the Theologies of Time and the Liturgy of the Hours in pre-Viking Ireland* (T & T Clark, London and New York, 2007).

33 Charles Plummer, *Irish Litanies: Text and Translation* (Henry Bradshaw Society LXII, London, 1925).

34 Plummer, *Irish Litanies*, p. 41.

O God of the waves from the bottomless house of the ocean,
O God of the constellations, and all the bright stars . . .[35]

And the Litany of Creation:

I entreat Thee by the tenth order in the compact earth;
I entreat laud-worthy Michael to help me against demons . . .
I entreat Thee by water and the cruel air; I entreat Thee by fire,
I entreat Thee by earth.[36]

In commenting on these litanies, Plummer observed that many of them illustrate the tendency common to almost all Irish literature, especially in its later stages, 'to heap up alliterating verbs and epithets'.[37] Much is lost in translation, but the extravagant and imaginative imagery stands out. However, Plummer, pointing out that they are all products of private devotion, observed: 'There is no hint that they were ever used, or intended to be used, in the public service of the Church, for which most of them are quite unsuited.'[38] Hence I refer to them as para-liturgical forms.

Only a small sample of what we do know of Celtic public worship, as it is reflected in contemporary Celtic worship, can be considered here. John Birch's *heart2heart* has a good number of prayers he composed himself. The supposed Celtic concern for creation is given full rein, with 'Creator God' and 'Creating God' being favoured epithets. Much of the material is personal devotion rather than public prayer, and a few litanies are included. A short and pleasing litany addressed to the Spirit begins: 'Holy Spirit, giver of life, creative breath of God through whom this world was breathed into existence and is sustained', with the response, 'Blow through the parched earth of our existence, and breathe Your Life into our lives.'

As noted above, in the preface Birch appeals to the Celtic Church, explaining that since he lives in Wales, it is difficult not to be influenced by the vision and prayer life of the early Christian saints. No claim is made specifically about the litanies, which, like his prayers, vary in literary quality. It is therefore difficult to know what is specifically

---

35 Plummer, *Irish Litanies*, p. 79.
36 Plummer, *Irish Litanies*, p. 103.
37 Plummer, *Irish Litanies*, p. xvi.
38 Plummer, *Irish Litanies*, p. xv.

Celtic about them, especially since there is no attempt to base them on the Celtic litanies we do have.

More widely known is the work of the Northumbria Community, and here I turn to this community's *Celtic Daily Prayer*. In this volume, services are provided for Morning, Midday and Evening Prayer, while a separate collection caters to Night Prayer. The orders of service take the form of prayers, meditations and Scripture readings. There are opening sentences with versicles and responses entitled 'Call and Response'. There is a short declaration of faith, a psalm, and Old and New Testament readings, a meditation and prayer, a canticle and a blessing. Although these are devotional, short and refreshing, they bear no resemblance at all to the ancient liturgical sources. There is no set psalmody, and no traditional canticles. So what makes it Celtic? The canticle 'Christ as a light' is inspired by 'St Patrick's Breastplate', but the canticle 'In the shadow of your wings' is a 1985 compilation. The meditations are from a wide range of authors, including Rowan Williams, who, though Welsh, is not a Celtic divine. Although these are delightful short Offices, we are still left with the unanswered question: what is it that makes these delightful short Offices 'Celtic'?

CELTIC EUCHARISTS

My main focus, however, is with Celtic Eucharists. The first, entitled 'An Order for Holy Communion', is described as 'a resource' and comes from the Northumbria Community's *Celtic Daily Prayer*. An opening sentence is followed by the Preparation said by all, and then Prayers of Penitence introduced by the leader. The Confession certainly recalls the idea of humanity in the Irish Penitentials:

> We are guilty and polluted, O God, in spirit, in heart, and in flesh, in thought, in word, in act, we are hard in thy sight in sin. Put thou forth to us the power of thy love, be thou leaping over the mountains of our transgressions, and wash us in the true blood of conciliation.[39]

The rather antiquated language perhaps adds to the idea that this is Celtic. The Canticle, 'I praise the wounds and the blood of the Lamb',

---

39 *Celtic Daily Prayer*, p. 58.

is a fine piece of work, but has no acknowledged source.[40] The rite includes, as a declaration of faith, the Creed recorded by St Patrick, which is thought to be a form of an early British creed. Free intercessions are concluded with the Lord's Prayer. The Peace has:

> Christ, King of Tenderness
> Christ, King of Tenderness
> Bind us with a bond
> That cannot be broken
> Bind us with a bond of love
> That cannot be broken.
> My brothers and sisters
> The peace of our Lord Jesus Christ
> Be with you.[41]

The Eucharistic Prayer is short, Protestant, Western, and not Stowe! The post narrative requests:

> Almighty God, our heavenly Father,
> in your tender mercy,
> send us the Spirit of the Lamb,
> and us the loving Spirit of the Lamb.[42]

This is followed by the G. J. Cuming 'Agnus Dei', said by all.

More archaisms appear in the post-communion congregational prayer, and the final blessing includes the petitions, 'may the sun be bright upon you, may the night call down peace and when you come to his household may the door be open wide for you to go in to your joy'. It seems somewhat strange that the single source we have for a Celtic Mass is hardly used at all in this Celtic Holy Communion.

Next is Ray Simpson's *Celtic Worship through the Year*. In the notes, only two sources are acknowledged – one from David Adam, and for the Preface of the Eucharistic Prayer, the Stowe Missal. The rite begins with singing, and a call to worship or gathering, the language of which evokes the familiar coupling of Celtic and nature. The leader thus remarks: 'Let this wondrous creation, plundered by alien forces, open

40 *Celtic Daily Prayer*, p. 58.
41 *Celtic Daily Prayer*, p. 61.
42 *Celtic Daily Prayer*, p. 64.

wide its arms to its returning Saviour.'[43] A reader says to God – though God is not addressed as such – 'As the birds brought food to your people in the parched deserts, so now you bring food to our parched and hungry souls.'[44] A rubric then allows more singing, the speaking of good things of God or God's creation, and at longer celebrations, dancing, creative arts, eating or sharing of news. Again, it is difficult to understand what is Celtic about these elements.

The penitential section is called 'Lamentation', and asks God to give us tears for various ends. This is a good and imaginative piece of prose, and is designed to be followed by the Kyries, though it also allows for personal expression of sorrow, pain or hurt, prior to the Kyries. A form of declaration of loving reconciliation to the soul follows. The Liturgy of the Word gives three lections of contemporary lectionary provision. The Gospel may be followed by teaching, singing, silence or more creative activities which, with candles and incense, may be brought up with the bread, wine and gift of money. The Peace, which echoes slightly two of the 'Peace' declarations in *Carmina Gadelica*, mimics the formulaic repetitive style that Bowman noted of this genre. The offering section includes the *Trisagion*, and quite imaginative and poetic table prayers, which continue to pick up the theme of creation with which the rite began. It is difficult to see much connection between the short Eucharistic Prayer in this rite and that of the Stowe Missal, despite Simpson's claim. It is free flowing, and does have a petition for conse-cration in the old *Quam oblationem* position. The post narrative reads:

> Risen Christ we welcome you. You are the flowering bough of creation; from you cascades music like a million stars, truth to cleanse a myriad souls. From you flee demons, omens and all ill-will; around you rejoice the angels of light. Father, send us the tender Spirit of the Lamb; Feed us with the Bread of Heaven; May we become drunk with your holiness.[45]

This has dramatic imagery, the mention of demons, omens and ill-will has an archaic sound, and echoes the charms found in the Stowe Missal. In an overly rational age, it is a reminder that postmodernism is open to an enchanted world, and readers of J. R. R. Tolkien, C. S. Lewis, J. K.

---

43 Simpson, *Celtic Worship*, p. 75.
44 Simpson, *Celtic Worship*, p. 75.
45 Simpson, *Celtic Worship*, p. 79.

Rowling and Philip Pullman will feel at home, yet it is certainly not following the Stowe *canon missae*. More puzzling, however, is the fact that although in the Stowe Missal, the fraction is clearly an important and elaborate ritual, there is no reference to the fraction at all in Simpson's rite. After communion, a statement of faith and commitment to Christ is said by all, and the leader pronounces the following blessing:

> The saving streams from the pierced heart of Christ save you.
> The Sacred Three shield you from all ill-will; protect you
> from all that destroys; and lead you always along Christ's paths.
> Go in peace to love and serve the Lord.[46]

It has a certain freshness, and its reference to the 'Sacred Three' certainly echoes the types of private blessings found in *Carmina Gadelica*. The final sentence of dismissal betrays the Anglican background of the compiler, and immediately after the text of the rite there are notes which explain how this could be used in a Church of England service without breaking canon law.

Brendan O'Malley, a former Cistercian monk and now Anglican priest, has published *A Celtic Eucharist* in his *A Celtic Primer*, and as a separate service booklet. The former has certain alternatives which are not found in the separate booklet, and it is the fuller version that I am outlining here. O'Malley is of Irish descent, Scottish by birth, and is a chaplain in Wales. In his compilation he worked closely with Professor Thomas O'Loughlin who teaches Celtic studies. This rite begins with 'St Patrick's Breastplate' or 'Deer's Cry', either chanted or with a hymnic version. An optional Ceremony of Light is provided for evening celebrations. The Gloria is sung, then the Collect of the Day is prayed, and there is provision for three eucharistic lections and a homily. Two creeds are provided – the first is the Creed of Tirechan, and the second is St Patrick's Confession of Faith. There follow Bidding Prayers of St Martin from Stowe, though there they precede the Gospel. This is followed by a Litany of the Trinity, adapted from Plummer. Alternative formulae for the Peace are provided, including one that is Stowe. Two rather elegant table prayers are provided, the first centring on creation, and the second on humanity. There is provision for naming the departed. The Stowe

---

46 Simpson, *Celtic Worship*, p. 80.

Preface is given, and the canon from Stowe, slightly emended for non-Roman usage, and with the addition of the names of Celtic saints. However, as alternatives, a Gallican Eucharistic Prayer is given and, oddly, Hippolytus, in the belief that this is to be dated 215 CE. The Lord's Prayer follows with embolism, though not that of Stowe. O'Malley faithfully reproduces the formula for the fraction from Stowe, though not the detailed instructions for its execution. Agnus Dei is followed by the Stowe communion anthems, though a bizarre alternative is the eschatological piece, 'If anyone is holy', from *Didache*. The Prayer Book blessing is provided, though a 'Celtish'-flavoured alternative is given.

With the exceptions of the inclusion of Hippolytus, and pieces from the *Didache* and the Book of Common Prayer, O'Malley has attempted a Eucharist that is directly patterned on the Stowe Mass. The use of one of the Irish litanies, adapted, is an example of using what was private devotion in public prayer, but it cannot be denied that it is a genuine Celtic liturgical piece and works well.

Another example, from *The Iona Community Worship Book* (1991), begins the Sunday Morning Communion with Opening Responses and a Song, which is a contemporary composition. A Prayer of Confession and Invocation follow, both of which are couched in *Carmina Gadelica* style – 'O hidden mystery, Sun behind all suns, Soul behind all souls, In everything we touch, In everyone we meet, Your presence is round us, And we give you thanks.'[47] A short version of the *Trisagion* is provided, followed by the readings and homily. A contemporary Creed, 'We believe in God above us', or the Apostles' Creed, are given. The Invitation begins, 'The Table of bread and wine is now made ready', and the second half reads:

So, come to this table,
You who have much faith
And you who would like to have more;
You who have been to this sacrament often,
And you who have not been for a long time;
You who have tried to follow Jesus,

---

47 The Iona Community, *The Iona Community Worship Book: The Abbey Services of the Iona Community* (Wild Goose Publications, Glasgow, 1991), p. 65.

And you who have failed.
Come.
It is Christ who invites us to meet him here.[48]

The Story of the Last Supper, which includes the institution narrative, is narrated prior to the Eucharistic Prayer. The Preface includes joining with nature and named Celtic saints to sing the Sanctus. Christ is asked to breathe his Spirit on us and the bread and wine, and intercessions follow. The final blessing begins, 'May the everlasting God shield you.'[49] The hymn 'Shout for Joy!' concludes the rite.

The style of the *Carmina Gadelica* is present in a good number of the compositions. The Eucharistic Prayer reflects Presbyterian usage, but the inclusion of saints in the Preface, and the intercessions at the end, do at least give a nod to the structure of the Stowe's Roman *canon missae*. No claim is made that this is a Celtic Eucharist, but coming from Iona it is perceived as such, and it might be argued, of course, that anything coming from this Scottish-based community is de facto Celtic. However, Kathy Galloway, herself a member of the Iona Community, writes:

The Iona Community and its worship have often been described as 'Celtic', and in recent years we have seen an explosion of interest in all things considered Celtic. But this is not an accurate description of our community. Our membership is not primarily composed of Gaels (Irish or Highlands Scots); and what can, with any legitimacy, today be termed Celtic is held in the Celtic languages: Scots and Irish Gaelic, Welsh, Breton. We do not worship in any of these languages. Our community is Lowland more than Highland Scottish, and has many non-Scottish members. It started in Glasgow, not Iona. But we share with the Columban church an incarnational and creaturely spirituality, and in fact it is this which people see and name incorrectly as Celtic.[50]

---

48 *The Iona Community Worship Book*, p. 66.
49 *The Iona Community Worship Book*, p. 24.
50 Kathy Galloway, 'The Worship of the Iona Community' in Thomas F. Best and Dagmar Heller (eds), *Worship Today: Understanding, Practice, Ecumenical Implications* (WCC Publications, Geneva, 2004), pp. 222–8, p. 226.

Still another example is a celebration of 'Celtic Evensong and Communion' celebrated on 17 November 2006 at St Stephen's Episcopal Church, Richmond, Virginia, at a conference entitled 'Going Forward Together: Third Millennium Christianity'.[51] The rite has some things in common with the Celtic Eucharist published on the website of another Episcopal church, the Church of the Holy Communion, Memphis, Tennessee, and this latter may have been a source.

The rite begins with opening sentences which seem to be addressed to the Holy Spirit with such titles as Breath of God, Breath of Life, Comforter, Disturber, Midwife of Change, and, given the popular motel chain in the USA, the unfortunate term 'Lamplighter'. The hymn was 'Look Well Within, Wake to Your Soul', which is a modern compilation concerned with realizing 'the wonder of your soul'. A Prayer for the Evening began, 'We seek the grace of healing, O God', which had more the form of a statement of intent to God rather than a prayer. The single reading was followed by a reflection and then music for meditation, the 'Arran Boat Song'. The intercessions all began with the statement, 'We hold before God', and were followed by further music for meditation, 'Buchal an Eire', a traditional Irish Air. A second hymn was 'How Deep the Silence of the Soul' by Sylvia Dunston to the tune 'Resignation'. The sections entitled Grace and The Peace were a statement to be at peace and follow the example of good men and women of old, and are taken from the Blessing at the end of the Evening Service in *Celtic Daily Prayer*. The Eucharistic Prayer was written by the Revd Janet Vincent for the Order of the Holy Cross in Grahamstown, South Africa. The prayer itself displays the doctrinally questionable sentence, 'We bless you for Jesus, born of human love', and the epiclesis refers to the elements as these 'material things of bread and wine'. A setting of the Agnus Dei was sung to 'Blarney Pilgrim'. An invitation to communion is suggested by *The Iona Community Worship Book*:

This is the table, not of the Church, but of our Lord Jesus. It is made ready for those who love him and for those who want to love him more.

---

51 This service is no longer available online, but for other examples of this regular service at St Stephen's, see <www.eenonline.org/download/liturgy/CelticEvensong-Adv2C.pdf>.

So, come, you who have much faith and you who have little, you who have been here often and you who have not been here long, you who have tried to follow and you who have failed.

Come, because it is Jesus who invites you. It is his will that those who want him should meet him here.

A short post-communion prayer and a blessing centred on the Spirit were followed by the hymn 'Go My Children, with My Blessing' to the tune 'Ar Hyd y Nos' and a dismissal, with some further music for meditation.

Again, the puzzle here is what exactly made this a Celtic Eucharist, as distinct from any other type of Eucharist. The Eucharistic Prayer from South Africa is clearly not Celtic, and neither is the use of material from *A New Zealand Prayer Book*. 'Look Well Within' is a hymn of 2002, and is not Celtic. Acknowledged sources include prayers from the Northumbria Community's *Celtic Daily Prayer*, Philip Newell's *Celtic Benediction*, the *Iona Community Worship Book* and *A Wee Worship Book* of the Wild Goose Worship Group from Iona.[52] Does use of contemporary work published in Scotland, with some Irish and Scottish music, make it Celtic? Exactly what does the term 'Celtic' denote in the service held at Richmond, Virginia?

CONCLUSION

In terms of what we do know of Celtic public liturgy from the historical sources, it appears that only in the case of Brendan O'Malley is there a conscious effort to take the ancient sources seriously and draw on the Stowe Missal for his Celtic Eucharist. Most compilers seem to build on the contemporary claims and styles of others, such as those of David Adam, the Northumbria Community and the Iona Community. These in turn seem to be more inspired by the style of *Carmina Gadelica*, and even the Irish litanies, than acknowledged liturgical sources of the Celtic Churches. In other words, what most contemporary compilers find attractive seems to be the quaint vocabulary and style of material that was for private prayer and the quasi-devotional folklore collected

---

52 Wild Goose Resource Group, *A Wee Worship Book* (Wild Goose Publications, Glasgow, 1999).

by Carmichael.[53] Most of the new material inspired by this genre seems to be written in English by Celtophiles rather than in Celtic languages by those who can claim to be of Celtic descent. This, of course, is also true of the Iona Community. Contemporary 'Celtic' worship services seem as much Celtic as Wedgwood china made in Hong Kong is Wedgwood, or Taco Bell fast food is Mexican. Furthermore, the 'Celtic' world and theology they presuppose is mainly a projection backward of postmodernity. Donald Meek astutely observes:

> Among its postmodern characteristics are: its low factual base and lack of historical rationale; its tendency to rely on a motley collection of snapshots and images of the past, which are assembled to meet the needs of the collector, and made to bear a very large element of subjective interpretation; and the localized focus of much of the material, which stresses Britain and Ireland as its matrix.[54]

Bradley notes that Tolkien, who knew what myth-making was, wrote in 1963 that the term Celtic was 'a magic bag, into which anything may be put, and out of which almost anything may come . . . Anything is possible in the fabulous Celtic twilight, which is not so much a twilight of the gods as of the reason.'[55] However, it is precisely because the postmodern condition is a twilight of the reason that the contemporary industry in Celtic spirituality and Celtic worship resources flourishes. One of the contrasts between modernity and postmodernity is that unlike Enlightenment culture, reason does not hold sway in postmodernity. It is what stirs the heart, soul and spirit in an individual and works for that individual that makes a commodity marketable, not whether it is rational or historically authentic.

We live in a 'pick-and-mix' and *bricolage* culture, and so why not place a eucharistic prayer by a South African woman with some pieces from *A New Zealand Prayer Book* and some Scottish and Irish music, and call it Celtic? If the contemporary Celtic liturgies speak to and feed

---

53 It is this folklore style, and not the poetry of the Celtic monks themselves, that inspires contemporary 'Celtic' prayers. See T. O. Clancy and G. Márkus, *Iona: The Earliest Poetry of a Celtic Monastery* (Edinburgh University Press, Edinburgh, 1995).
54 Meek, *Quest*, p. 24.
55 J. R. R. Tolkien, *Angles and Britons* (University of Wales Press, Cardiff, 1963), pp. 29–30, cited in Bradley, *Celtic Christianity*, p. 226.

a spiritual hunger that prayers and hymns of other genres do not, then all is well and good. After all, liturgy is ultimately about prayer forms and their liturgical performance, which together allow a community to experience and worship God, regardless of the pedigree of those forms and their performance. I am therefore less critical of contemporary things Celtic than is Donald Meek. What we have, though, are forms which although they sport the title Celtic, are mostly simulacra. At least in terms of a scholarly taxonomy, contemporary 'Celtic' forms may perhaps more accurately be described as 'postmodern Celtish'. Due to the fact that this term is not very attractive for marketing to a potential congregation – not nearly as mysterious, appealing and sellable as 'Celtic' – those who write and market such forms will no doubt continue to call their products 'Celtic'. Like contemporary medieval fairs, they can be fun, people seem to enjoy them, and what is more, they also frequently make money.

Chapter 7

Second-guessing post-Vatican II liturgies

In the worship mall, the largest and most well-known anchor store is the Roman Catholic Church. The liturgical reforms that flowed from the Second Vatican Council's *Sacrosanctum Concilium* (*SC*), promulgated on 4 December 1963, not only revolutionized both the textual provisions and styles of celebration in the Roman Catholic Church, but also affected, directly and indirectly, worship in most mainstream Western Protestant churches. In the immediate aftermath of *Sacrosanctum Concilium*, J. D. Crichton could euphorically write: 'The findings and experiences of the liturgical movement of the last sixty years form the underlying basis of the document and a window is opened on to a future the end of which no man can see.'[1]

Crichton was, on the whole, an enthusiastic receiver and interpreter of the new rites that resulted.[2] More recently, in contrast, Denis Crouan claimed that 'Never in the course of history has the implementation of the Roman rite been the cause of so many difficulties and so many divisions as it has been since the Second Vatican Council.'[3] In a similar vein, Brian W. Harrison asserts that 'what we have witnessed in these thirty years [since Vatican II] has been a tragic polarization and fragmentation among Catholics in regard to the liturgy'.[4] In the context of this polarization, M. Francis Mannion has suggested that there are at least five distinct liturgical agendas in the English-speaking Catholic

---

1 J. D. Crichton, *The Church's Worship* (Geoffrey Chapman, London, 1964), p. 3.

2 J. D. Crichton, *Christian Celebration: The Mass, the Sacraments, the Prayer of the Church* (Geoffrey Chapman, London, 1981).

3 Denis Crouan, *The History and the Future of the Roman Liturgy*, ET (Ignatius Press, San Francisco CA, 2005), p. 239.

4 In Thomas M. Kocik (ed.), *The Reform of the Reform? A Liturgical Debate: Reform or Return* (Ignatius Press, San Francisco CA, 2003), p. 154.

world: 'advancing official reform; restoring the pre-conciliar; reforming the reform; inculturating the reform; and recatholicising the reform'.[5] More recently, John Baldovin has surveyed the 'critics' under the heads of the philosophical, the historical, the theological, and sociological/ anthropological.[6] Our consideration of some of these critiques and agendas here will mainly focus on the English-speaking Catholic world.

FROM GUÉRANGER TO THE POST-VATICAN II LITURGICAL RITES

Whether legitimate or illegitimate, the liturgical reforms that followed Vatican II were the outcome of the Liturgical Movement, which is usually traced to the work of Dom Prosper Guéranger at the Abbey of Solesmes, and the *motu proprio* of Pius X, *Tra le sollecitudini* of 1903.[7] Guéranger, reacting against both neo-Gallicanism and Quietism, worked to bring the clergy back to a love and knowledge of the Roman rite, as derived from the 1570 missal and the Tridentine liturgical reforms; and through teaching on the liturgical year, to unite the faithful with the celebration of the rites. His emphasis could be described as a contemplative one, whereby people are formed by praying the 'official' liturgy. He was particularly keen on restoring Gregorian chant to the liturgy. The work of Guéranger and his successors at Solesmes found some encouragement in the 1903 *motu proprio* of Pius X, which, in calling for a fuller restoration of Gregorian chant, noted:

> Filled as We are with a most ardent desire to see the true Christian spirit flourish in every respect and be preserved by all the faithful, We deem it necessary to provide before anything else for the sanctity and dignity of the temple, in which the faithful assemble for no other object than that of acquiring this spirit from its

---

5 M. Francis Mannion, 'The Catholicity of the Liturgy: Shaping a new agenda' in Stratford Caldecott (ed.), *Beyond the Prosaic: Renewing the Liturgical Movement* (T & T Clark, Edinburgh, 1998), pp. 11–48, p. 11.

6 John F. Baldovin, *Reforming the Liturgy: A Response to the Critics* (Liturgical Press, Collegeville MN, 2008).

7 Only the briefest summary of this important movement, its personages, and the crucial documents can be given here. See John Fenwick and Bryan Spinks, *Worship in Transition: The Liturgical Movement in the Twentieth Century* (T & T Clark, Edinburgh, 1995), and the bibliographies listed there.

foremost and indispensable font, which is the active participation [*la partecipazione attiva*] in the most holy mysteries and in the public and solemn prayer of the Church.[8]

The term 'active participation' would be a recurring theme in the Liturgical Movement and post-Vatican II reforms, with sharply differing views on its meaning and implications.

The continuing concerns of Guéranger can be seen in the lay missal produced by Anselm Schott of the Abbey of Beuron, and more particularly by the work of Dom Lambert Beauduin in Belgium, and the abbeys of Mont César and Maredsous. With Beauduin and the Belgian movement there was an emphasis on the pastoral aspect of liturgy, with the need for understanding and therefore the need for instruction.[9] This added emphasis was taken up also by the German exponents of the Liturgical Movement, such as Dom Ildephonse Herwegen at Maria Laach Abbey, and Odo Casel who emphasized the 'mystery' dimension of the liturgy; and Pius Parsch of Klosterneuberg in Austria, who emphasized the need for a biblical renewal. In the USA it was the social justice dimension of the liturgy that found expression in the writings of Dom Virgil Michel.[10] Teresa Berger has drawn attention to the lesser-known role that Catholic women played in this Liturgical Movement.[11] Hand in hand with the contemplative, pastoral, biblical and social concerns for renewal went scholarly research, uncovering the development of the Roman liturgies.

Official recognition, as well as a condemnation of some of its extremes, was forthcoming in the important encyclical of Pius XII, *Mediator Dei*. This document was critical of those who introduced novelty or tried to revive obsolete rites. It was concerned to stress mystical participation of the faithful, and indicated the means of

---

8 ET, <http://www.adoremus.org/TraLeSollecitudini.html> (accessed 26/11/08). It is slightly curious that a document extolling the Latin text (III.7) should have been promulgated in Italian.

9 Sonya A. Quitslund, *Beauduin: A Prophet Vindicated* (Newman Press, New York, 1973).

10 R. W. Franklin and Robert L. Spaeth, *Virgil Michel: American Catholic* (Liturgical Press, Collegeville MN, 1988); Keith F. Pecklers, *The Unread Vision: The Liturgical Movement in the United States of America 1926–1955* (Liturgical Press, Collegeville MN, 1998).

11 Teresa Berger, *Women's Ways of Worship: Gender Analysis and Liturgical History* (Liturgical Press, Collegeville MN, 1999).

promoting participation as the use of missals, joining in the chants, and the dialogue Mass. The encyclical encouraged the pioneers of the Liturgical Movement, particularly when it noted that certain things in the liturgy are divine, and do not change; but some are human, and do change. In 1948 the Pope created a Pontifical Commission for the Reform of the Liturgy, and between 1951 and 1955 the rites for Holy Week were revised, and rules on fasting before communion were relaxed. Pius XII was succeeded by John XXIII who embarked upon a path of *aggiornamento*, and called an Ecumenical Council to equip the Church for its twentieth-century mission. His death in 1963 meant that it was his successor Paul VI who had to oversee the Council, and the liturgical reforms that resulted. *Sacrosanctum Concilium* certainly called for reforms, the simplification of rites, the removal of duplications, and allowed for the vernacular. However, voices such as Crouan question whether in fact the new rites that resulted were a distortion of *Sacrosanctum Concilium* rather than a faithful expression. Following the promulgation of *Sacrosanctum Concilium*, the *Consilium ad Exsequendam Constitutionem de Sacra Liturgia* was established in February 1964 to carry out the reforms that the document was thought to envisage. This Consilium was under the presidency of Cardinal Lercaro and the secretary-ship of Fr Annibale Bugnini. It consisted of cardinals and bishops who had voting rights, and many liturgical scholars and experts who would carry out the work. The members of the Consilium were divided into study groups called *coetus*, and each of these was responsible for a particular liturgical rite or subject, such as the missal, or the calendar and lectionary. An interim reform of the Mass took place in 1965, but the new missal was promulgated in 1969, and included not only a revision of the canon missae but three new eucharistic prayers. The Ordinal was completely revised (1968), as were the rites of Christian initiation (1969, 1971, 1972).[12] Although liturgical scholars and theologians were critical of some aspects of the various new rites, it has been the revisions of the Mass and the new missal of Paul VI (*Ordo missae*, 1969; *Missale Romanum*, 1970) that have attracted most controversy and discussion, both in the Latin

---

12 See Annibale Bugnini, *The Reform of the Liturgy 1948–1975*, ET (Liturgical Press, Collegeville MN, 1990); Piero Marini, *A Challenging Reform: Realizing the Vision of the Liturgical Movement* (Liturgical Press, Collegeville MN, 2007). Both authors were involved in the implementation of the reforms, and thus represent the official view of reform at that time.

typica edition, and more particularly in the translations adopted for the English-speaking world.

Some of the discussion has been openly polemical in style and content. Michael Davies, whose obituary described him as 'the Traditionalist's Traditionalist', believed that what took place after Vatican II was not a general restoration 'of the existing rite but the creation of a new Order of Mass, *Novus Ordo Missae*, something which the Constitution on the Liturgy did not authorize'.[13] Davies attacks the banal music that has replaced Latin chant, irreverent and informal style of celebrations of the Mass, and what he sees as the playing down of transubstantiation and the sacrifice of the Mass. In his view, 'Pope Paul VI presided over and authorized a liturgical revolution which has destroyed the Roman Mass – the greatest treasure of the Latin Church and possibly the greatest achievement of Western Civilization.'[14] Davies argued that the reforms were a sell out to Protestantism on the grounds that even if the Protestant Observers at Vatican II did not influence the reforms, anything in the new rite that is acceptable to Protestants must represent a departure from Catholic dogmas. Although Pope Paul VI must take responsibility for destroying the Mass, Davies at times suggests that he was misled by Fr (later Archbishop) Bugnini, who it was rumoured was a Freemason, and so the new Mass is tainted by Freemasonry. The English translation, so he argued, was entirely the work of Fr Frederick McManus of the USA.

Equally polemical is the otherwise useful summary of the Liturgical Movement by Didier Bonneterre. In his view, the Liturgical Movement was a praiseworthy endeavour as conceived by Dom Prosper Guéranger and as endorsed by Pius X. However, subsequent exponents began to lead the Movement astray, beginning with Beauduin who exalted the pastoral dimensions of liturgy above its doxological nature. He wrote:

> [T]he period between the wars saw the growth of the most serious theological deviations of the Liturgical Movement. Dom Beauduin is dragging it on to the path of a false ecumenism, Maria Laach is misleading it into archaeologism, Dom Parsch is

---

13 Michael Davies, *Liturgical Revolution: Vol. III, Pope Paul's New Mass* (Angelus Press, Dickenson TX, 1980), p. 16. Davies has written several books on the same theme with dramatic titles such as *Liturgical Time Bombs in Vatican II: The Destruction of Catholic Faith through Changes in Catholic Worship* (Tan Books, Rockford IL, 2003).

14 Davies, *Liturgical Revolution*, p. 69.

making common cause with a judaizing biblicism. On the eve of the Second World War, the forces of Modernism hold the movement in their hands.[15]

According to Bonneterre, Beauduin, Herwegen, Casel and Parsch all distorted the original Liturgical Movement. The Centre de Pastorale Liturgique – 'the cesspool of all (anti-liturgical) heresies' – added to the distortions by encouraging 'the inversion of the ratio of worship to pastorate, archaeologism, contempt for "rubricism", the primacy of the Word of God, an activist conception of participation, collectivism in liturgical assemblies, etc.'.[16] In Bonneterre's view, Pius XII tried to stem the tide in *Mediator Dei*, but was misled, and delivered himself bound hand and foot to the revolutionary leaders of the Movement when he established the Pontifical Commission for the Reform of the Liturgy. He notes that John XXIII had known Beauduin since the 1920s, and was a willing accomplice. Paul VI and the chief architect, Annibale Bugnini, put the final nails in the coffin. 'The plan would unfold thus: moderate reforming tendency (1964), progressively becoming more pronounced (1967) in order to give place eventually to the "ultra-reformers" (1969).'[17] The new liturgies, and particularly the Mass, were a sell out to Modernism, Freemasonry, and the Protestantism of the Taizé liturgy, which Bonneterre believed influenced the reform of the Roman Mass.[18]

SOCIOLOGICAL, LINGUISTIC, PHILOSOPHICAL AND ANTHROPOLOGICAL CRITIQUES

Both Davies and Bonneterre represent a traditionalist position which views any change from the pre-1962 Roman Missal as a change in doctrine and a betrayal of Catholic faith, although their polemical tone and scare-mongering are open invitations for them not to be taken too seriously. However, deeper questioning of the nature and tone of the Vatican II reforms have been made by those writing from a sociological,

---

15 Didier Bonneterre, *The Liturgical Movement from Dom Guéranger to Annibale Bugnini: The Trojan Horse in the City of God*, ET (Angelus Press, Kansas City MO, 2002), pp. 30–1. Cf. p. 3.
16 Bonneterre, *The Liturgical Movement*, p. 38.
17 Bonneterre, *The Liturgical Movement*, p. 86.
18 Bonneterre, *The Liturgical Movement*, Appendix, pp. 97–119.

anthropological and cultural-theological standpoint, suggesting that the reformed liturgies are expressions of modernity and appeared just when the world was passing to postmodernity.

One of the first to pose this question was Kieran Flanagan, in *Sociology and Liturgy*. Flanagan's central argument was that Vatican II adopted a theological strategy of modernization that was misconceived in sociological terms. Modernity was seen as a solution to liturgical problems rather than a symptom of them.[19] He wrote:

> What were the cultural assumptions used by liturgists in the past two decades in making alteration to forms of rite and how sociologically adequate were these? When rites were ordered according to objective criteria, where discretion in performance was denied, the issue of the social hardly emerged. But if cultural elements were imputed to rites, that indicated how they ought to be shaped, then an exercise in sociology of knowledge is required to investigate the indices used by liturgists that governed their expectations of rite. Many of their ideas were secular and ideological and owed little either to sociology or theology. The marginal position of liturgists within theology, and their clerical place on the edge of society, has often made them poor judges of what will convince in contemporary cultural circumstances. They managed to back modernity as a winning ticket, just at the point when it became converted into post-modernism. They found a solution in modern culture, just when it failed in sociology.[20]

This embracing of modernity

> led to the rise of consumer friendly rites and a demand for loose and lax 'happy clappy' events full of meet and greet transactions. These trivialize the social, preclude deeper meanings being read into the action and skate along the surface of some very thin ice where all attention to danger, awe and reverence is bracketed. They are rites of the immediate that demand instantaneous theological results.[21]

---

19 Kieran Flanagan, *Sociology and Liturgy: Re-Presentations of the Holy* (Macmillan, Basingstoke and London, 1991), p. 24.
20 Flanagan, *Sociology and Liturgy*, p. 42.
21 Flanagan, *Sociology and Liturgy*, p. 13.

Here Flanagan has in mind not only the simplification of the rites and removal of redundancies, and the flat English translations, but also the failure to observe the rules of enactment found in the General Instructions on the Roman Missal, resulting in 'liturgical uncertainty in which the middle classes, used to dealing with indeterminate situations, have been the main beneficiaries'.[22] Flanagan noted that, for Guéranger, liturgy was strong and found its witness within its ritual apparatus; 'rites achieve their sense of community less through processes of adaptation, than through the power of the instruments they use'.[23] Flanagan does not suggest a return to the pre-Vatican II rites – indeed, he admits that often the older rites were performed in a careless and unacceptably meaningless manner that few would care to see revived. Rather, he is concerned with the importance of gesture and symbol in ritual, which convey a divine purpose. For sociologists, the important questions about rites are concerned with how they secure their plausibility, and not their pliability. Had the liturgical reformers heeded some lessons of sociology, the resulting rites might have been rather different:

> The link between the sacred and the secular carries qualities of incommensurability. The religious rituals of Christianity have always displayed signs of contradictions to the surrounding cultural landscape. The improbable mysteries they display, the ambiguous and indeterminate qualities of their styles of enactment, all suggest they do not fit easily into the modern mind operating in advanced industrialized societies. The problem of incompatibility has been at the heart of efforts of liberal theologians to make religion consonant with the assumptions of contemporary culture.[24]

However, wittingly or unwittingly, the Constitution on the Sacred Liturgy and the resulting new liturgies were the expression of modernity.

> Modernity embodies a particular plight, a blindness that disables an appreciation of liturgical transactions. Liberal theologians have sought to adjust Christian forms and styles of belief to the fashions of modernity, but in so doing, they simply assimilate its ills into

---

22 Flanagan, *Sociology and Liturgy*, p. 50.
23 Flanagan, *Sociology and Liturgy*, p. 49.
24 Flanagan, *Sociology and Liturgy*, p. 270.

liturgical enactments. With the growth of post-modernism, they find themselves orphans of the times, plodding up a road to see sociologists coming running down in the opposite direction seeking 'signals of transcendence' elsewhere.[25]

The result of the reforms was thus: 'Rites no longer grip, symbols seem thin rather than thick and an unproductive uncertainty mixed with a disillusion at the outcome of the liturgical reforms. Too much got cast away in the decade following Vatican II.'[26] For Flanagan, it is simplification of rite and symbol, together with an informal and banal performance of the liturgy, that is the major problem.

A critique from a linguistic philosophical approach is represented by the Anglican lay philosophical theologian Catherine Pickstock, who with John Milbank and Graham Ward has developed 'radical orthodoxy', though 'neo-Romanticism' might be an equally apt term. In an extremely densely written and argued book, Pickstock sees postmodernity as simply the logical outcome of modernity's concern with power. Responding to postmodern deconstruction, the radical orthodoxy group attempt to revisit and revive Augustine's Neoplatonism, and the theological confidence of Aquinas. In a rereading of Plato's *Phaedrus*, Pickstock argues for the priority of the oral over the written, and doxology as the ultimate expression of the oral. A large section of the book is concerned with a narrative of how Duns Scotus followed by Pierre Ramus led to the privileging of static analysis and charts – 'spatialization' – over temporality. Lists take priority over verbs, and 'asyndeton' – syntax characterized by the absence of co-ordinating and subordinating conjunctions – destroys narrative. Modernity's love of nouns leads to 'necrophilia':

> [M]odernity less seeks to banish death, than to prise death and life apart in order to preserve life immune from death in pure sterility. For in seeking *only* life, in the form of pseudo-eternal permanence, the 'modern' gesture is secretly doomed to necrophilia, a love of what has to die, can only die. In seeking only life, modernity gives life over to death, removing all traces of death only to find that life has vanished with it.[27]

---

25 Flanagan, *Sociology and Liturgy*, p. 286.
26 Flanagan, *Sociology and Liturgy*, p. 325.
27 Catherine Pickstock, *After Writing: On the Liturgical Consummation of Philosophy* (Blackwell, Malden MA and Oxford, 1998), p. 104.

It is in the third part of her work that Pickstock turns to investigate what she calls the medieval Roman Mass. Charging the Vatican II reformers of the 1960s with regarding the Mass then in use as representing a corruption of an 'original liturgy', she asserts:

> In being too eager to find secularization in any forms of repetition or apophatic re-beginnings which it associated with a decadent epoch, the liturgical revisers of Vatican II chose as a liturgical paradigm a text [the so-called Apostolic Tradition attributed to Hippolytus] which, as being more of a treatise *on* liturgy than a liturgy as such, would in the end prove misleading for the programme of liturgical recovery. Moreover, in rejecting the features of multiple repetition, complexity of genre, instability of the worshipping subject, and continued interruption of progress by renewed prayers of penitence, under the assumption that these were secular interpolations, they ironically perpetuated certain features of the truly secularizing modern epoch . . . they ironed-out the liturgical stammer and constant re-beginning; they simplified the narrative and generic strategy of the liturgy in conformity with recognizably secular structures, and rendered simple, constant and self-present the identity of the worshipper . . . above all, the liturgical reformers of Vatican II failed to realize that one cannot simply 'return' to an earlier form, because the earlier liturgies only existed as part of a culture which was itself ritual (ecclesial-sacramental-historical) in character.
>
> A genuine liturgical reform, therefore, would either have to overthrow our anti-ritual modernity, or, that being impossible, devise a liturgy that *refused* to be enculturated in our modern habits of thought and speech.[28]

Pickstock's reading of the medieval Mass, which has been embraced by some Catholic writers, is problematic. David Brown has pointed out that her proposed reading of the 'stammers', 'journeys', 'returns' and 'repetitions' is too cerebral, and is probably far from how it was ever experienced by the clergy, let alone the laity.[29] He is also concerned by the fact that it is entirely concerned with words and text rather than the

---

28 Pickstock, *After Writing*, pp. 175–6.
29 David Brown, *God and Mystery in Words: Experience through Metaphor and Drama* (Oxford University Press, Oxford, 2008), p. 256.

Eucharist as an experience.[30] Julie Gittoes has been critical of the fact that Pickstock's discussion remains abstract, with no prognosis offered, or any practical social application.[31] However, a far more serious problem is the fact that her reading purports to be of the medieval Roman Mass. There was no such thing as the medieval Roman Mass, but only diocesan or regional medieval 'Western' Masses. A reading of such a Mass would have required a particular medieval manuscript or printed missal, as well as the customary, and use of the other liturgical books needed for the performance of the specific service. What Pickstock uses is the critical edition of Botte and Mohrmann – a generic scholars' text rather than a medieval Mass. What in fact is presented as the medieval Roman Mass is a Romantic postmodern simulacrum, which is as medieval as a Disney castle. Although not spelled out, the implication of Pickstock would seem to be that there can be no adequate modern or postmodern liturgies, since both these cultures are alien to such possibilities; hence there can only be the pre-modern liturgy.

A not too dissimilar criticism is found in David Torevell's *Losing the Sacred*.[32] Writing after both Flanagan and Pickstock, Torevell was able to draw on both of those writers in addition to considering the implications of the work of anthropologists. He argued that in both *Sacrosanctum Concilium* and in the new liturgical rites that resulted, the Roman Catholic bishops, theologians and liturgists seriously misunderstood the importance of ritual and the human body, and merely reflected the passing fashion of the 1960s. He suggests that his work might be viewed as a kind of postmodern critique of the modern Roman Catholic liturgical rites that have given precedence to a cerebral approach (active participation meaning rational understanding), and elevated modernity's preference for mind over body. Drawing on the works of Durkheim, Weber, Turner, Tambiah and Rappaport, Torevell stresses the importance of ritual in religious formation, and the importance of understanding the person as body and soul, or body and mind. The Enlightenment and modernity have elevated the individual over the collective, and the mind over the body. This was not understood by the Vatican II reformers, who also misunderstood the original Liturgical

---

30 Brown, *God and Mystery in Words*, p. 256.
31 Julie Gittoes, *Anamnesis and the Eucharist: Contemporary Anglican Approaches* (Ashgate, Aldershot, 2008), p. 97.
32 David Torevell, *Losing the Sacred: Ritual, Modernity and Liturgical Reform* (T & T Clark, Edinburgh, 2000).

Movement of Guéranger. The resulting rites represent a surrender of divine transcendence in favour of anthropocentricity, which even led, in 1985, to permission for the celebrant of the Mass to add his own commentary and explanation of the rite as it proceeds. He particularly notes the loss of the sacred, the loss of the ordained priest's authority, and a loss of reverence in the celebration of the liturgy:

> [W]hat emerged during the 1960s was an emphasis on the pastoral nature of liturgy underpinned by a more personalist, anthropocentric and individualistic approach to worship. The secular and theological culture of the time had clearly encouraged this far more rationalist, classificatory and subjective approach to worship. The challenge (never signalled at the time by the Church reformers) was to meet the demands of pastoral liturgical sensitivity while preserving the liturgy of the Church as an objective ritual performance whose form, by its very nature, resisted alteration. It is not surprising that such a task proved increasingly difficult to achieve.[33]

In his judgement, 'The mistakes which have been made in worship had been seen before in the cultural and political programmes which dominated the post-Enlightenment era. Many postmodern critiques have helped liturgists to re-think the direction worship might take in the future.'[34] Torevell called for a new liturgical movement which will conserve the gains of Vatican II, but which will rectify the mistakes of modernity.

Flanagan is a Catholic layman, and Master of Ceremonies at Clifton Cathedral; Pickstock is an Anglican laywoman; and Torevell is a Catholic layman. Some of their concerns find clerical articulation in critiques by Jonathan Robinson and Aidan Nichols.[35] Nichols appealed to Walter Trapp's assessment of the Enlightenment, and concluded that it is the spirit of the Enlightenment that drives the approach to liturgy in the Anglo-Saxon sphere: 'anthropocentric, moralizing, voluntaristic, didactic and subjectivist'.[36] In his view, liturgical reform was decided by

---

33 Torevell, *Losing the Sacred*, p. 145.
34 Torevell, *Losing the Sacred*, p. 201.
35 Aidan Nichols, *Looking at the Liturgy: A Critical View of Its Contemporary Form* (Ignatius Press, San Francisco CA, 1996). He writes before Torevell's book, but draws on Flanagan and the doctoral dissertation version of Catherine Pickstock's book.
36 Nichols, *Looking at the Liturgy*, pp. 28–9.

'reunions of technicians', and church authority gave the professionals what amounted to a blank cheque to redesign the liturgy in an inorganic manner.[37] His solution is for the Church to take measures to prevent further erosion of the liturgy, and to ensure prayerful, dignified, correct and, where appropriate, solemn celebrations of the *Novus Ordo*. A moderate reform of the pre-Vatican II Mass would address the concerns of the traditionalists. The Missal of 1969/70 would be designated as *ritus communis*, which could be adapted to particular cultures.

A rather more sophisticated philosophical critique is mounted by Jonathan Robinson in *The Mass and Modernity: Walking to Heaven Backward*.[38] Although there were important benefits from the Enlightenment, its rejection of revelation and mystery, and even the rejection of a deity, have had a profound impact on liturgy. The faith in experts, typified by Auguste Comte, leads directly to the post-Vatican II reforms, which were carried out by experts. Postmodernity, in Robinson's view, is also unhelpful because it rejects metanarratives, and Christianity is founded on a metanarrative. In his view, the old rite of the Mass was like a country house, in need of refurbishing and even some reconstruction, but it fulfilled its stated function – the worship of God.[39] However, instead of improvement there has been a loss, and the 'deformation of the liturgy has to be understood as the result of cultural and intellectual forces that will have to be recognized before anything very serious can be accomplished in the way of serious liturgical reform'.[40] Robinson does not advocate a return to the old rite, but rather a celebration of the present rite which is concerned with the transcendence of God rather than simply a ritual addressed to the local community.

Although not agreed on the answer, what unites these writers is the conviction that the Vatican II reforms were an expression of modernity, and the basic assumptions of modernity are not compatible with the social order that is at the base of Christian liturgy. This is endorsed with reference to modernist architecture by the English Catholic architect Moyra Doorly. She argues that the Church adopted modernist ideas about space, which are in keeping with contemporary ideals of self-reverence:

---

37 Nichols, *Looking at the Liturgy*, p. 47–55.
38 Jonathan Robinson, *The Mass and Modernity: Walking to Heaven Backward* (Ignatius Press, San Francisco CA, 2005).
39 Robinson, *The Mass and Modernity*, p. 300.
40 Robinson, *The Mass and Modernity*, p. 307.

When the Church adopted the new liturgy, existing churches began to be 'reordered' so that they could best reflect new ideas about the celebration of the Mass, and new church buildings were designed with an internal layout that had never been seen before in the history of the Church . . . The most obvious has been the reorientation of the priest so that Mass is said facing the people. This innovation says loud and clear that there is nothing to look forward to that is outside the community. It represents a denial of the transcendent in favour of the immanent. This is even more marked in churches where seating is arranged to create a circular or semicircular layout, where there is nothing beyond the priest at the altar than more people facing the altar. Circles by their very nature are inward-looking forms.[41]

HISTORICAL CRITIQUES

The Consilium responsible for formulating the new rites contained many distinguished liturgical scholars. However, as in all disciplines, there are differences of opinions between 'experts', and not all Roman Catholic liturgical scholars felt able to endorse the new rites. Klaus Gamber, the Regensburg scholar who had made significant contributions on the history of the Roman Mass, was one such critic, and his collected essays, *The Reform of the Roman Liturgy: Its Problems and Background*, have been very influential. For Gamber, although the Mass needed reform, liturgical studies were only in their early stages, and thus the 'experts' were not sufficiently equipped for the task they were given. The results have 'turned out to be a liturgical destruction of startling proportions – a debacle worsening with each passing year', not to mention a 'shocking assimilation of Protestant ideas' introduced under the guise of ecumenism; 'a destruction of the forms of the Mass which had developed organically during the course of many centuries'.[42]

---

41 Moyra Doorly, *No Place for God: The Denial of the Transcendent in Modern Church Architecture* (Ignatius Press, San Francisco CA, 2007), p. 5. Doorly describes the hallmarks of Modernist architecture as rejecting all forms of embellishment and decoration, and opting for a universal architectural aesthetic to be found in geometry, mass production and the use of honestly expressed materials. The Weissenhof Estate, Stuttgart, 1927, is given as an example of the results (pp. 36, 38).

42 Klaus Gamber, *The Reform of the Roman Liturgy: Its Problems and Background*, ET (Una Voce Press, San Juan Capistrano CA, 1993), p. 9.

Convinced that the Roman liturgy is the oldest Christian rite, Gamber argued that individual piety began to creep in during the Gothic period, and even by the 1400s, in Germany, popular church song had started to supplant the Latin chants.[43] However, the pre-eminent root cause of today's liturgical distress is to be found in the age of the Enlightenment.[44] Gamber outlined the history of the development of the Roman Mass as he understood it, and regarded the 1965 *Ordo Missae* as being a true expression of the reform envisaged in *Sacrosanctum Concilium*. This evolution could be described as an 'organic' development.

In contrast, that of 1969/70 marks a complete break, or a revolution rather than evolution. Among the micro criticisms, Gamber complained that the new eucharistic prayers were 'Eastern', and it is not correct for the West to use Eastern prayers any more than it is for the East to use Western prayers. In his view, Paul VI should have allowed the old order (1962 or 1965?) alongside the new rite, as a simple gesture of pluralism and inclusiveness. He was critical of the almost universal move to face the congregation for celebrating Mass, which he noted was not mandated by the Council or any other official document. Gamber drew attention to the fact that in those ancient basilicas where the altar appears to be free-standing so the celebrant could stand behind it, it was because the entrance doors faced East, and the tradition was for celebrant and people to face East for the eucharistic prayer. The celebrant was oriented not for the people, but for the East, and the congregation probably also faced East with their backs to the celebrant – a concern recently also taken up by U. M. Lang.[45] Gamber posed the question, 'What exactly was to be gained with all the petty changes? Was it just to realize the pet ideas of some liturgy experts at the expense of a rite founded on a tradition of 1,500 years?'[46]

The whole contrast between 'organic' development and 'revolution' is at the heart of Alcuin Reid's *The Organic Development of the Liturgy*. This is a much fuller consideration of the development of the rite than Gamber's essays, and has a detailed discussion of the gradual changes that were made from the beginnings of the Liturgical Movement to

---

43 Gamber, *The Reform of the Roman Liturgy*, pp. 13 and 15.
44 Gamber, *The Reform of the Roman Liturgy*, p. 20.
45 Gamber, *The Reform of the Roman Liturgy*, Part II, pp. 117–79. See also U. M. Lang, *Turning towards the Lord: Orientation in Liturgical Prayer* (Ignatius Press, San Francisco CA, 2004).
46 Gamber, *The Reform of the Roman Liturgy*, p. 58.

1948, and from 1948 to 1962, because 'In determining whether the rites promulgated by Paul VI herald the apotheosis of liturgical history, or its nadir, we must know the mind of Guéranger. St. Pius X, Beauduin, Guardini, Parsch, Casel, and others.'[47] In his conclusion he observed:

> Catholic liturgical reform cannot, therefore, be an archaeologism or a pastoral expediency. It may not be hurried. Nor may it be a scholarly revision, nor even may that which is authorised, nay initiated, by the Pope or the College of Bishops, unless it respect the one fundamental principle of liturgical reform in which all Catholic liturgical reform finds its legitimacy. That principle is the principle of organic development.[48]

Implicit in his conclusion is that the new rites of Vatican II are far from being an organic development, and are the result of the Liturgical Movement's activist pressuring for a reform that moved beyond the bound.[49]

REFORMING THE REFORM

The critiques of Gamber and Reid find some support in Joseph Cardinal Ratzinger, now Pope Benedict XVI. According to Ratzinger, 'at all times and in all religions, the fundamental law of liturgy has been the law of organic growth within the universality of the common tradition'. In spite of many advantages,

> the new Missal was published as if it were a book put together by professors, not a phase in a continual growth process. Such a thing has never happened before. It is absolutely contrary to the laws of liturgical growth, and it has resulted in the nonsensical notion that Trent and Pius V had 'produced' a Missal four hundred years ago. The Catholic liturgy was thus reduced to the level of a mere product of modern times.[50]

---

47 Alcuin Reid, *The Organic Development of the Liturgy* (Saint Michael's Abbey Press, Farnborough, 2004), p. 8.
48 Reid, *The Organic Development*, p. 289.
49 Reid, *The Organic Development*, p. 292.
50 Joseph Ratzinger, *The Feast of Faith: Approaches to a Theology of the Liturgy*, ET (Ignatius Press, San Francisco CA, 1986), pp. 66, 86.

However, he is probably to be placed among those who, though not uncritical of the haste in which the new rites were written and implemented, believe that it is the ethos of the rites and the mentality of many of the celebrants where the real problems lie. He noted what he calls the 'new view' on liturgy which is concerned with creativity, freedom, celebration and community. Quoting from an article by Elisabeth Bickl, Ratzinger observes:

> The fundamental idea here is that liturgy is a community celebration, an act in which the community forms and experiences itself as such. In fact this means that the liturgy more and more acquires a 'party' character and atmosphere, as we see for instance in the increased importance attached to the words of greeting and dismissal and in the search for elements with 'entertainment' value. A 'successful' liturgical celebration is judged by the effects achieved in this way. Liturgy is thus dependent on the 'creativity', the 'ideas' of those who organize it.[51]

Ratzinger draws attention to those priests who, 'following the etiquette of polite society, feel that they must not receive Communion until all others have been "served"; or they no longer feel able to say "I bless *you*".'[52] The need for novelty results in 'the unhappy multiplication of eucharistic prayers', the quality and the theological content of which are often poor.[53] Nevertheless, he affirms:

> I am very grateful for the new Missal, for the way it has enriched the treasury of prayers and prefaces, for the new eucharistic prayers and the increased number of texts for use on weekdays, etc., quite apart from the availability of the vernacular.[54]

What Ratzinger argues for is a God-centred rite, with dignity and awe. There is no need for the whole eucharistic prayer to be prayed aloud each time, and every need to recapture the eastward facing for that prayer. There is a need for good church music, and the more frequent

---

51 Ratzinger, *The Feast of Faith*, p. 62. The article is Elisabeth Bickl, 'Zur Rezeption des "Gotteslob". Einführungsschwierigkeiten und Lesungsvorschläge', *Singende Kirche* 25 (1977/8), pp. 115–18.
52 Ratzinger, *The Feast of Faith*, pp. 84–5.
53 Ratzinger, *The Feast of Faith*, p. 73.
54 Ratzinger, *The Feast of Faith*, p. 87.

use of Latin. He also advocated (and, when Pope, gave permission) for much more regular use of the 1962 missal. Active participation in the liturgy is not about everyone having a role, but about praying the liturgy, using signs and symbols such as bows, crossings and genuflections (community ritual) as well as the use of silence.[55] Claiming Ratzinger as his inspiration, Laurence Hemming has developed a liturgical theology in which he argues that in contrast to the rationalism of twentieth-century liturgical reforms, true worship is grounded in how God reveals himself, and how in worship God brings humanity back from exile to a place where the divine can be truly known. His liturgical books for this enterprise are the 1884 Missale Romanum and the 1623 Breviarum Romanum, which, given that both belong to the modern period, seem odd choices.[56]

Ratzinger takes a theological approach to liturgy, whereas Denis Crouan, an organist and chant specialist, takes a historical approach. In contrast to Gamber and Reid, Crouan has no quarrel with the new rites themselves, but rather, like Ratzinger, with the way they were, and are, performed: 'What was the problem and what continues to be the problem is the manner in which the magisterial documents have been hijacked and used to take the Roman liturgy where the Church never wanted it to go.'[57] Crouan asserts that never in all its history has the implementation of the Roman liturgy been the cause of so many difficulties as it has since Vatican II. He lays the blame at the feet of clergy who ignore the rubrics and instructions on the Mass, and who preside in an informal manner, give banal commentaries on the rite, and also the often poor and banal music that displaces the more classical repertoire of the Church. He points the finger, not at the Vatican II Council or the experts who wrote the rites but (probably correctly) on liturgical formation:

> The crisis that the liturgy has been going through since the end of the last Council cannot be resolved, therefore, until those in high places decide to provide serious liturgical formation in the semi-

---

55 See in addition to *The Feast of Faith*, Joseph Cardinal Ratzinger, *The Spirit of the Liturgy*, ET (Ignatius Press, San Francisco CA, 2000), which has specific chapters on some of these subjects.
56 Laurence Paul Hemming, *Worship as a Revelation: The Past, Present and Future of Catholic Liturgy* (Burns & Oates, London, 2008).
57 Crouan, *The History and the Future*, p. 199.

naries; until they put a stop to the spread of the 'liturgical planning magazines' that are invading the sacristies and the rectories, to the point where they have more influence on the priests than the missal itself; and until the pressure groups accept the fact that the Latin and Gregorian form of the current liturgy can have its rightful place in the parishes.[58]

ENGLISH LANGUAGE PROBLEMS

The *Sacrosanctum Concilium* gave encouragement for the revised rites to be in the vernacular. In fact, all the new rites were written first in Latin (edition typica), and it was the task of the bishops of the various countries to see that the texts were properly translated into the vernacular. However, different countries using the same language were to have a common, shared text. In the English-speaking world this task was undertaken by the International Commission on English in the Liturgy (ICEL), which was based in Washington DC, USA. The procedure was that the ICEL's draft text, the Green Book, was submitted to the bishops, and their vetted version, the White Book, was then submitted to Rome for authorization. Local bishops' conferences could, and did, make their own alterations, but in general the ICEL translations were the ones in use in the English-speaking world. The ICEL translations have had a fair number of critics. Some have suggested that there was an inbuilt preference for American English, overseen by Fred McManus, and it is certainly true that at one time pressure was put on the English hierarchy to abandon their objections to some of the ICEL translation.[59] Translating is a notoriously difficult undertaking, since any translation tends to be an approximation, and can suffer from being either too literal, or too free – it has generally been the latter accusation that has been made against the 1973 ICEL translations. It is unclear whether Catherine Pickstock's blanket criticism of the language of the new Roman rites as being an expression of modernity had in mind the Vatican Latin or the ICEL, and her detailed published criticism was of the ICET (Ecumenical) version of the Nicene Creed rather than any of the Roman prayer texts. That is not the case with Eamon Duffy, the

58 Crouan, *The History and the Future*, p. 262.
59 Davies, *Liturgical Revolution*: vol. III, pp. 614–15. See also the essays by Frederick McManus and John Page in Peter C. Finn and James M. Schellman (eds), prepared by ICEL, *Shaping English Liturgy* (Pastoral Press, Washington DC, 1990).

Catholic revisionist church historian at Cambridge. Prefacing his examination of some of the Latin originals over against the ICEL versions,
Duffy noted:

> [I]t seems to me that the actual moment at which the transition to
> the vernacular occurred could hardly have been less propitious. The
> post-conciliar transformation of Catholic liturgy, theology and
> ecclesiology coincided with a period of profound cultural disloca-
> tion in the West. Genuine theological renewal became inextricably
> entangled with a shallow and philistine repudiation of the past
> which was to have consequences as disastrous in theology as they
> were in the fine arts, architecture and city planning.[60]

This 'cultural dislocation' (the end of modernity?) gave rise to a particular method in translation which Duffy views as more than just
unfortunate. In the Roman canon missae,

> the distinctive and very prominent humility of address to God
> which is such a feature of the Roman Canon was systematically
> removed, and qualifying adverbs and adjectives which increased
> this deference of address – like 'most merciful', 'holy', 'venerable'
> and so on – were not translated. So, for example, in the opening
> lines of the prayer the phrase 'supplices rogamus ac petimus' was
> rendered, baldly, 'we ask', setting a benchmark for translation
> practice throughout the rest of the missal.[61]

Duffy is by no means critical of all the ICEL translations, but notes a
tendency to render the Latin in such a way that there is a loss of
resonance and theological context, with a 'Pelagian' concern for 'us' and
'we' rather than God, which goes beyond 'well-meaning liberalism'. He
concludes that for a whole generation the splendour of the paradoxes of
grace in the Latin has been buried behind unworthy and vapid substi-
tutes posing as translations.[62]

---

60 Eamon Duffy, 'Rewriting the Liturgy: The theological implications of translation' in
Caldecott (ed.), *Beyond the Prosaic*, pp. 97–126.
61 Duffy, 'Rewriting the Liturgy', pp. 102–3.
62 Duffy, 'Rewriting the Liturgy', p. 122.

The several detailed examples Duffy discusses are less important than his concern that the ICEL translations, in trying to speak in common language, have transposed serious theological principles into the banalities of the English language of the 1960s, which was culturally unsuited for conveying such deep principles. Lauren Pristas has subjected the new Lenten collects to a close examination, comparing them with the foci of Lent set forth in *Sacrosanctum Concilium* 109. Her conclusion is that the preparatory character of Lent is given greater prominence than in the collects of 1962, but the penitential character, and the intimate relationship between body and soul that is integral to ascetical theology, are muted.[63]

POSTMODERN RESPONSES?

As previously noted, a common accusation made against the Vatican II rites has been that they express the concerns of modernity and were compiled just as the culture was passing into postmodernity. Since liturgy, by its nature, is always a product of its time, any changes made in the late 1960s and early 1970s could not help but be a product of modernity. I had argued this in a UK context with respect to the Roman Catholic, Church of England, Methodist and United Reformed Church rites in an article published as long ago as 1977.[64] There I noted:

Western culture has been described as scientific, technological, democratic, industrial and classless. Some of these categories apply very well to some of the new English Eucharistic liturgies:

(a) *Scientific and technological.* The revision of the liturgy was, in the main, placed in the hands of scholars and experts to be revised in accordance with scientific scholarship of liturgical history.

(b) *Democratic.* In the Church of England Series 2 was subjected to debate by the Church Assembly, and Series 3 by the new General Synod. The members of these two bodies

---

63 Lauren Pristas, 'The Post-Vatican II Revision of the Lenten Collects' in Uwe Michael Lang (ed.), *Ever Directed towards the Lord: The Love of God in the Liturgy of the Eucharist Past, Present, and Hoped For*, Proceedings of the Society of St Catherine of Siena Conference held in Oxford, 29 October 2005 (T & T Clark, London, 2007), pp. 62–89.

64 Bryan D. Spinks, 'Christian Worship or Cultural Incantations?', *Studia Liturgica* 12 (1977), pp. 1–19.

represented either a Church 'party' or merely themselves. The little amount of time available for full discussion, and the amount of uninformed criticism that occurred, have an interesting parallel in the debates in Western parliamentary legislation. Series 3 was drafted after those other strange phenomena of modern society, 'opinion polls' and 'fact-finding missions' among the consumer society, had been undertaken.

(c) *Industrial.* It is noticeable that the Eucharistic revisions of all the various denominations are very similar. Perhaps this is less a triumph for ecumenism and the Liturgical Movement than for modern mass production and egalitarianism.

(d) *Classless.* New groups of liturgical commissions and committees sprang into existence to manufacture new liturgies for the consumer society. Possibly we have here a parallel to the 'classless' aristocracy of English society in the 1960s.

What is being suggested here is that far from ignoring the culture patterns of modern Western society, the new English Eucharistic liturgies, at least those represented by the Church of England, but possibly those of other denominations as well, have been a product of those culture patterns. What in fact we may have are not new eucharistic liturgies at all, but 'cultural incantations'. By this term we mean that the 'liturgies' spring from the culture of modern society and not primarily from the demands of Christian theology. We would endorse the comment made by U. Simon on the Church of England's Series 3 eucharist:

> The sociologist will certainly identify this work with the generation from which it has sprung and which it serves. Here is the liturgy of the Western middle class, full of good intentions, decent, and just a little dull . . . 1971 must be reckoned to be petty bourgeois to the point of nausea.[65]

What was said then regarding the Church of England rites is for the most part also applicable to the Vatican II new rites. However, the new liturgies could hardly be other since no liturgy is a-cultural or a-temporal in its composition. If, then, the Vatican II reforms are an expression of modernity, how can this be corrected? Given that official

---

65 Spinks, 'Christian Worship', pp. 10–11; Ulrich Simon, 'Alternative Services', *View Review*, vol. 22:4 (SPCK, November 1971), pp. 18–19, p. 18.

reform in the Roman Catholic Church can only come from Rome, have any of the documents and changes in recent years done anything to mitigate the modernity detected in the 1970 rites? Three documents are of some significance in this respect.

I *Liturgiam Authenticam* and the new ICEL translations

A complaint from the English-speaking world was the poor quality of the ICEL translation of the 1970s. A new translation of the missal was started in 1981, but fresh ICEL translations of the Psalter, ordination rites and the Roman Missal, submitted to the Congregation for Divine Worship and the Discipline of the Sacraments, were all rejected during 1997 and 1998. ICEL itself underwent a complete restructuring, seen by many as a coup by a more conservative group which included Cardinal Francis George of Chicago, and Cuthbert Johnson and Anthony Ward from England. On 28 March 2001 the document *Liturgiam Authenticam* was published. This document was concerned with an authentic Roman rite, and gave new rules to govern translation. The document called for liturgical books which are 'marked by sound doctrine, which are exact in wording, free from ideological influence'.[66] It has an idealized view of what constituted the Roman rite, and in the light of its glaring historical inaccuracies, chant scholar Peter Jeffery has concluded: 'Inaccuracies, misrepresentations and contradictions so abound in *LA* that anyone who tried to obey it religiously would find himself hopelessly mired in absurdities, demonstrating fidelity to Roman tradition by doing things that are neither Roman nor traditional.'[67] Whatever its merits and faults, it laid down the principles that were followed by the newly constituted ICEL, and the new, and now approved, translations in draft that will replace the present English forms.[68] For example, 'the fellowship of the Holy Spirit' becomes 'the communion of the Holy Spirit', and the response to 'the Lord be with you' changes from 'And also with you' to 'And with your spirit'. In the Gloria in excelsis, the old and new first few lines are placed in parallel for comparison:

---

66 *Liturgiam Authenticam*, para. 3.
67 Peter Jeffery, *Translating Tradition: A Chant Historian Reads Liturgiam Authenticam* (Liturgical Press, Collegeville MN, 2005), p. 22. He has described it as 'the most ignorant statement on liturgy ever issued by a modern Vatican congregation' (p. 98).
68 English translation of The Order of the Mass I (ICEL Inc., Washington DC, 2006, 2008).

1970	2008
Glory to God in the highest And peace to his people on earth.	Glory to God in the highest and on earth peace to people of good will.

Lord God, heavenly King,
almighty God and Father,
we worship you, we give you thanks,
we praise you for your glory.
	We praise you,
	we bless you,
	we adore you,
	we glorify you,
	   we give you thanks
	   for your great glory,
	   Lord God, heavenly King,
	   O God, almighty Father.

Changes in translation have been made in the Ordinary such as the Creed and the Sanctus where 'God of Power and Might' reverts to 'Lord God of hosts', as in the Church of England's old prayer books. The old and new rendering of the opening words of Eucharistic Prayer III further serve to show the impact of *Liturgiam Authenticam*:

1970	2008
Father, you are holy indeed,	You are indeed Holy, O Lord,

And all creation rightly gives you
   praise
All life, all holiness comes from you
through your Son, Jesus Christ
   our Lord,
by the working of the Holy Spirit.
	and all you have created
	rightly gives you praise,
	
	for through your Son our
	   Lord Jesus Christ,
	You give life to all things
	and make them holy,

From age to age you gather a people
   to yourself,
so that from east to west
	and you never cease to
	   gather a people to yourself,
	so that from the rising of
	the sun to its setting

a perfect offering may be made	a pure offering may be offered
to the glory of your name.	to your name.

This is, of course, a new translation from the Latin and the latter remains unchanged from Vatican II. While some of the new changes seem irritating, others are much closer to the Latin than was the case with the 1973 texts. The question to consider, however, is whether or not the new prose represents a re-enchantment and expresses mystery and transcendence. As far as the Ordinary is concerned, there is an irony. ICEL eschewed much of the older English translations of the Church of England, and wanted a more contemporary form of English. Many English-speaking Churches then adopted or slightly adapted (e.g. the Lord's Prayer) the ICEL forms as shared ecumenical texts in common. The new translation leaves the 1973 texts in Protestant Churches, while Roman Catholics revert to many of the older, more archaic formulae. If there is any gain in mitigating modernity it has been bought at considerable ecumenical cost.[69]

2 Pope Benedict XVI's *Motu Proprio Summorum Pontificum*

When he was Vatican Prefect of the Congregation for the Doctrine of the Faith, Cardinal Joseph Ratzinger made some significant contributions to the debate about the Vatican II liturgical reforms. Although he could refer to the reforms following only 20 years after the encyclical *Mediator Dei* as a 'silent landslide', his criticisms have been less about the actual rites than an unwarranted liberal approach to their celebration and interpretation.[70] Comparing the liturgy to a fresco, he suggested:

> [I]t was largely concealed beneath instructions for and forms of private prayer. The fresco was laid bare by the Liturgical Movement and, in a definitive way by the Second Vatican Council. For a moment its colors and figures fascinated us. But since then the fresco has been endangered by climatic conditions as well as by various restorations and reconstructions. In fact, it is threatened with destruction, if the necessary steps are not taken to stop these damaging influences. Of course, there must be no question of its being covered with whitewash again, but what is

---

69 Maxwell E. Johnson, 'The Loss of a Common Language: The end of ecumenical-liturgical convergence', *Studia Liturgica* 37 (2007), pp. 55–72.
70 Ratzinger, *The Feast of Faith*, p. 83.

imperative is a new reverence in the way we treat it, a new under-standing of its message and its reality, so that rediscovery does not become the first stage of irreparable loss.[71]

Some traditionalists have urged the restoration of the pre-Vatican II Mass, sometimes wrongly called the 'Tridentine' rite. Although this rite was never absolutely forbidden, during the pontificate of Paul VI, most bishops strongly discouraged its use. Under John Paul II wider permis-sion was granted for its celebration. On 7 July 2007 Pope Benedict XVI (formerly Joseph Cardinal Ratzinger) extended the provisions for the celebration of the pre-Vatican II rite as contained in the 1962 edition. This *Motu Proprio Summorum Pontificum* stated:

> In more recent times, Vatican Council II expressed a desire that the respectful reverence due to divine worship should be renewed and adapted to the needs of our time. Moved by this desire our predecessor, the Supreme Pontiff Paul VI, approved, in 1970, reformed and partly renewed liturgical books for the Latin Church. These, translated into the various languages of the world, were willingly accepted by bishops, priests and faithful. John Paul II amended the third typical edition of the Roman Missal. Thus Roman pontiffs have operated to ensure that 'this kind of liturgi-cal edifice . . . should again appear resplendent for its dignity and harmony.'
>
> But in some regions, no small numbers of faithful adhered and continue to adhere with great love and affection to the earlier liturgical forms. These had so deeply marked their culture and their spirit that in 1984 the Supreme Pontiff John Paul II, moved by a concern for the pastoral care of these faithful, with the special indult 'Quattuor abhinc anno,' issued by the Congregation for Divine Worship, granted permission to use the Roman Missal published by Blessed John XXIII in the year 1962. Later, in the year 1988, John Paul II with the Apostolic Letter given as Motu Proprio, 'Ecclesia Dei,' exhorted bishops to make generous use of this power in favour of all the faithful who so desired.
>
> Following the insistent prayers of these faithful, long deliber-ated upon by our predecessor John Paul II, and after having

---

71 Ratzinger, *The Spirit of the Liturgy*, p. 8.

listened to the views of the Cardinal Fathers of the Consistory of 22 March 2006, having reflected deeply upon all aspects of the question, invoked the Holy Spirit and trusting in the help of God, with these Apostolic Letters we establish the following:

Art 1. The Roman Missal promulgated by Paul VI is the ordinary expression of the 'Lex orandi' (Law of prayer) of the Catholic Church of the Latin rite. Nonetheless, the Roman Missal promulgated by St. Pius V and reissued by Bl. John XXIII is to be considered as an extraordinary expression of that same 'Lex orandi,' and must be given due honour for its venerable and ancient usage. These two expressions of the Church's Lex orandi will in no way lead to a division in the Church's 'Lex credendi' (Law of belief). They are, in fact two usages of the one Roman rite.

It is, therefore, permissible to celebrate the Sacrifice of the Mass following the typical edition of the Roman Missal promulgated by Bl. John XXIII in 1962 and never abrogated, as an extraordinary form of the Liturgy of the Church.[72]

The accompanying letter to the bishops explained that the two versions, 1962 and 1969/70, were not two rites, but instead a twofold use of one and the same Roman rite, and that each would enrich the other. It would also, he hoped, serve to reconcile the disaffected traditionalists. Apart from the Easter Triduum, either missal can be used at Masses celebrated without the people. Religious communities are allowed to use 1962, and in parishes where a group of the faithful exists that is strongly attached to the pre-Vatican II rite, it may be used, but it should only be used once on a Sunday. The older rites for other services, such as marriage and baptism, as well as the Daily Office, may also be used.

It is quite possible to see this move as thoroughly postmodern, where pluriformity is expected, with personal preference and choice, though the rite itself is not. Given the history of the pre-Vatican II missal, it is, at best, modernity's version of a more ancient tradition.

---

72 <http://www.summorumpontificum.net/2007/07/summorum-pontificum-english.html>.

3 Inculturation

Sacrosanctum Concilium 37–40 had encouraged inculturation of the liturgy, or adaptations to different cultures. The possible implications of this have been the subject of a number of studies by Anscar Chupungco, in which he has differentiated between adaptation or acculturation, inculturation, and 'liturgical creativity'.[73] Among the most notable results have been the (Australian) Aboriginal Eucharistic Prayer, the Swiss Synod Eucharistic Prayer and the Zaire Mass. The Mass for India was given only partial approval, and the ICEL Eucharistic Prayer failed to be approved. In the meantime, one document in particular has been concerned with liturgical inculturation, *Varietates Legitimae* (1994). This document has been regarded as privileging the Roman rite, and trimming the vision of *Sacrosanctum Concilium*, and placing many restrictions on the possibility of any further substantial incultured rites. Paragraph 30 states that when considering inculturation, episcopal conferences should call upon people who are competent both in the liturgical tradition of the Roman rite and in the appreciation of local cultural values. The limits of such ventures are posited in paragraph 36, namely 'to maintain the substantial unity of the Roman rite'. The end result should not be the creation of new families of rites (*novas familias rituales*), and it will be the Apostolic See (the Congregation for Divine Worship and Discipline of the Sacraments) which shall oversee such proposals. Although reference is made to language, gestures, postures, music, singing, art and furnishings, paragraph 63 stated that the adaptations referred to in *Sacrosanctum Concilium* 40 'do not envisage a transformation of the Roman rite, but are made within the context of the Roman rite'. The Zaire Mass, for example, which was approved in 1988, is regarded as the Roman Missal for the Dioceses of Zaire, and not a Zaire rite on a par with the Visigothic rite or Chaldean Eastern rite. The concern with the Roman rite to the exclusion of any newer rite is reiterated in *Liturgiam Authenticam*, which affirms that the Roman rite itself is a precious example and instrument of true inculturation, 'a harmonious unity that transcends the boundaries of any single region' (para. 5). Paragraph 107 was clear to insist that new texts composed in a vernacular language are to contain nothing that is inconsistent with the meaning, structure, style,

---

73 Anscar J. Chupungco, *Liturgies of the Future: The Process and Methods of Inculturation* (Paulist Press, New York, 1989).

theological content, traditional vocabulary or other important qualities of the texts found in the Latin *editiones typicae*. It would seem that any new compilations can only be variations of the Roman rite – a cultural veneer on a Latin (Roman) superstructure. Such concern with Latin, the Roman rite, and centralized control by the Roman Curia would suggest that modernity is alive and well, and that views on liturgical inculturation are at best paternalistic and at worst hegemonic and colonial. Pope Benedict XVI regards the missal of Paul VI as providing a framework for adaptation to local variation,[74] and the Zaire Mass as the Roman rite 'in the Zairean mode':

> It still belongs within the great fellowship of the apostolically rooted Roman rite, but that rite is now, so to speak, clad in Congolese garments, with the addition – this seems to me to make perfect sense – of certain elements from the Christian East.[75]

However, he has been particularly critical of 'creativity' which often takes the form of entertainment and homespun liturgies. True liturgy cannot be manufactured.[76]

CONCLUDING NOTE

In so far as the present plurality is a pick-and-mix, 'treasures old and new', and offers the consumer choice, Roman Catholic worship is certainly in keeping with postmodern culture. However, whether either the 1962 Mass, consolidated in early modernity, or the Mass of Paul VI, created in modernity, can claim itself to be postmodern will perhaps provoke a new debate. For the present and immediate future, one thing seems certain – since no new major liturgical revisions seem to be envisaged, whatever enchanting texts and rituals might or might not have emerged had the Vatican II reforms taken place twenty years later will now never be known. The Roman Catholic Church has liturgies *in* a postmodern world, but cannot claim to have liturgies *for* a postmodern world.

---

74 Ratzinger, *The Feast of Faith*, p. 80.
75 Ratzinger, *The Spirit of the Liturgy*, p. 170.
76 Ratzinger, *The Spirit of the Liturgy*, pp. 168 and 166.

Concluding remarks

This visit to the Worship Mall has come to an end. Like most visits to malls, not every store received our attention and we could have lingered longer in those that were visited. Our peek inside those featured here is not a definitive visit, but we have visited the main anchor stores, and some of the more esoteric ones. Thus perhaps Roman Catholic worship is likened to Target or Tesco Extras, and the megachurches to J. C. Penny or Debenhams. Blended worship might be Macys or John Lewis, whereas alt.worship could be either Pacsun or Hollister, or Topshop. Some emergent worship is more like a visit to Home Depot or B&Q, where do-it-yourselfers who know what they are doing can be successfully creative, and those who don't end up with a jerry-rigged mess. Multi-sensory worship may be the Apple Store or CompUSA or PC World. Many US malls have a store that sells Amish products, and there are always exotic stores that offer African and Asian goods. Perhaps the snake-handlers are The Pet Company or Petco or Pets at Home; though as I tell my Anglican students, we too have something akin to snake-handling, but we call it handling bishops.

Some consumers prefer not to go to the mall, but instead order online. Online and virtual worship is another postmodern phenomenon which is not considered here.[1] However, this somewhat limited visit to what is going on in worship in our postmodern, global culture poses the question of whether or not any of them are really 'postmodern worship' as distinct from 'worship in a postmodern era'. Roman Catholic critics see the Vatican II reforms as an expression of modernity, and megachurch worship, as well as seeker services, were most certainly spawned in modernity. We have suggested that much emergent worship

---

1 <http://www.cnn.com/2009/TECH/11/13/online.church.services/>.

seems 'retro', doing things that were done in the 1960s but are now being done with the latest technology.

In an article concerned with worship and secularization in 1970, Charles Davis made the point that our worship is outdated because worship itself is outdated: 'our faith and worship are not part of the modern secular world in which we live, not part of its socially shared and confirmed reality'.[2] Here Davis did not mean that worship should cease, but that it comes from a pre-modern world, and thus could not be modernized. Although postmodernity is hailed as being a culture that gives space for an enchanted world, and thus less hostile to belief and worship, that does not necessarily mean that the culture *itself* is any more conducive to engendering liturgical forms than was modernity. That may not be what 'emergents' want to hear. However, Aidan Kavanagh reminds us that liturgy has a habit of inculturating itself without us having to be self-conscious about it.[3] Kavanagh writes:

> For in one sense inculturation is nothing other than the continuation of God's own humble incarnation in our midst by Word, faith, and sacrament – an incarnation which reached its peak, to be sure, in Jesus the Christ, but which began already in the genesis of the world and continues, as the Pauline corpus implies, in the Spirit-filled Body corporate of Christ which is the Church. Inculturation in this sense is a precious mystery in itself of which God is the agent: a pregnant grace which, like every other grace, gestates according to God's pleasure rather than that of some ecclesiastical bureaucracy or ideologically pure committee. God's will cannot be gainsaid but at our peril; nor can it be forced, but only served. This is not a call for *laissez-faire* on our part, but it is a small encouragement of patience and reverence, because faithful inculturation is at its deepest level a divine, not a human, benevolence.[4]

In other words, organic development of liturgy, *providing the liturgical tradition is open to change*, will probably be more successful than liturgi-

---

2 Charles Davis, 'Ghetto or Desert: Liturgy in a cultural dilemma', *Studia Liturgica* 7 (1970), pp. 10–27, p. 17.
3 Aidan Kavanagh, 'Liturgical Inculturation: Looking to the future', *Studia Liturgica* 20 (1990), pp. 95–106.
4 Kavanagh, 'Liturgical Inculturation', pp. 104–5.

cal genetic engineering where we are always intervening to *make* the liturgy contemporary. The medieval Western rites were able to develop regionally and locally because there was no central body to which every single change had to be submitted for approval; it gave rise to 'glocaliza-tion'.[5] The Roman Catholic Western rite today is not able to develop organically because reform is centralized and controlled, as are the litur-gical forms in many other churches. Yet if at one end of the spectrum inculturation is hindered by curial or synodical control, at the other end organic inculturation is destroyed by the worship committees and tech-nocrats who plan a new thing every week to entice and entertain the congregation, and thereby impose their own ritual self-expressions. If worship can be described as entertainment, that entertainment is primarily for an audience of Three – the triune God, not the audience of postmodern consumers. Furthermore, one of Robert Wuthnow's findings needs to be carefully considered:

> Some of the young people journalists interview say the innovative worship styles that appealed to baby boomers do not appeal to them. They think church services should feel like church. They say the so-called seeker services that were geared towards people who disliked church are now passé. In the major research project I did a few years ago on the uses of music and the arts in congrega-tions, I observed, too, that young adults are often as interested in preserving traditional worship as they were in changing it.[6]

In his recent book *Desiring the Kingdom*, James K. A. Smith has accused the churches of trying to *in*form in worship rather than form, and of adopting the Enlightenment philosophy of seeing humans as just thinking beings.[7] He contrasts the approaches of humans as thinkers and believers – both concerned with the mind and information – with

5 For this postmodern term, see David Lyon, *Postmodernity*, second edn (University of Minnesota Press, Minneapolis, 2005), p. 64. For medieval 'glocalization', see Richard W. Pfaff, *The Liturgy in Medieval England: A History* (Cambridge University Press, Cambridge, 2009). Such development became more difficult in modernity with printing and centralization of authority, but with material now available on the web, custom-ization is easier in postmodernity.
6 Robert Wuthnow, *After the Baby Boomers: How Twenty- and Thirty-Somethings are Shaping the Future of American Religion* (Princeton University Press, Princeton NJ, 2007), p. 223–4.
7 James K. A. Smith, *Desiring the Kingdom: Worship, Worldview, and Cultural Formation* (Baker Academic, Grand Rapids MI, 2009).

humans as lovers, concerned with all the senses. Drawing on the theology of Charles Williams, he urges that humans are at root erotic beings, and have desire and love, which becomes desire and love of the kingdom.[8] Contrasting the Church with the mall, he writes:

> While Victoria's Secret [UK = La Senza] is fanning a flame in our *kardia*, the church is trucking water to our minds. While secular liturgies are enticing us with affective images of a good life, the church is trying to convince us otherwise by depositing ideas.[9]

In an Alcuin publication of 1991 I wrote, and repeat now: 'Liturgy needs to be powerful enough to allow the worshippers to grow in love – even fall in love – with the Bridegroom, and to make love.'[10] Making love is very different from a lecture on sex – and all too often it is the latter that worship resembles, be it emergent, seeker service, Praise and Worship or an instructed Vatican II parish Mass. Earlier in this work I drew attention to Frank Senn's call for enchantment rather than entertainment, and in the re-enchanted world of postmodernity that should be possible. The immanent and transcendent; the mind, soul and body; the informal and formal; the everyday and mystery should all be able to be juxtaposed in worship. Liturgy should entice and enchant us not only to desire, but also to fall in love with God the Trinity, and thereby love our neighbours. Regardless of what we may think of Smith's analogy with Victoria's Secret (or La Senza), serious postmodern worship, whatever its actual form, and wherever it takes place, should ravish the heart, and wound the soul with love (Song of Songs 4.9; 5.8). Such a foundation transcends the changes and chances of this mortal life, whatever the cultural epoch.

---

8 He refers to Charles Williams, *Outlines of Romantic Theology*, ed. Alice M. Hadfield (Eerdmans, Grand Rapids MI, 1990). For a more recent approach, see J. Harold Ellens, *The Spirituality of Sex* (Praeger, Westport CT, 2009), especially chs 4, 5 and 6.
9 Williams, *Outlines*, p. 127.
10 Bryan D. Spinks, 'Worship and Evangelism' in Michael Perham (ed.), *Liturgy for a New Century* (SPCK/Alcuin Club, London, 1991), pp. 101–5, p. 104.

Bibliography

Adam, David, *The Edge of Glory: Prayers in the Celtic Tradition*, London: Triangle/SPCK, 1985.

Adam, David, *Tides and Seasons: Modern Prayers in the Celtic Tradition*, London: Triangle/SPCK, 1989.

Ai-Ling Sun, Irene, 'Songs of Canaan: Hymnody of the house-church Christians in China', *Studia Liturgica* 37 (2007), pp. 98–116.

Albrecht, Daniel E., *Rites in the Spirit: A Ritual Approach to Pentecostal/Charismatic Spirituality*, Sheffield: Sheffield Academic Press, 1999.

Allchin, Donald, *God's Presence Makes the World: The Celtic Vision through the Centuries in Wales*, London: Darton, Longman & Todd, 1997.

Allchin, Donald and de Waal, Esther, *Threshold of Light*, London: Darton, Longman & Todd, 1986.

Ashley, Jennifer with Bickle, Mike, Driscoll, Mark and Howerton, Mike, *The Relevant Church: A New Vision for Communities of Faith*, Lake Mary FL: Relevant Books, 2004.

Bachman, Calvin George, *The Old Order Amish of Lancaster County*, Lancaster PA: Pennsylvania German Society, 1961.

Baker, Jonny, 'Alternative Worship and the Significance of Popular Culture', <http://www.freshworship.org/node/94>.

Baker, Jonny and Gay, Doug with Jenny Brown, *Alternative Worship: Resources from and for the Emerging Church*, Grand Rapids MI: Baker Books, 2003.

Baldovin, John F., *Reforming the Liturgy: A Response to the Critics*, Collegeville MN: Liturgical Press, 2008.

Bauman, Zygmunt, *Intimations of Postmodernity*, London: Routledge, 1992.

Bauman, Zygmunt, *Liquid Modernity*, Malden MA: Polity Press, 2000.

Beach, Nancy, *An Hour on Sunday: Creating Moments of Transformation and Wonder*, Grand Rapids MI: Zondervan, 2004.

Beall, Patricia and Keys Barker, Martha, *The Folk Arts in Renewal: Creativity in Worship, Teaching and Festivity as Developed by the Fisherfolk*, London: Hodder & Stoughton, 1980.

Bender, Harold S., 'The First Edition of the Ausbund', *The Mennonite Quarterly Review* 3 (1929), pp. 147–50.

Berger, Teresa, *Women's Way of Worship: Gender Analysis and Liturgical History*, Collegeville MN: Liturgical Press, 1999.

Birch, John, *heart2heart: Contemporary Prayers, Litanies and Liturgies for Christian Worship*, Ilkeston: Moorley's, 2004.

Blair, Paige, 'What is a U2 Eucharist (or U2charist) as celebrated at St. George's Episcopal Church', at <http://s3.amazonaws.com/dfc_attachments/public/documents/414/What_is_a_U2charist.pdf>.

Blanchard, John and Lucarini, Dan, *Can We Rock the Gospel? Rock Music's Impact on Worship and Evangelism*, Darlington: Evangelical Press, 2006.

Blank, Benuel S., *The Amazing Story of the Ausbund*, Sugarcreek OH: Carlisle Printing, 2001.

Bloom, Allan, *The Closing of the American Mind*, New York: Simon & Schuster, 1987.

Bonneterre, Didier, *The Liturgical Movement from Dom Guéranger to Annibale Bugnini: The Trojan Horse in the City of God*, Kansas City MO: Angelus Press, 2002.

Boschman, LaMar, *Future Worship: How a Changing World Can Enter God's Presence in the New Millennium*, Ventura CA: Renew Books, 1999.

Bowman, Marion, 'Contemporary Celtic Spirituality' in Joanne Pearson (ed.), *Belief Beyond Boundaries: Wicca, Celtic Spirituality and the New Age*, Aldershot and Milton Keynes: Ashgate/Open University, 2002, pp. 55–101.

Bradley, Ian, *Celtic Christianity: Making Myths and Chasing Dreams*, Edinburgh: Edinburgh University Press, 1999.

Bradley, Ian, *Colonies of Heaven: Celtic Models for Today's Church*, London: Darton, Longman & Todd, 2000.

Brain, Chris, 'The Nine O'Clock Service' in David Gillett and Michael Scott-Joynt (eds), *Treasure in the Field: The Archbishop's Companion for the Decade of Evangelism*, London: Fount Paperbacks, 1993, pp. 163–75.

Brown, David, *God and Grace of Body: Sacrament in Ordinary*, Oxford: Oxford University Press, 2007.

Brown, David, *God and Mystery in Words: Experience through Metaphor and Drama*, Oxford: Oxford University Press, 2008.

Brown, Fred and McDonald, Jeanne, *The Serpent Handlers: Three Families and Their Faith*, Winston-Salem NC: John F. Blair, 2000.

Bugnini, Annibale, *The Reform of the Liturgy 1948–1975*, ET, Collegeville MN: Liturgical Press, 2007.

Burkhart, Charles, 'The Church Music of the Old Order Amish and Old Colony Mennonites', *The Mennonite Quarterly Review* 27 (1953), pp. 34–54.

Burns, Stephen and Monro, Anita (eds), *Christian Worship in Australia: Inculturating the Liturgical Tradition*, Strathfield NSW: St Pauls Publications, 2009.

Burton, Thomas, *Serpent-Handling Believers*, Knoxville: University of Tennessee Press, 1993.

Bush, Trudy, 'Back to the Future: Fourth-century style reaches Bay Area seekers', *Christian Century*, vol. 119, no. 24 (20 November–3 December 2002), pp. 18–22.

Caldecott, Stratford (ed.), *Beyond the Prosaic: Renewing the Liturgical Movement*, Edinburgh: T & T Clark, 1998.

Carmichael, Alexander, *Carmina Gadelica: Hymns and Incantations*, ed. C. J. Moore, Edinburgh: Floris Books, 1992.

Carson, D. A., *Becoming Conversant with the Emerging Church: Understanding a Movement and Its Implications*, Grand Rapids MI: Zondervan, 2005.

Celtic Missal, ET and rubrication by Kristopher G. Dowling, Akron OH: Ascension Western Rite Orthodox Church, 1997.

Chadwick, Nora, *The Celts*, Harmondsworth: Penguin Books, 1971.

Chatháin, Próinséas Ní, 'The Liturgical Background of the Derrynavlan Altar Service', *Journal of the Royal Society of Antiquaries of Ireland* 110 (1980), pp. 127–48.

Chupungco, Anscar J., *Liturgies of the Future: The Process and Methods of Inculturation*, New York: Paulist Press, 1989.

Clammer, John, 'Aesthetics of the Self: Shopping and social being in contemporary urban Japan' in Rob Shields (ed.), *Lifestyle Shopping: The Subject of Consumption*, London: Routledge, 1992, pp. 195–215.

Clancy, Thomas Owen and Márkus, Gilbert, *Iona: The Earliest Poetry of a Celtic Monastery*, Edinburgh: Edinburgh University Press, 1995.

Commission on Theological Concerns of the Christian Conference of Asia (ed.), *Minjung Theology: People as the Subject of History*, Maryknoll NY: Orbis Books, 1983.

Connor, Steven, *Postmodernist Culture: An Introduction to Theories of the Contemporary*, 2nd edn, Oxford: Blackwell, 1997.

Cornwall, Judson, *Let Us Worship*, Plainfield NJ: Bridge Publishing Inc., 1983.

Costen, Melva Wilson, *In Spirit and in Truth: The Music of African American Worship*, Louisville KY: Westminster John Knox Press, 2004.

Covington, Dennis, *Salvation on Sand Mountain: Snake Handling and Redemption in Southern Appalachia*, New York: Penguin Books, 1995.

Cray, Graham (chair), *Mission-Shaped Church: Church Planting and Fresh Expressions of Church in a Changing Context*, London: Church House Publishing, 2004.

Crichton, J. D., *The Church's Worship: Considerations on the Liturgical Constitution of the Second Vatican Council*, London: Geoffrey Chapman, 1964.

Crichton, J. D., *Christian Celebration: The Mass, the Sacraments, the Prayer of the Church*, London: Geoffrey Chapman, 1981.

Croft, Steven, 'What Counts as a Fresh Expression of Church and Who Decides?' in Louise Nelstrop and Martyn Percy (eds), *Evaluating Fresh Expressions: Explorations in Emerging Church*, Norwich: Canterbury Press, 2008, pp. 3–14.

Crouan, Denis, *The Liturgy Betrayed*, trans. Marc Sebanc, San Francisco CA: Ignatius Press, 2000.

Crouan, Denis, *The History and the Future of the Roman Liturgy*, trans. Michael Miller, San Francisco CA: Ignatius Press, 2005.

Curran, Michael, *The Antiphonary of Bangor and the Early Irish Monastic Liturgy*, Dublin: Irish Academic Press, 1984.

Cusic, Don, *The Sound of Light: A History of Gospel and Christian Music*, Milwaukee WI: Hal Leonard, 2002.

Daugherty, Mary Lee, 'Serpent Handlers: When the sacrament comes alive' in Bill J. Leonard (ed.), *Christianity in Appalachia: Profiles in Regional Pluralism*, Knoxville: University of Tennessee Press, 1999, pp. 138–52.

Davies, Michael, *Liturgical Revolution, Vol. III: Pope Paul's New Mass*, Dickinson TX: Angelus Press, 1980.

Davies, Michael, *Liturgical Time Bombs in Vatican II: The Destruction of Catholic Faith through Changes in Catholic Worship*, Rockford IL: Tan Books, 2003.

Davies, Oliver, *Celtic Christianity in Early Medieval Wales: The Origins of the Welsh Spiritual Tradition*, Cardiff: University of Wales Press, 1996.

Davis, Charles, 'Ghetto or Desert: Liturgy in a cultural dilemma', *Studia Liturgica* 7 (1970) pp. 10–17.

Delanty, Gerard, *Modernity and Postmodernity: Knowledge, Power and the Self*, London: Sage Publications, 2000.

de Waal, Esther, *God Under My Roof*, Abingdon: Fairacres Publications, 1984.

de Waal, Esther, *The Celtic Vision*, London: Darton, Longman & Todd, 1988.

Doorly, Moyra, *No Place for God: The Denial of the Transcendent in Modern Church Architecture*, San Francisco CA: Ignatius Press, 2007.

Dorgan, Howard, *Giving Glory to God in Appalachia: Worship Practices of Six Baptist Subdenominations*, Knoxville: University of Tennessee Press, 1987.

Drane, John, *The McDonaldization of the Church: Consumer Culture and the Church's Future*, Macon GA: Smyth & Helwys Publishing Inc., 2001.

Draper, Brian and Draper, Kevin, *Refreshing Worship*, Oxford: Bible Reading Fellowship, 2000.

Drury, Keith, 'I'm Desperate for You: Male perception of romantic lyrics in contemporary worship music' in Robert Woods and Brian Walrath (eds), *The Message in the Music: Studying Contemporary Praise & Worship*, Nashville TN: Abingdon Press, 2007, pp. 54–64.

Duffy, Eamon, 'Rewriting the Liturgy: The theological implications of translation' in Stratford Caldecott (ed.), *Beyond the Prosaic: Renewing the Liturgical Movement*, Edinburgh: T & T Clark, 1998.

Ellens, J. Harold, *The Spirituality of Sex*, Westport CT: Praeger, 2009.

Ellingson, Stephen, *The Megachurch and the Mainline: Remaking Religious Tradition in the Twenty-First Century*, Chicago IL: University of Chicago Press, 2007.

Ellington, Edward Kennedy, *Music Is My Mistress*, New York: Da Capo, 1973.

Emanuel, Frank, 'An Incarnational Theology of the Emerging Church', a research paper toward the degree of MTh, Saint Paul University, Ottawa, 2008.

Enninger, Werner and Raith, Joachim, *An Ethnography-of-Communication Approach to Ceremonial Situations: A Study on Communication in Institutionalized Social Contexts: The Old Order Amish Church Service*, Wiesbaden: Franz Steiner Verlag GMBH, 1982.

Enriching Our Worship, New York: Church Publishing Inc., 1997; vol. 2, 2000.

Episcopal Church Women of the Diocese of Virginia, 'A Prayer and Worship Retreat', <www.rlva.org/documents/2008/AprilHarbinger.doc>.

Fabian, Richard (comp.), pamphlet: 'The Book of Common Prayer at St. Gregory's', 1988.

Farrell, James J., *One Nation under Goods: Malls and the Seduction of American Shopping*, Washington DC: Smithsonian Books, 2003.

Fenwick, John and Spinks, Bryan, *Worship in Transition: The Liturgical Movement in the Twentieth Century*, Edinburgh: T & T Clark, 1995.

Finn, Peter C. and Schellman, James M. (eds), prepared by ICEL, *Shaping English Liturgy*, Washington DC: Pastoral Press, 1990.

Finney, Charles Grandison, *Lectures on Revivals of Religion*, ed. William G. McLoughlin, Cambridge MA: The Belknap Press of Harvard University Press, 1960.

Flanagan, Kieran, *Sociology and Liturgy: Re-Presentations of the Holy*, Basingstoke and London: Macmillan, 1991.

Flannagan, Andy, *Distinctive Worship: How a New Generation Connects with God*, Carlisle: Authentic Media, 2004.

Frame, John M., *Contemporary Worship Music: A Biblical Defense*, Phillipsburg NJ: P & R Publishing, 1997.

Franklin, R. W. and Spaeth, Robert L., *Virgil Michel: American Catholic*, Collegeville MN: Liturgical Press, 1988.

Friedmann, Robert, 'Mennonite Prayer Books', *The Mennonite Quarterly Review* 17 (1943), pp. 179–206.

Gabriel, Yiannis and Lang, Tim. *The Unmanageable Consumer: Contemporary Consumption and Its Fragmentation*, London: Sage Publications, 1995.

Galloway, Kathy, 'The Worship of the Iona Community' in Thomas F. Best and Dagmar Heller (eds), *Worship Today: Understanding, Practice, Ecumenical Implications*, Geneva: WCC Publications, 2004, pp. 222–8.

Gamber, Klaus, *The Reform of the Roman Liturgy: Its Problems and Background*, trans. Klaus D. Grimm, San Juan Capistrano CA: Una Voce Press, and Harrison NY: The Foundation for Catholic Reform, 1993.

Gamble, Robin, 'Mixed Economy: Nice slogan or working reality?' in Louise Nelstrop and Martyn Percy (eds), *Evaluating Fresh Expressions*, Explorations in Emerging Church, Norwich: Canterbury Press, 2008, pp. 15–23.

Gascho, Milton, 'The Amish Division of 1693–1697 in Switzerland and Alsace', *The Mennonite Quarterly Review* 11 (1937), pp. 235–66.

Gibbs, Eddie, *Churchmorph: How Megatrends are Reshaping Christian Communities*, Grand Rapids MI: Baker Academic, 2009.

Gibbs, Eddie and Bolger, Ryan K. (eds), *Emerging Churches: Creating Christian Community in Postmodern Cultures*, Grand Rapids MI: Baker Academic, 2005.

Giles, Richard, *Re-Pitching the Tent: Re-ordering the Church Building for Worship and Mission in the New Millennium*, Norwich: Canterbury Press, 1997.

Gillespie, Paul F. (ed.), *Foxfire 7*, Garden City: Anchor Press, 1982.

Gittoes, Julie, *Anamnesis and the Eucharist: Contemporary Anglican Approaches*, Aldershot: Ashgate, 2008.

Goldie, Mark, *God's Bordello: Storm over a Chapel*, Cambridge: Churchill College, 2007.

Grace, Pocket Liturgies, Proost, <www.proost.co.uk>, 2007.

Grenz, Stanley J., *A Primer on Postmodernism*, Grand Rapids MI: Eerdmans, 1996.

Gross, Leonard (ed. and trans.), *Prayer Book for Earnest Christians*, Scottsdale PA: Herald Press, 1997.

Grubbs, Lucas Michael, 'Emerging Church Liturgy: Three examples of post-modern worship', an extended paper (with CD recording) toward the degree of STM, Yale University, March 2008.

Halgren Kilde, Jeanne, *When Church Became Theatre: The Transformation of Evangelical Architecture and Worship in Nineteenth-Century America*, New York: Oxford University Press, 2002.

Halgren Kilde, Jeanne, 'Reading Megachurches: Investigating the religious and cultural work of church architecture' in Louis P. Nelson (ed.), *American Sanctuary: Understanding Sacred Spaces*, Bloomington and Indianapolis: Indiana University Press, 2006.

Hall, Bill, 'Jazz – Lewd or Ludens?' in Jeff Astley, Timothy Hone and Mark Savage (eds), *Creative Chords: Studies in Music, Theology and Christian Formation*, Leominster: Gracewing, 2000, pp. 194–209.

Ham, Ken and Beemer, Britt, with Hillard, Todd, *Already Gone: Why Your Kids Will Quit Church and What You Can Do to Stop It*, Green Forest AR: Master Books, 2009.

Hamilton, Reid and Rush, Stephen, *Better Get It in Your Soul: What Liturgists Can Learn from Jazz*, New York: Church Publishing Inc., 2008.

Harries, Jim (lecturer), *Visits to AICs, submitted to the African Literature Profile of Kima International School of Theology*, January to March 2006, <http://www.jim-mission.org.uk/articles/visits-to-aics.pdf>

Hayes, Stephen, *Black Charismatic Anglicans: The Iviyo loFakazi bataKristu and Its Relations with Other Renewal Movements*, Pretoria: Studia Specialia, University of South Africa Press, 1990.

Heelas, Paul and Woodhead, Linda et al., *The Spiritual Revolution: Why Religion is Giving Way to Spirituality*, Oxford: Blackwell, 2005.

Hemming, Laurence Paul, *Worship as a Revelation: The Past, Present and Future of Catholic Liturgy*, London: Burns & Oates, 2008.

Hilborn, David (ed.), '*Toronto' in Perspective: Papers on the New Charismatic Wave of the Mid 1990s*, Carlisle: ACUTE, Paternoster Press, 2001.

Hoehler-Fatton, Cynthia, *Women of Fire and Spirit: History, Faith, and Gender in Roho Religion in Western Kenya*, New York: Oxford University Press, 1996.

Holder, Timothy, *The Hip Hop Prayer Book with Holy Bible Stories*, New York: Church Publishing, 2006.

Horton, Michael, *Christless Christianity: The Alternative Gospel of the American Church*, Grand Rapids MI: Baker Books, 2008.

Hostetler, John A., *Amish Society*, 3rd edn, Baltimore and London: Johns Hopkins University Press, 1980.

Howard, Jay R. and Streck, John M., *Apostles of Rock: The Splintered World of Contemporary Christian Music*, Lexington: University of Kentucky Press, 1999.

Howard, Roland, *The Rise and Fall of the Nine O'Clock Service: A Cult within the Church?* London: Mowbray, 1996.

Huizinga, Johan, *Homo Ludens*, London: Paladin, 1970.

Iona Community, *The Iona Community Worship Book. The Abbey Services of the Iona Community*, Glasgow: Wild Goose Publications, 1991.

Iona Community, *Iona Abbey Worship Book*, Glasgow: Bell & Bain, 2007.

Jackson, Bill, *The Quest for the Radical Middle: A History of the Vineyard*, Cape Town: Vineyard International Publishing, 1999.

Jeffery, Peter, 'Eastern and Western Elements in the Irish Monastic Prayer of the Hours' in Margot E. Fassler and Rebecca A. Baltzer (eds), *The Divine Office in the Latin Middle Ages: Methodology and Source Studies, Regional Developments, Hagiography*, Oxford: Oxford University Press, 2000, pp. 99–143.

Jeffery, Peter, *Translating Tradition: A Chant Historian Reads Liturgiam Authenticam*, Collegeville MN: Liturgical Press, 2005.

Jencks, Charles A., *The Language of Post-Modern Architecture*, 4th edn, London: Academy Editions, 1984.

Jewell, Derek, *Duke: A Portrait of Duke Ellington*, New York: W. W. Norton & Co. Inc., 1977.

Johnson, Maxwell E., 'The Loss of a Common Language: The end of ecumenical-liturgical convergence?', *Studia Liturgica* 37 (2007), pp. 55–72.

Johnson, Todd E., 'Disconnected Rituals: The origins of the seeker service movement' in Todd E. Johnson (ed.), *The Conviction of Things Not Seen: Worship and Ministry in the 21st Century*, Grand Rapids MI: Brazos Press, 2002, pp. 53–66.

Jolly, Karen Louise, *Popular Religion in Late Saxon England: Elf Charms in Context*, Chapel Hill: University of North Carolina Press, 1996.

Jones, Tony, *The New Christians: Dispatches from the Emergent Frontier*, San Francisco CA: Jossey-Bass, 2008.

Joseph, Mark, *Faith, God and Rock + Roll, from Bono to Jars of Clay: How People of Faith are Transforming American Popular Music*, Grand Rapids MI: Baker Books, 2003.

Kallestad, Walt, *Entertainment Evangelism: Taking the Church Public*, Nashville TN: Abingdon Press, 1996.

Kauppinen, Juha, *The Thomas Mass: Case Study of an Urban Church Service*, publication no. 43 of the Research Institute of the Lutheran Church in Finland, Tampere, 1992.

Kavanagh, Aidan, 'Liturgical Inculturation: Looking to the future', *Studia Liturgica* 20 (1990), pp. 95–106.

Kendrick, Graham, *Worship*, Eastbourne: Kingsway Publications, 1984.

Kendrick, Graham, 'Worship in Spirit and in Truth' in Stephen Darlington and Alan Kreider (eds), *Composing Music for Worship*, Norwich: Canterbury Press, 2003, pp. 86–103.

Kendrick, Graham with Price, Clive, *Behind the Songs*, Stowmarket: Kevin Mayhew, 2001.

Kiernan, Jim, 'African Independent Churches and Modernity' in Dawid Venter (ed.), *Engaging Modernity: Methods and Cases for Studying African Independent Churches in South Africa*, Westport CT: Praeger, 2004, pp. 45–58.

Killinger, John, *Leave It to the Spirit: A Handbook for Experimental Worship*, London: SCM Press, 1971.

Kim, Dong-sun, *The Bread for Today and the Bread for Tomorrow: The Ethical Significance of the Lord's Supper in the Korean Context*, Frankfurt am Main: Peter Lang, 2001.

Kimball, Dan, *Emerging Worship: Creating Worship Gatherings for New Generations*, Grand Rapids MI: Zondervan, 2004.

Kimbrough, David, *Taking Up Serpents: Snake Handlers of Eastern Kentucky*, Macon GA: Mercer University Press, 2002.

Kinnaman, David and Lyons, Gabe, *UnChristian: What a New Generation Really Thinks about Christianity . . . and Why It Matters*, Grand Rapids MI: Baker Books, 2007.

Kock, Thomas M., *The Reform of the Reform? A Liturgical Debate: Reform or Return*, San Francisco CA: Ignatius Press, 2003.

Kocik, Thomas M. (ed.), *The Reform of the Reform? A Liturgical Debate: Reform or Return*, San Francisco CA: Ignatius Press, 2003.

Koenig, Sarah, 'This Is My Daily Bread: Toward a sacramental theology of evangelical praise and worship', *Worship* 82 (2008), pp. 141–61.

Kraybill, Donald B. and Hurd, James P., *Horse-and-Buggy Mennonites: Hoofbeats of Humility in a Postmodern World*, University Park PA: Pennsylvania State University Press, 2006.

Lang, Uwe Michael, *Turning Towards the Lord: Orientation in Liturgical Prayer*, San Francisco CA: Ignatius Press, 2004.

Lang, Uwe Michael (ed.), *Ever Directed Towards the Lord: The Love of God in the Liturgy of the Eucharist Past, Present, and Hoped For*, Proceedings of the

Society of St Catherine of Siena Conference held in Oxford, 29 October 2005, London and New York: T & T Clark, 2007.

Lathrop, Gordon W., 'New Pentecost or Joseph's Britches? Reflections on the history and meaning of the worship ordo in the megachurches', *Worship* 72 (1998), pp. 521–38.

Lee, Shayne and Sinitiere, Phillip Luke, *Holy Mavericks: Evangelical Innovators and the Spiritual Marketplace*, New York and London: New York University Press, 2009.

Lee, Yeong Mee, 'A Political Reception of the Bible: Korean minjung theological interpretation of the Bible', *SBL Forum* (cited October 2005), <http://sbl-site.org/Article.aspx?ArticleID=457>.

Liesch, Barry, *The New Worship: Straight Talk on Music and the Church*, Grand Rapids MI: Baker Books, 2001.

Lippy, Charles H., 'Popular Religiosity in Central Appalachia' in Bill J. Leonard (ed.), *Christianity in Appalachia: Profiles in Regional Pluralism*, Knoxville: University of Tennessee Press, 1999, pp. 40–51.

Lomax, Tim and Moynagh, Michael, *Liquid Worship*, Grove Worship Book 181, Cambridge: Grove Books, 2004.

Lyon, David, *Postmodernity*, 2nd edn, Minneapolis: University of Minnesota Press, 2005.

MacCarthy, B. (ed.), *On the Stowe Missal: The Transactions of the Royal Irish Academy*, vol. XXVII, 1886.

Macnair, Wilmer E., *Unraveling the Mega-Church: True Faith or False Promises?*, Westport CT: Praeger, 2009.

Male, David, 'Who Are Fresh Expressions Really For? Do they really reach the unchurched?' in Louise Nelstrop and Martyn Percy (eds), *Evaluating Fresh Expressions: Explorations in Emerging Church*, Norwich: Canterbury Press, 2008, pp. 148–60.

Mannheim, Karl, 'The Problem of Generations' in *Essays on the Sociology of Knowledge*, cited in Sara Savage et al., *Making Sense of Generation Y: The World View of 15–25-year-olds*, London: Church House Publishing, 2006.

Mansur, Fatma, *Process of Independence*, London: Routledge & Paul; New York, Humanities Press, 1962.

Marini, Piero, *A Challenging Reform: Realizing the Vision of the Liturgical Movement*, Collegeville MN: Liturgical Press, 2007.

Martin, William, 'Prime Minister', *Texas Monthly*, August 2005, <http://www.texasmonthly.com/2005-08-01/feature.php>

Maynard, Beth, 'A Brief History of U2 for Novices' in Raewynne J. Whiteley and Beth Maynard (eds), *Get Up Off Your Knees: Preaching the U2 Catalog*, Cambridge MA: Cowley Publications, 2003, pp. 167–76.

McLean, G. R. D., *Poems of the West Highlands*, London: SPCK, 1961.

Meek, Donald E., *The Quest for Celtic Christianity*, Edinburgh: The Handsel Press Ltd., 2000.

Merricks, Trenton, 'U2 and the Problem of Evil', in Mark A. Wrathall (ed.),

U2 and Philosophy: How to Decipher an Atomic Band, Chicago IL: Open Court, 2006, pp. 99–108.

Micklem, Caryl et al., *Contemporary Prayers for Public Worship*, London: SCM Press, 1967.

Micklem, Caryl et al., *More Contemporary Prayers*, London: SCM Press, 1970.

Miles, Sara, *Take This Bread: A Radical Conversion*, New York: Ballantine Books, 2007.

Miller, Kim, *Designing Worship: Creating and Integrating Powerful God Experiences*, Loveland CO: Group Publishing, 2004.

Miller, Kim and the Ginghamsburg Church Worship Team, *Handbook for Multi-Sensory Worship*, Nashville TN: Abingdon Press, 1999.

Miller, Kim and the Ginghamsburg Church Worship Team, *Handbook for Multi-Sensory Worship*, vol. 2, Nashville TN: Abingdon Press, 2001.

Miller, Steve, *The Contemporary Christian Music Debate: Worldly Compromise or Agent of Renewal?*, Waynesboro GA: OM Literature, 1993.

Miller, Vincent J., *Consuming Religion: Christian Faith and Practice in a Consumer Culture*, London and New York: Continuum, 2005.

Mitton, Michael, *Restoring the Woven Cord: Strands of Celtic Christianity for the Church Today*, London: Darton, Longman & Todd, 1995.

Mobsby, Ian, 'Liquid Modernity and the Need for Transcendent Encounter', paper, 3 February 2003, <http://www.moot.uk.net/docs/fluid.pdf>.

Mobsby, Ian, Mcleary, Mark, Radcliffe, Carey and Radcliffe, Michael L. (comp.), *Moot Community Little and Compline Services*, Pocket Liturgies, Proost, 2009, <www.proost.co.uk>.

Morgenthaler, Sally, 'An Emerging Worship Response' in Paul Basden (ed.), *Exploring the Worship Spectrum*, Grand Rapids MI: Zondervan, 2004, pp. 208–13.

Morrow, Jimmy with Hood, Ralph W., Jr., *Handling Serpents: Pastor Jimmy Morrow's Narrative History of His Appalachian Jesus' Name Tradition*, Macon GA: Mercer University Press, 2005.

Newell, J. Philip, *Celtic Prayers from Iona*, New York: Paulist Press, 1997.

New Moon of the Season, London: Christian Community Press, 1960.

New Patterns for Worship, London: Church House Publishing, 2005.

New Zealand Prayer Book, A, London: Collins, 1989.

Nichols, Aidan, *Looking at the Liturgy: A Critical View of Its Contemporary Form*, San Francisco CA: Ignatius Press, 1996.

Nichols, Aidan, *A Pope and a Council on the Sacred Liturgy*, Farnborough: St Michael's Abbey Press, 2002.

Northumbria Community (comp.), *Celtic Daily Prayer*, London: Marshall Pickering, 1994.

Northumbria Community (comp.), *Celtic Night Prayer*, London: Marshall Pickering, 1996.

Ó Cróinín, Dáibhí, *Early Medieval Ireland, 400–1200*, London: Longmans, 1995.

O'Loughlin, Thomas, *Celtic Theology: Humanity, World and God in Early Irish Writings*, London and New York: Continuum, 2000.

O'Malley, Brendan (ed.), *A Celtic Eucharist*, Harrisburg PA: Morehouse Publishing, 2002.

O'Malley, Brendan (ed.), *A Celtic Primer: The Complete Celtic Worship Resource and Collection*, Harrisburg PA: Morehouse Publishing, 2002.

Omoyajowo, J. Akinyele, *Cherubim and Seraphim: The History of an African Independent Church*, New York and Lagos: NOK Publishers, 1982.

Page, Nick, *And Now Let's Move into a Time of Nonsense . . . Why Worship Songs are Failing the Church*, Bletchley: Authentic Media, 2004.

Pagitt, Doug and Jones, Tony (eds), *An Emergent Manifesto of Hope*, Grand Rapids MI: Baker Books, 2007.

Pagitt, Doug and the Solomon's Porch Community, *Reimagining Spiritual Formation: A Week in the Life of an Experimental Church*, Grand Rapids MI: Zondervan, 2003.

Paris, Jenell Williams, 'I Could Sing of Your Love Forever: American romance in contemporary worship music' in Robert Woods and Brian Walrath (eds), *The Message in the Music: Studying Contemporary Praise & Worship*, Nashville TN: Abingdon Press, 2007, pp. 43–53.

Park, Andy, *To Know You More: Cultivating the Heart of the Worship Leader*, Downers Grove IL: InterVarsity Press, 2002.

Park, Jooil, 'Kuk-ak Worship in Korea', unpublished essay, Yale Divinity School, May 2009.

Park, Seong-Won, *Worship in the Presbyterian Church in Korea: Its History and Implications*, Frankfurt am Main: Peter Lang, 2001.

Parry, Robin, *Worshipping Trinity: Coming Back to the Heart of Worship*, Bletchley: Paternoster Press, 2005.

Paul Winter Consort, <http://www.livingmusic.com/biographies/pwconsort. html>.

Peacock, Charlie with Nicholas, Molly, *At the Crossroads: Inside the Past, Present, and Future of Contemporary Christian Music*, Colorado Springs: Shaw Books, 1998, 2004.

Pecklers, Keith F., *The Unread Vision: The Liturgical Movement in the United States of America 1926–1955*, Collegeville MN: Liturgical Press, 1998.

Pecklers, Keith F. (ed.), *Liturgy in a Postmodern World*, London and New York: Continuum, 2003.

Percy, Martyn, *Words, Wonders and Power: Understanding Contemporary Christian Fundamentalism and Revivalism*, London: SPCK, 1996.

Percy, Martyn, 'Sweet Rapture: Subliminal eroticism in contemporary charismatic worship', *Theology and Sexuality* 6 (1997), pp. 71–106.

Percy, Martyn, 'Old Tricks for New Dogs? A critique of fresh expressions' in Louise Nelstrop and Martyn Percy (eds), *Evaluating Fresh Expressions: Explorations in Emerging Church*, Norwich: Canterbury Press, 2008, pp. 27–39.

Peterson, Eugene H., *The Message//Remix: The Bible in Contemporary Language*, Colorado Springs: NavPress Publishing, 2003.

Pettit, Edward, *Anglo-Saxon Remedies, Charms, and Prayers from British Library Ms. Harley 585*, Lewiston, Queenston and Lampeter: The Edwin Mellen Press, 2001.

Pfaff, Richard W., *The Liturgy in Medieval England: A History*, Cambridge: Cambridge University Press, 2009.

Piatt, Christian and Piatt, Amy, *MySpace to Sacred Space: God for a New Generation*, St Louis MO: Chalice Press, 2007.

Pickstock, Catherine, *After Writing: On the Liturgical Consummation of Philosophy*, Malden MA and Oxford: Blackwell, 1998.

Plummer, Charles (ed.), *Irish Litanies: Text and Translation*, London: Harrison & Sons Ltd., 1925.

Polman, Bert, 'Praise the Name of Jesus: Are all Praise and Worship songs for the congregation?' in Robert Woods and Brian Walrath (eds), *The Message in the Music: Studying Contemporary Praise and Worship*, Nashville TN: Abingdon Press, 2007, pp. 127–37.

Powell, Mark Allen, *Encyclopedia of Contemporary Christian Music*, Peabody MA: Hendrickson, 2002.

Pristas, Lauren, 'The Post-Vatican II Revision of the Lenten Collects', in Uwe Michael Lang (ed.), *Ever Directed Towards the Lord: The Love of God in the Liturgy of the Eucharist Past, Present, and Hoped For*, Proceedings of the Society of St Catherine of Siena Conference held in Oxford, 29 October 2005, London and New York: T & T Clark, 2007.

Pritchard, G. A., *Willow Creek Seeker Services: Evaluating a New Way of Doing Church*, Grand Rapids MI: Baker Books, 1996.

Puthangara, P., 'Liturgical Renewal in India', *Ephemerides Liturgicae* 91 (1977), pp. 350–66.

Pytches, David, 'A Man Called John' in David Pytches (ed.), *John Wimber: His Influence and Legacy*, Guildford: Eagle, 1996, pp. 9–39.

Quitslund, Sonya A., *Beauduin: A Prophet Vindicated*, New York: Newman Press, 1973.

Quoist, Michel, *Prayers of Life*, London: Gill & Macmillan Ltd, 1965.

Raine, Andy and Skinner, John T. (comp.), *Celtic Daily Prayer: A Northumbrian Office*, London: Marshall Pickering, 1994.

Ramaker, A. J., 'Hymns and Hymn Writers among the Anabaptists of the Sixteenth Century', *The Mennonite Quarterly Review* 3 (1929), pp. 93–131.

Rasmussen, Ane Marie Bak, *Modern African Spirituality: The Independent Holy Spirit Churches in East Africa 1902–1976*, London and New York: British Academic Press, 1996 (published posthumously).

Ratzinger, Joseph Cardinal, *The Feast of Faith: Approaches to a Theology of the Liturgy*, trans. Graham Harrison, San Francisco CA: Ignatius Press, 1986.

Ratzinger, Joseph Cardinal, *The Spirit of the Liturgy*, trans. John Saward, San

Francisco CA: Ignatius Press, 2000.

Redman, Matt, 'Worshipper and Musician' in David Pytches (ed.), *John Wimber: His Influence and Legacy*, Guildford: Eagle, 1996, pp. 62–70.

Redman, Matt, *The Unquenchable Worshipper: Coming Back to the Heart of Worship*, Ventura CA: Regal, 2001.

Redman, Matt (comp.), *The Heart of Worship Files*, Ventura CA: Regal, 2003.

Redman, Robb, *The Great Worship Awakening: Singing a New Song in the Postmodern Church*, San Francisco CA: Jossey-Bass, 2002.

Reid, Alcuin, *The Organic Development of the Liturgy*, Farnborough: St Michael's Abbey Press, 2004.

Reid, Alcuin (ed.), *Looking Again at the Question of the Liturgy with Cardinal Ratzinger: Proceedings of the July 2001 Fontgombault Liturgical Conference*, ET, Farnborough: Saint Michael's Abbey Press, 2003.

Riddell, Mike, Pierson, Mark and Kirkpatrick, Cathy, *The Prodigal Project: Journey into the Emerging Church*, London: SPCK, 2000.

Ritzer, George, *The McDonaldization of Society*, rev. New Century edn, Thousand Oaks CA: Pine Forge Press, 1995.

Robeck, Jr., Cecil M., *The Azusa Street Mission & Revival: The Birth of the Global Pentecostal Movement*, Nashville TN: Nelson Reference & Electronic, 2006.

Roberts, Paul, 'Liturgy and Mission in Postmodern Culture: Some reflections arising from "Alternative" services and communities', 1995, <http://seaspray.trinity-bris.ac.uk/~robertsp/papers/lambeth.html> (this site is no longer available).

Roberts, Paul, 'Thoroughly modern worship, thoroughly postmodern culture', a paper given at a conference at King's College, London, December 1996.

Roberts, Paul, *Alternative Worship in the Church of England*, Grove Worship Book 155, Cambridge: Grove Books, 1999.

Robinson, Jonathan, *The Mass and Modernity: Walking to Heaven Backward*, San Francisco CA: Ignatius Press, 2005.

Ross, Melanie, 'Joseph's Britches Revisited: Reflections on method in liturgical theology', *Worship* 80 (2006), pp. 528–50.

Rumsey, Patricia M., *Sacred Time in Early Christian Ireland: The Monks of the Navigatio and the Céli Dé in Dialogue to Explore the Theologies of Time and the Liturgy of the Hours in Pre-Viking Ireland*, London and New York: T & T Clark, 2007.

Rundell, Simon, 'Blesséd: A sacramental perspective of alternative worship with young people' in Stephen Croft and Ian Mobsby (eds), *Fresh Expressions in the Sacramental Tradition*, Norwich: Canterbury Press, 2009, pp. 132–9.

Ruth, Lester, 'Lex Agendi, Lex Orandi: Toward an understanding of seeker services as a new kind of liturgy', *Worship* 70 (1996), pp. 386–405.

Ruth, Lester, *A Little Heaven Below: Worship at Early Methodist Quarterly Meetings*, Nashville TN: Abingdon Press, 2000.

Ruth, Lester, 'Reconsidering the Emergence of the Second Great Awakening and Camp Meetings Among Early Methodists', *Worship* 75 (2001), pp. 334–55.

Ruth, Lester, 'How Great Is Our God: The Trinity in contemporary Christian worship music' in Robert Woods and Brian Walrath (eds), *The Message in the Music: Studying Contemporary Praise and Worship*, Nashville TN: Abingdon Press, 2007, pp. 29–42.

Ruth, Lester, 'Lex Amandi, Lex Orandi: The Trinity in the Most-Used Contemporary Christian Worship Songs' in Bryan D. Spinks (ed.), *The Place of Christ in Liturgical Prayer: Trinity, Christology, and Liturgical Theology*, Collegeville: Liturgical Press, 2008, pp. 342–59.

Sanctus 1, Pocket Liturgies, Proost, 2008,<www.proost.co.uk>.

Sargeant, Kimon Howland, *Seeker Churches: Promoting Traditional Religion in a Nontraditional Way*, New Brunswick NJ: Rutgers University Press, 2000.

Scharen, Christian, *One Step Closer: Why U2 Matters to Those Seeking God*, Grand Rapids MI: Brazos Press, 2006.

Schell, Donald, '"Public Work" at Ground Zero', *Open*, Associated Parishes for Liturgy and Mission (Spring 2008), pp. 3–4.

Schmidt, Leigh Eric, *Holy Fairs: Scotland and the Making of American Revivalism*, 2nd edn, Grand Rapids MI: Eerdmans, 2001.

Schofield Clark, Lyn, *From Angels to Aliens: Teenagers, the Media and the Supernatural*, New York: Oxford University Press, 2003.

Schuller, Robert H., *Your Church Has Real Possibilities*, Glendale CA: Regal Books, 1976.

Schuller, Robert H., *Self-Esteem: The New Reformation*, Nashville TN: W Publishing Group, 1982.

Schuller, Robert H., *My Journey: From an Iowa Farm to a Cathedral of Dreams*, San Francisco CA: HarperOne, 2001.

Schultze, Quentin J., *High-Tech Worship? Using Presentational Technologies Wisely*, Grand Rapids MI: Baker Books, 2004.

Schwartz, Scott W., 'Music of the Serpent-Handling Service' in Thomas Burton (ed.), *Serpent-Handling Believers*, Knoxville: University of Tennessee Press, 1993, pp. 146–8.

Scott, Stephen, *The Amish Wedding and Other Special Occasions of the Old Order Communities*, Intercourse PA: Good Books, 1988.

Senn, Frank C., *Christian Liturgy: Catholic and Evangelical*, Minneapolis MN: Fortress Press, 1997.

Simon, Ulrich, 'Alternative Services', *View Review* 22:4 (1971), pp. 18–19.

Simpson, Ray (comp.), *Celtic Worship through the Year: Prayers, Readings and Creative Activities for Ordinary Days and Saints' Days*, London: Hodder & Stoughton, 1998.

Slaughter, Michael, *Out on the Edge: A Wake-Up Call for Church Leaders on the Edge of the Media Reformation*, Nashville TN: Abingdon Press, 1998.

Slaughter, Michael with Bird, Warren, *Unlearning Church: Just When You*

Thought You Had Leadership All Figured Out, Loveland CO: Group Publishing Inc., 2002.

Smith, Efrem and Jackson, Phil, *The Hip-Hop Church: Connecting with the Movement Shaping Our Culture*, Downers Grove IL: InterVarsity Press, 2005.

Smith, James K. A., *Desiring the Kingdom: Worship, Worldview, and Cultural Formation*, Grand Rapids MI: Baker Academic, 2009.

Smith, R. Scott, *Truth and the New Kind of Christian: The Emerging Effects of Postmodernism in the Church*, Wheaton IL: Crossway Books, 2005.

Spinks, Bryan D., 'Christian Worship or Cultural Incantations?' *Studia Liturgica* 12 (1977), pp. 1–19.

Spinks, Bryan D., 'The Anaphora for India: Some theological objections to an attempt at inculturation', *Ephemerides Liturgicae* 95 (1981), pp. 529–49.

Spinks, Bryan D., 'Worship and Evangelism' in Michael Perham (ed.), *Liturgy for a New Century*, London: SPCK/Alcuin Club, 1991.

Steven, James, *Worship in the Restoration Movement*, Grove Worship Series 110, Bramcote: Grove Books, 1989.

Stevenson, Jane and Warren, F. E., *The Liturgy and Ritual of the Celtic Church*, Woodbridge: The Boydell Press, 1987.

Stockman, Steve, *Walk On: The Spiritual Journey of U2*, Orlando: Relevant Books, 2005.

Stratford, Tim (ed.), *Worship: Window of the Urban Church*, London: SPCK, 2006.

Sun Dances, The, London: Christian Community Press, 1960.

Sun, Irene Ai-Ling, 'Songs of Canaan: Hymnody of the house-church Christians in China', *Studia Liturgica* 37 (2007), pp. 98–116.

Taylor, Steve, *The Out of Bounds Church? Learning to Create a Community of Faith in a Culture of Change*, Grand Rapids MI: Zondervan, 2005.

Thomson, Iain, '"Even Better than the Real Thing"? Postmodernity, the triumph of the simulacra, and U2' in Mark A. Wrathall (ed.), *U2 and Philosophy: How to Decipher an Atomic Band*, Chicago IL: Open Court, 2006, pp. 73–95.

Thornton, Sarah, *Club Cultures: Music, Media and Subcultural Capita*, Hanover and London: Wesleyan University Press, 1996.

Thumma, Scott and Travis, Dave, *Beyond Megachurch Myths: What We Can Learn from America's Largest Churches*, San Francisco CA: Jossey-Bass, 2007.

Titon, Jeff Todd, *Powerhouse for God: Speech, Chant, and Song in an Appalachian Baptist Church*, Austin: University of Texas Press, 1988.

Torevell, David, *Losing the Sacred: Ritual, Modernity and Liturgical Reform*, Edinburgh: T & T Clark, 2000.

U2 Eucharist, cited at <http://www.e4gr.org/pray/u2services.html>.

Umble, John, 'Amish Service Manuals', *The Mennonite Quarterly Review* 15 (1941), pp. 26–32.

Umble, John (ed.), 'An Amish Minister's Manual', *The Mennonite Quarterly Review* 15 (1941), pp. 95–117.

Van de Wyer, Robert, *Celtic Fire*, London: Darton, Longman & Todd, 1990.

Vansau McCauley, Deborah, *Appalachian Mountain Religion: A History*, Urbana and Chicago: University of Illinois Press, 1995.

Venter, Dawid, 'Concepts and Theories in the Study of African Independent Churches' in Dawid Venter (ed.), *Engaging Modernity: Methods and Cases for Studying African Independent Churches in South Africa*, Westport CT: Praeger, 2004, pp. 13–43.

Vineyard Music Group, *Let Your Glory Fall: Songs and Essays*, Anaheim CA: Mercy/Vineyard Publishing, nd *c.* 1994.

Voskuil, Dennis, *Mountains into Goldmines: Robert Schuller and the Gospel of Success*, Grand Rapids MI: Eerdmans, 1983.

Wagner, C. Peter, *The Third Wave of the Holy Spirit: Encountering the Power of Signs and Wonders*, Ann Arbor MI: Vine Books, 1988.

Walker, Andrew, 'Thoroughly Modern: Sociological reflections on the charismatic movement from the end of the twentieth century' in Stephen Hunt, Malcolm Hamilton and Tony Walter (eds), *Charismatic Christianity: Sociological Perspectives*, New York: St Martin's Press, 1997, pp. 17–42.

Walker, Andrew, *Restoring the Kingdom: The Radical Christianity of the House Church Movement*, rev. edn, Guildford: Eagle, 1998.

Walker, G. M. S., *Sancti Columbani Opera*, Dublin: Dublin Institute for Advanced Studies, 1957 (Columbanus, Epistle V.3).

Wallace, Sue, *Multi-Sensory Prayer*, Bletchley: Scripture Union [2000] 2005.

Wallace, Sue, 'Alternative Worship and the Story of Visions in York' in Steven Croft and Ian Mobsby (eds), *Fresh Expressions in the Sacramental Tradition*, Norwich: Canterbury Press, 2009, pp. 9–15.

Ward, Karen, 'A Story of Anglimergence: Community, covenant, Eucharist and mission at Church of the Apostles' in Stephen Croft and Ian Mobsby (eds), *Fresh Expressions in the Sacramental Tradition*, Norwich: Canterbury Press, 2009, pp. 156–61.

Ward, Pete, *Growing Up Evangelical: Youthwork and the Making of a Subculture*, London: SPCK, 1996.

Ward, Pete, *Liquid Church*, Carlisle: Paternoster Press, 2002.

Ward, Pete, *Selling Worship: How What We Sing Has Changed the Church*, Bletchley: Paternoster Press, 2005.

Ward, Pete (ed.), *Mass Culture: Eucharist and Mission in a Post-modern World*, Oxford: Bible Reading Fellowship, 1999.

Ward, Pete (ed.), *The Rite Stuff: Ritual in Contemporary Christian Worship and Mission*, Oxford: Bible Reading Fellowship, 1999.

Warren, F. E., *The Liturgy and Ritual of the Celtic Church*, Willits CA: Eastern Orthodox Books, 1979.

Warren, F. E., *The Liturgy and Ritual of the Celtic Church*, 2nd edn with introduction and bibliography by J. Stevenson, Woodbridge: The Boydell Press, 1987.

Warren, Rick, *The Purpose-Driven Church: Growth without Compromising Your Message and Mission*, Grand Rapids MI: Zondervan, 1995.

Webber, Robert, *Planning Blended Worship: The Creative Mixture of Old and New*, Nashville TN: Abingdon Press, 1998.

Webber, Robert, *The Younger Evangelicals: Facing the Challenges of the New World*, Grand Rapids MI: Baker Books, 2002.

Webber, Robert, 'Blended Worship' in Paul A. Basden (ed.), *Exploring the Worship Spectrum: 6 Views*, Grand Rapids MI: Zondervan, 2004, pp. 175–91.

Wild Goose Resource Group, *A Wee Worship Book*, Glasgow: Wild Goose Publications, 1999.

Williams, Charles, *Outlines of Romantic Theology*, ed. Alice M. Hadfield, Grand Rapids MI: Eerdmans, 1990.

Wimber, John (ed.), *Thoughts on Worship*, Anaheim CA: Vineyard Music Group, 1996.

Woods, Robert and Walrath, Brian (eds), *The Message in the Music: Studying Contemporary Praise and Worship*, Nashville TN: Abingdon Press, 2007.

Wright, Nigel, 'The Nature and Variety of Restorationism and the "House Church" Movement' in Stephen Hunt, Malcolm Hamilton and Tony Walter (eds), *Charismatic Christianity: Sociological Perspectives*, New York: St Martin's Press, 1997, pp. 60–76.

Wright, Timothy, *A Community of Joy: How to Create Contemporary Worship*, Nashville TN: Abingdon Press, 1994.

Wuthnow, Robert, *After the Baby Boomers: How Twenty- and Thirty-Somethings Are Shaping the Future of American Religion*, Princeton NJ: Princeton University Press, 2007.

York, Terry W., *America's Worship Wars*, Peabody MA: Hendrickson Publishers, 2003.

Young, Richard, *The Rise of Lakewood Church and Joel Osteen*, New Kensington PA: Whitaker House, 2007.

Zinchini, Cassandra, 'Taking Revival to the World', *Christianity Today*, October 2007.

Zschech, Darlene, *Extravagant Worship*, Minneapolis MN: Bethany House, 2001.

Zschech, Darlene, *The Kiss of Heaven: God's Favor to Empower Your Life Dream*, Minneapolis MN: Bethany House, 2003.

Zschech, Darlene, 'The Role of the Holy Spirit in Worship: An introduction to the Hillsong Church, Sydney, Australia' in Teresa Berger and Bryan D. Spinks (eds), *The Spirit in Worship – Worship in the Spirit*, Collegeville MN: Liturgical Press, 2009, pp. 285–92.

Discography

Durham Cathedral, *Duke Ellington: The Durham Connection, Selection from the Sacred Concerts*, Stan Tracey Orchestra, 2000.

Hillsong, *Songs for Communion*, Hillsong Church, Hillsong Music Australia, 2006.

McKennitt, Loreena, *The Mask and the Mirror*, Quinlan Road, 1994 and 2004.

Redman, Matt, *Beautiful News*, Sparrow, 2006.

Redman, Matt, *We Shall Not Be Shaken*, Sparrow, 2009.

Rhinehart, Laura, *The Soaking Room*, vol. 1, Laura Rhinehart Music, 2007.

Park, Andy, *Wonder Working God*, Ion Records, 2009.

Zschech, Darlene, *Kiss of Heaven*, Extravagant Worship, 2003.

Index